FITTING THE
PIECES TOGETHER

PUBLISHED BY
BRITISH AGENCIES FOR
ADOPTION & FOSTERING
11 SOUTHWARK STREET
LONDON SE1 1RQ
© VERA FAHLBERG 1988
ISBN 0 903534 78 9
DESIGNED BY ANDREW HAIG
TYPESET BY INTERTYPE
PRINTED AND BOUND IN ENGLAND

PRACTICE SERIES: 17

Fitting the pieces together

Attachment & separation
Child development
Helping children when they must move
The child in placement:
common behavioural problems

Vera Fahlberg

BRITISH AGENCIES FOR
ADOPTION & FOSTERING

The workbooks in this volume were originally published in America by Michigan Department of Social Services. They were the result of a project, *Training of children in foster care*, co-sponsored by the Michigan Department of Social Services, Spaulding for Children of Michigan, and Forest Heights Lodge, Evergreen, Colorado, with a grant from the Edna McConnell Foundation. All four books have also been published separately by BAAF.

BAAF is grateful to Dr Vera Fahlberg for permission to publish these books in this new volume and to make some minor changes to the text so that it is more applicable to the British scene. This has involved changes in spelling and some descriptions of procedures and facilities. In no way, however, has the core of the work been changed.

Contents

References appear at the end of each individual book. We have added an up-to-date *Further reading* list at the end which relates to all four books.

Foreword

Vera Fahlberg must be a familiar name to most child care workers in Britain. It is almost ten years since BAAF first published the three purple workbooks that have proved so useful to anyone whose job is to help children in distress. Their publication was followed by Dr Fahlberg's visits to Britain in 1982 and 1988, when many of us benefitted directly from her unique blend of insight, imagination and commonsense. In both speaking and writing, Dr Fahlberg draws freely on the wisdom of experienced carers and social workers as well as on her own extensive clinical knowledge, and it is this interdisciplinary approach, expressed in simple but vivid language, that is so effective.

BAAF is grateful for the opportunity to publish the three workbooks, *Attachment and separation*, *Child development* and *Helping children when they must move* in this omnibus edition, and especially so in that we have been able to include a fourth book *The child in placement: common behavioural problems*. While we must emphasise that intensive work with children should never be undertaken without the help of a supervisor or a consultant, we have to recognise that workers are frequently confronted with a child's difficult and perhaps mystifying behaviour when help is not immediately to hand. This fourth book offers a bridge over the gap between interpreting the origins of the behaviour and dealing with its manifestations in the here and now.

Publishing all four books in this one cover emphasises that they are, in fact, four sections of one work and should be treated as such. Several important points underline this quartet:

- Dr Fahlberg states: 'negative behaviour can stem from a healthy need'. We should perceive behaviour as a child's way of communicating need rather than as an inconvenient problem in the path of an adult

- children should be seen in their historical context and within their total environment if they are to be understood and helped. Similar behaviour in different children may stem from different roots

- pain often recurs at different stages of development; this does not mean that earlier work was wasted, rather that further progress depends on further work

- expert advice may well be available and should be sought when children persistently cannot respond to the help offered, even when their behaviour does not appear to be severely disturbed.

Daphne Batty
Secretary, BAAF Medical Group

WORKBOOK ONE
Attachment and separation

CONTENTS

About this workbook

Every child who comes into care is in crisis. These children have been removed from the homes of their parents, often unexpectedly and abruptly. If these children have a bond or an attachment to their parents, they are in crisis because of this separation. Some of these abused or neglected children may have no attachment to their parents or may have attachments that are extremely problematic. This means it is likely that they have serious developmental problems.

Attachment between humans is a complex matter. The way attachments develop and function is not yet completely understood. However, we believe it is essential that professionals who serve children and families and participate in major decisions about their lives understand as much as possible about attachment. Helping children and families handle problems with attachment and separation is at the heart of child care.

In this workbook, we attempt to present material about attachment and separation in a way that is useful to people in the field. We attempt to tie theoretical material to the practical questions asked by social workers, mental health practitioners, school personnel, and others.

We have had extensive experiences in presenting this material to child care staff. They have taught us that it is easy to feel overwhelmed by the content and immobilised by guilt about past mistakes. It is our hope that the reader will use this material to think about new ways of dealing with children currently on a caseload rather than focusing on the past.

We hope that upon a first reading you will be able to identify a new technique or idea to use with a child who is handling an attachment and/or separation issue. In addition, we hope it will also stand as a reference to which one can return when faced with problems.

This workbook has five major sections. The first defines attachment and explores its relevance in child care. Section 2, on the 'Development of attachment between parent and child' describes the normal way that bonding occurs. This information serves as a base for the practical material in the rest of the workbook.

Section 3 offers checklists for 'Assessing attachment'. 'Separation' is the topic of Section 4. In this section, we discuss things that influence a child's reaction to separation and ways to help a child handle a move from one family to another. Finally Section 5 is entitled 'Identifying and overcoming attachment problems'. In it we review signs and symptoms of faulty attachment in children and suggest ways to enhance bonding.

Exercises have been interspersed throughout the text. They ask the reader to apply the material to practice. We think these exercises can be useful to the individual who wishes to use this material as a workbook. We have also found that the exercises may be used in a staff meeting with groups of foster parents or serve as a basis for training workshops on this material.

1 Introduction

What is attachment?

Attachment has been defined as 'an affectionate bond between two individuals that endures through space and time and serves to join them emotionally' (Kennell[1]). A strong and healthy bond to a parent allows a child to develop both trust in others and self-reliance. The bond that a child develops to the person who cares for him or her in their early years is the foundation of their future psychological, physical, and cognitive development and for their future relationships with others. Below we highlight the many positive effects of a child's strong attachment to the parent. Many children who come into care are in jeopardy of losing all these strengths. Selma Fraiberg[2] has noted that children who do not have an attachment 'have been deprived of their humanity'.

Attachment helps the child:
- attain full intellectual potential;
- sort out what he or she perceives;
- think logically;
- develop a conscience;
- become self-reliant;
- cope with stress and frustration;
- handle fear and worry;
- develop future relationships;
- reduce jealousy.

Attachment in abused and neglected children

A basic psychological task faced by every individual is to find a healthy and comfortable balance between autonomy or self reliance, and dependency or trust in others. No one achieves this balance once and for all. It is, instead, shifted and negotiated throughout life. The balance between autonomy and dependency is affected by major events such as marriage, the birth of a child, or the death of a loved one.

The kinds of needs each of us has for dependency and autonomy and the way we achieve a balance between them seems to be strongly influenced by the way we were parented.

Many parents who abuse and neglect their children seem to have an imbalance in needs for dependency and autonomy. Some abusive parents appear to have an excessive urge for autonomy and independence. They have difficulty asking for help or receiving it when it is offered. They don't seem able to trust others; they equate any form of dependency with loss of control. This excessive autonomy is frequently compensation for the fact that their early dependency needs were not met by their own parents.

On the other hand, some abusive and neglectful parents are very dependent on others to meet their needs. They cannot meet the needs of their own children, and many in fact require the child to help them. When the children are unable to meet the parents' unreasonable needs, the parents may become frustrated, angry and abusive.

Most children who come into care have come from families in which the needs of the parents have made it difficult for the children to learn to achieve a healthy balance between needs for dependency and autonomy. Without other kinds of experiences, these foster children will eventually become parents who will have difficulty helping their own children with these issues. Thus, one of the objectives of foster care should be to recognise these imbalances in the needs of the children and to help foster parents create an environment that allows the child to form a healthy bond to a parent and go on to other developmental tasks.

Attachment and children in foster care

Foster care can help children develop a sense of trust and a sense of self-reliance. It can be an opportunity for children to have some experiences with parents that can improve the way they function and the way that they are able to relate to others. If this is to happen, however, children need to be helped to develop healthy attachments.

The social worker's first responsibility is to maintain the child in his or her family and to work to improve the child's attachment to the biological parents. If, however, the child must be removed from the birth family and placed in a foster family, the foster parents' roles ought to be twofold: to help the child develop healthy attachments and to aid in transferring these attachments to the permanent caretakers of the child who may be either birth parents or adoptive parents.

In order to do this effectively, foster parents and foster children need to develop bonds. In the past, the growth of such attachments has often been discouraged. Those who discourage such bonds between foster parents and children are encouraging emotional neglect of the children involved.

This means that foster parents must be selected and trained who have the ability to form normal attachments. Social workers must develop their abilities to assess attachment in children, to identify attachment problems and to help families develop and transfer attachments.

Attachment and permanent planning

In human societies the initial bonding occurs between the infant and the primary caretaker who is usually the infant's mother figure. The primary caretaker may be a birth mother, foster mother, or adoptive mother. In some cases, the primary caretaker is the father. Neither blood ties to the child nor sex of the primary caretaker seem to be as important as the relationship this person has to the child. In most societies both infant and mother are members of a larger unit, the family. This family provides an excellent context in which attachments with the child can grow. The following highlights the functions the family plays in relation to children.

Things the family provides for children:
- a primary caretaker for the child;
- care by specific adults to whom the child can become attached;
- continuous contact with these adults on a day-to-day basis;
- continuous but changing relationships with a small number of individuals over a lifetime;
- safety and security;
- stimulation and encouragement for growth;
- reasonable expectations;
- experience in identifying and expressing emotions;
- support in times of stress.

Studies done of children raised in institutions have shown that adequate physical care is not enough to lead to the development of a physically and psychologically healthy child. A primary person to whom the child can become attached, who responds to the child's needs and who initiates positive activities with the child seems to be indispensable. Although this primary caretaker doesn't have to meet all the child's needs all the time, usually she or he is responsible for the child most of the time and makes arrangements for the child's care in their absence.

This kind of day-to-day care by a primary caretaker provided in a family context has traditionally been provided for children in foster care. However, there are other aspects of family care that foster children have been denied. Many children in foster care have moved from one family to another and have not experienced relationships to members of a family over a long period of time.

This continuous but constantly changing contact with a small number of individuals is important. The relationship between a parent and an infant changes when that child becomes a toddler. When the child is of school age the relationship changes once more. It is transformed again when the child becomes an adolescent and when the adolescent leaves home.

Relationships continue to change when the children become parents of the next generation of the family. Many people upon reaching middle age find their parents have more and more dependency needs. In many cultures, the elderly become quite dependent on their children, thus completing a cycle.

It is this long-range relationship over time and space that truly defines attachment. The continually changing nature of such a lifetime bond helps individuals achieve a strong sense of identity and of responsibility. People who lack such long-term attachments may have more difficulty sorting out what to attribute to their own actions and what to attribute to changes in the environment.

Most families provide growing children with memories of their past and help them keep memories alive. This helps children develop a sense of self. In foster care, we often minimise the past of children. Sometimes, we minimise their future as well. Often we do this because we are not sure what will happen in the future. This uncertainty may extend so far that we can't even tell the child who will be taking care of him or her next year. We focus only on the here and now.

We believe that all those involved in foster care need to do all that is possible to ensure that the child has a stable family to whom he or she can relate throughout their lifetime. If we do not do this we are neither meeting one of the child's most basic needs nor are we modelling the importance of foresight, planning and responsibility for one's own actions.

In this introduction we have reviewed the relevance of attachment to child care. In order to deal with the attachment issues that are such a key to this work, one must understand how bonding normally occurs. In Section 2, we turn our attention to the way that attachment usually develops between parent and child.

2 Development of attachment between parent and child

Introduction

This section of the workbook describes the way attachment normally develops between parent and child. An understanding of this normal process must underlie much of what the social worker does with families and children.

Workers often find that they must assess the degree to which a child is attached to a family in order to make decisions about the case. An understanding of how child and parent behave when there is a normal attachment between them serves as a basis for such an assessment. Another important role workers need to play is to help a child develop a strong attachment to a parent. Sometimes this means helping to strengthen a faulty parent-child attachment; sometimes it means helping a child bond to a new foster or adoptive parent. Again, an understanding of the normal bonding process is critical.

In this section we discuss that normal process. First we look at the kinds of interactions that occur between parent and child and at the way these interactions change as the child develops. Then, we take a close look at how these parent-child interactions work to build attachment between them.

The attachment process and child development
Setting the stage for bonding
The stage is set for bonding between parents and child during the period between the child's conception and birth, called the pre-natal period. During this period, parents begin to develop images of what the unborn child will be like. They form expectations and hopes for their child, for themselves as parents, and for their relationship with their child.

Many conditions of the pre-natal period affect the kind of attachment that will develop between parent and child. Some of these factors include characteristics of the pregnancy itself such as the timing of the pregnancy, the mother's condition during the pregnancy, and the presence or absence of pre-natal complications.

In addition, the relationship between the child's parents during pregnancy affects the bonding that will occur with the child. The kind of parenting that the parents themselves received strongly influences the kind of images that they will develop of their child and of themselves as parents. Characteristics of the infant *in utero* come into play as well. Mothers of more than one child by birth sometimes notice marked differences in infants *in utero*; one may rarely move and another may kick and turn frequently. The characteristics of the child and the way the mother perceives them affect the bonds that will develop.

Adoptive parents can benefit from a period of 'psychological pregnancy'. During this time, they, too, can fantasise about what it will be like to be parents in a variety of situations. A very short pre-placement waiting period precludes this kind of preparation. On the other hand, waits of one to three years are too long and tend to erode the benefits of a psychological pregnancy.

Bonding at birth
Direct bonding between mother and child begins during the very first moments of the child's life. Desmond[3] found that during the first hour of an infant's life he or she is wide awake with both eyes wide open. After this, the infant falls into a deep sleep. Most mothers use their first contact with their newborn children to explore them, to count fingers and toes, and just generally to see if they are physically normal.

A newborn infant who is held horizontally will reflexively turn his or her head towards the person who is doing the holding. The mother is pleased when the infant looks at her. She tends to caress the child gently.

All of this exploring is part of the claiming process. During this process the mother is consciously and unconsciously looking for ways to tell her child from others. Studies based on videotapes of mother and child interactions made during deliveries and post-partum hospital stays indicate that when the mother doesn't take an active part in this claiming process the family is at high risk for severe parent-child difficulties in future years.

Bonding in the first six months
When an infant is born, the nervous system is complete, but it is not

well organised. Especially during the first month of life, the newborn makes adjustments to life outside the mother's body. The perceptual threshold is high; that is, the infant is not sensitive to internal or external stimuli of which an older child would be clearly aware. The newborn is irregular in many areas, not eating, sleeping or eliminating on schedule. The infant startles on perceiving things, and moves in a jerky, unco-ordinated way.

During the first year of life and thereafter, the child's nervous system will become better organised. The interactions between the newborn and the parents are a major force in this process. The influence of parent-child interactions on the child's developing nervous system may explain why children who are not well attached often have poor cognitive development.

The interactions between parent and child are exchanges between them that involve touch, sound, or visual stimulation. The child has capacities to participate in these exchanges even in the first six months of life. Children do not initially have control over their voluntary muscles. There is a natural order in which control over these muscles comes. In general, the child acquires muscle control from the head downward and from the central part of the body outward.

Therefore, it is with the face muscles that the infant begins to respond to the bonding process. The infant first learns to focus the eyes on objects eight or nine inches (20 to 22.5 cm) away. This is the distance between the infant's eyes and the mother's face when the child is nursing at the breast. Thus, when children are held at the breast, they first become capable of focusing on their mother's face. From the age of four weeks, infants prefer looking at the human face to looking at other kinds of stimuli. By eight or nine weeks the infant is able to follow the movement of the human face and attend to it closely.

Face-to-face contact is very important in developing bonds with an infant. Parents need to be aware of its importance. Spitz[4] found that infants showed signs of pleasure even when they were presented with a mask of the human face. Covering up the lower part of the mask did not change their response. However, when the upper part of the mask was covered, even just one eye of it, the infants did not respond with pleasure. The infant's response to the human eye seems to be innate rather than learned.

By the time they are three or three and a half months old, most infants begin to prefer looking at their mother's face to looking at other faces. Though infants at this age continue to show pleasure at other faces, responses of pleasure occur more strongly and consistently in response to the mother's face. This preference for a specific face develops a full two months before the infant shows pleasure at the sight of a bottle or other object.

From the time of birth, loud noises distress and soft sounds quiet the infant. Wolff[5] has demonstrated infants turn towards sounds and that from the age of three to four weeks they recognise the mother's voice. By age four weeks the infant gurgles and coos in response to the human voice. When the mother or someone else responds to such vocalisations they increase. In fact, one of the functions of babbling seems to be to keep the mother close and to promote interaction between mother and child and thus to promote bonding.

Body contact between mother and child also contributes to bonding between them. In most societies children are in more frequent body contact with their mothers than they are in western industrialised countries. The rhythmic movements that the child experiences in being carried about by the mother are similar to those experienced before birth.

It has been found that experiencing rhythmic movement encourages growth among premature infants. Cradles and rocking chairs have long been used to help soothe fussy babies. In recent years an increasing number of mothers have been using a sling to permit closeness with their babies as they go about their daily housework and go out on excursions. This closeness seems to be particularly soothing to fussy babies.

We have seen that even in these early months the infant responds most to the particular sensations that promote contact with others. They prefer looking at the human face and listening to the human voice. They prefer the feel of soft clothes and the sense of rhythmical movement that they experience as their mother walks. They prefer the taste of their mother's milk. One might speculate that infants may prefer the smell of humans to other smells and even be able to identify their primary caretaker through smell although we know of no studies in this area.

Thus, infants are especially sensitive to developing attachment behaviour during the fourth, fifth and sixth months of their lives. This is confirmed by studies such as those done by Yarrow[6]. He found that 86 per cent of those infants in his study who were moved from a foster home to an adoptive home when they were six months old showed signs of disturbance. Every infant who was moved at the age of seven months or older showed marked disturbance.

Bonding from six months to 12 months
At the age of six to nine months the child can consistently distinguish between family members and strangers, and begins to demonstrate fear or anxiety when approached by a stranger. The strength and frequency of these fear reactions increase as the child nears one year of age. This makes it increasingly difficult for a child to develop an attachment to a new primary caretaker during this period.

By the age of eight months, the child plays a more active part in trying to keep the mother close by. The child obviously tries to catch the mother's attention. Since most children are somewhat mobile at this age, it becomes easier for them to achieve this aim. Such activities on the part of the child are a necessary part of forming an attachment and should not be discouraged. By the age of one year, the child and mother will have developed a unique balance between them in terms of who initiates interactions, how they are initiated, and how they are responded to.

Often, we can virtually see this kind of delicate balance being achieved. The infant's urge for closeness and attachment is so strong that if the mother does not stay close, the child behaves in a way that tends to draw her closer. Such infants are often clingy and whiney. If the parent rejects the child at these times, the clinging and whiney behaviour increases. In these cases, closeness to mother is maintained with primarily negative rather than positive interactions.

If, however, the mother shows the child that she is ready to remain close by, the child can relax and free energies for other activities. The nature of this balance between mother and child changes as the child develops. During the first year, attachment between mother and child should increase, but dependency should decrease. Attachment and dependency are not synonymous terms.

According to Ainsworth[7], the anxious, the insecure child may falsely appear more strongly attached to the mother than the secure child who can explore fairly freely in a strange situation using the mother as a secure base; who is not distressed by the appearance of a stranger; and who shows awareness of the mother's absence, greets her on her return, and then resumes previous activities.

In contrast, the insecure child is one who does not explore even when the mother is present; who becomes extremely alarmed by the appearance of a stranger; who seems helpless and in acute distress when the mother leaves, and on her return is either disinterested or in distress but in either case, incapable of making an organised attempt to reach her.

Bonding after one year

In general, one and two-year-old children continue to exhibit many kinds of attachment behaviour. The primary psychological task for a toddler is to recognise that he or she and the primary caretaker are two separate individuals. This is made easier because toddlers are increasingly able to get around without help. They are able to perceive more and more of what is in their environment and are developing speech which helps increase their autonomy and awareness of their own feelings and those of others. 'Me', 'mine', 'you', and 'no' are all words that help two-year-olds accomplish this task.

After the age of three, it becomes easier for the child to accept the mother's temporary absence. However, throughout life attachment behaviour increases during times of anxiety and stress. Observing children when they are tired, frightened, or not feeling well is often a useful way to find out about their attachment to their caretaker. Well-attached children will seek out their primary caretaker at this time and be comforted.

Even as adults, when we are sick, frightened , or vulnerable, we want to be close to the people to whom we are attached, and we may revert to dependent behaviour to keep them close.

Reciprocity between mother and child

We've seen that attachment between parent and child results from their interactions. These interactions begin at birth and continue and change as the child matures. We can analyse these interactions in terms of how they build the bond between mother and child.

Most of the interactions between a mother and her newborn child are initiated by the infant who fusses and cries when uncomfortable. The mother responds to these overtures. As the child gets older, an increasing percentage of interactions are initiated by the mother, and the child responds.

It is usual for many of the interactions between mother and child to be cyclical. In such cases the responses of one partner encourage the other to continue to respond. For example, the child cries when wet and uncomfortable and the mother responds by changing him or her. At the same time she talks and smiles at the child, who smiles and gurgles back. The interaction is pleasurable for both and is likely to continue through a series of activities.

Bowlby[8] says that there are two characteristics of the interactions between mother and child that strongly affect the kind and degree of attachment that will develop between them. These are the speed and intensity with which the mother responds to the infant's crying and the extent to which the mother initiates interactions with the infant. We will take a closer look at both interactions initiated by the child and those that the mother initiates and the way they contribute to attachment.

The arousal-relaxation cycle: its importance in bonding

We have noted that infants have a relatively high perceptual threshold. When, however, infants experience displeasure or tension, because of either internal or external stimuli, they discharge it. They move their arms and legs; they become red in the face; they cry; they squirm. It is clear to everyone that they are uncomfortable.

As long as they are discharging this tension, their perception of the outside world is blocked. Thus, if an infant or child continually experiences tension, his or her ability to perceive what is going on around them is seriously limited. As a result, intellectual development that depends on such perceptions is hampered or blocked.

The opposite of displeasure in an infant is not happiness or pleasure but is instead a state of quiescence or contentment. The parent's role when the infant is discharging this tension is to return the child to a quiescent state.

The following diagram depicts a typical, successful interaction between mother and child. The interaction is initiated by the child's need and consequent expression of displeasure and completed by the mother's response.

The cycle is what is called the 'arousal-relaxation cycle'. The repeated successful completion of this cycle is critical if the child is to develop a sense of trust and security and become attached to the mother.

Scrutiny of the diagram reveals several places where the successful completion of the arousal-relaxation cycle might break down for a

The arousal-relaxation cycle

mother and child pair. There is a tendency in our society today to blame parents, particularly the mothers, for any disturbances in their child's emotional development. It is true that some neglectful or abusive parents may fail consistently to respond to their children's overtures in a way that meets the child's needs and therefore disrupt this cycle of interactions.

This kind of parental lack of response is not, however, the only cause of disruption in the arousal-relaxation cycle. If for some reason the child does not experience states of discomfort, the cycle will not even be initiated. Parents of other children may try to respond to their infants but find themselves unable to relieve their discomfort. If a parent consistently meets the child's needs before he or she is uncomfortable or protects the child from any disturbing stimuli, the cycle is disrupted. Spitz[9] states that it is probably as harmful to deprive an infant of the feeling of discomfort as to deprive him or her of the feeling of displeasure.

Many premature infants are examples of children whose behaviour may not readily fit into a pattern that promotes attachment between mother and child. These children generally do not respond to environmental stimuli in the same way as other infants. Their perceptual thresholds are so high that they are not aware of internal discomfort; in fact they may have to be tube-fed on a regular schedule because they do not experience the same sensation of displeasure due to hunger. In addition, such infants are frequently isolated from other interactions such as being physically close to their mothers that lead to bonding.

Delacato [10] has speculated that children with certain organic problems may have abnormal perceptual thresholds; higher than normal in some cases or lower than normal in others. This means that these children may either rarely experience discomfort or experience it very frequently. In either case the child would not regularly experience the relief from an unpleasant state that is the key to forming an attachment to the mother. This theory may explain some cases of poor attachment between mother and child when mothering seems adequate.

A case example of a breakdown in the formation of attachment between mother and child that stemmed from abnormality in the child follows.

Case example
I was asked to see a three-year old boy who had delayed speech development and signs of lack of trust for his parents. The history revealed that this had been a planned pregnancy. The parents were hoping that this first child would be a boy; the marital situation was stable; and both parents seemed to be well-adjusted adults who had had their needs met as children.

However, the history also revealed that this child had developed seizures on the third day of life. They were rather a rare type with a poor prognosis. The parents were told that about one-third of the children with such seizures die within their first year; one-third are retarded and the remainder are normal.

The child was put on medication. The mother was advised that the prognosis for this particular child could be somewhat anticipated by the effectiveness of the medication in controlling the seizures. The mother noted that if she touched him a lot, he tended to have a seizure. Being a 'good' mother, her reaction was obviously to minimise the amount she stimulated him. Although she met his basic physical needs, she did not hold him, rock him or play with him during the first three months of his life.

His seizures ceased when he was six months old, but the child's disability had undermined his mother's confidence in her abilities to mother him. She undoubtedly continued to be somewhat restrained with him for fear she would reactivate the seizures.

We set up a programme that encouraged bonding between this three-year-old child and his parents. Despite a successful programme, some delays in the child's speech development remained. It will never be certain whether these delays resulted from brain damage that was related to the seizures or from the lack of stimulation he experienced in his first few months of life.

Initiation of positive interactions: its importance in bonding

We have seen that the arousal-relaxation cycle is initiated by the child's needs and that successful completion of the cycle contributes to bonding between mother and child. However, the extent to which the mother initiates interactions with the infant also influences the attachment between them. The diagram below illustrates the cycle of positive parent-child interaction that is initiated by the parent.

The positive interaction cycle

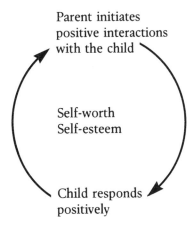

Parent initiates
positive interactions
with the child

Self-worth
Self-esteem

Child responds
positively

There is some evidence that these sorts of social interactions between mother and child contribute more to the bonds between them than do the kind of interactions that occur around meeting the child's physical needs. For example, Ainsworth[11] feels that social interactions, not routine care, are the most important part of mothering. The more social interactions an infant has with someone, the more strongly attached the infant becomes to that person.

In addition, it seems that a child who is well-attached to one person can more easily become attached to others. The fact that a child's strong attachment to one person eases the development of attachments to others is a critical one for foster care. It means that children can be helped to become attached to a foster parent and then to extend that attachment to natural family members, adoptive parents, or others.

3 Assessing attachment

As we try to assess attachment in various families we need to train ourselves to look at the children, the parents and the environment. When we look at the children, we need to observe their developmental functioning. We also need to look at the behaviour they exhibit, particularly in the home. As we observe in the home, we look at the interactions with adults in general and parents in particular and their interactions with siblings and peers.

Observing parents includes how they react to the child's overtures; the interactions that they initiate with the child; disciplinary techniques used in the home; and the parents' awareness of the children as separate individuals who have needs of their own rather than relating all of the behaviour to their needs. In addition, we need to know if the environment provides both adequate stimulation and safety measures appropriate to each child's age and stage of development.

The four Observation checklists that follow include some specific items to note in order to assess the child's attachment level. You may wish to add others in the blank spaces. In all cases, looking at the environment should be included with your observations of child and parents.

Observation checklist:
What to look for in assessing attachment

1: Birth to one year

Does the child . . .?
- appear alert?
- respond to humans?
- show interest in the human face?
- track with his/her eyes?
- vocalise frequently?
- exhibit expected motor development?
- enjoy close physical contact?
- exhibit discomfort?
- appear to be easily comforted?
- exhibit normal or excessive fussiness?
- appear outgoing or is passive and withdrawn?
- have good muscle tone?
  others:

Does the parent(s) . . . ?
- respond to the infant's vocalisations?
- change voice tone when talking to the infant or about the infant?
- show interest in face-to-face contact with the infant?
- exhibit interest in and encourage age-appropriate development?
- respond to the child's indications of discomfort?
- show the ability to comfort the child?
- enjoy close physical contact with the child?
- initiate positive interactions with the child?
- identify positive or negative qualities in the child that remind the parent of another family member?
  others:

Observation checklist:
What to look for in assessing attachment

2: One to five years

Does the child . . . ?
- explore the environment in a normal way?
- respond to parent(s)?
- keep occupied in a positive way?
- seem relaxed and happy?
- have the ability to express emotions?
- react to pain and pleasure?
- engage in age-appropriate activity?
- use speech appropiately?
- express frustration?
- respond to parental limit setting?
- exhibit observable fears?
- react positively to physical closeness?
- respond appropriately to separation from parent?
- respond appropriately to parent's return?
- exhibit body rigidity or relaxation?
others:

Does the parent(s) . . . ?
- use appropriate disciplinary measures?
- show interest in child's development?
- respond to child's overtures?
- encourage physical closeness with the child?
- comfort the child in a positive way?
- initiate positive interactions with the child?
- accept expressions of autonomy?
- see the child as 'taking after' someone? Is this positive or negative?
others:

Observation checklist:
What to look for in assessing attachment

3: Primary school children

Does the child . . . ?
- behave in a way which reflects a liking for him or herself?
- appear proud of accomplishments?
- share?
- perform well academically?
- always test limits?
- try new tasks?
- react realistically to making a mistake? Does the child show fear, anger, or acceptance?
- have the ability to express emotions?
- establish eye contact?
- exhibit confidence in own abilities or does he or she frequently say 'I don't know'?
- appear to be developing a conscience?
- move in a relaxed way or is there body rigidity?
- feel comfortable speaking to adults?
- smile easily?
- react to parent(s) being physically close?
- have positive interactions with siblings and/or peers?
- appear comfortable with his or her sexual identification?
  others:

Does the parent(s)?
- show interest in child's school performance?
- accept expression of negative feelings?
- respond to child's overtures?
- give support to child in terms of developing healthy peer relationships?
- handle problems between siblings equitably?
- initiate affectionate overtures?
- use appropriate disciplinary measures?
- assign age-appropriate responsibilities to the child?
  others:

4: Adolescents

Is the adolescent... ?
- aware of his or her strong points?
- aware of his or her weak points?
- comfortable with his or her sexuality?
- engaging in positive peer interactions?
- performing satisfactorily in school?
- exhibiting signs of conscience development?
- free from severe problems with the law?
- accepting and/or rejecting parents' value system?
- keeping occupied in appropriate ways?
- comfortable with reasonable limits or is he or she constantly involved in control issues?
- developing interests outside the home?
  others:

Does the parent(s)... ?
- set appropriate limits?
- encourage appropriate autonomy?
- trust the adolescent?
- show interest in and acceptance of adolescent's friends?
- display interest in adolescent's school performance?
- exhibit interest in adolescent's outside activities?
- have reasonable expectations of chores and/or responsibilities adolescents should assume?
- stand by the adolescent if he or she gets into trouble?
- show affection?
- think this child will 'turn out' okay?
  others:

Exercise 1:
Identifying signs of attachment

Instructions

Purpose
To help you learn what types of comments and/or observations in case records aid in assessing a child's attachment.

How to do it

1 Read Danny's case history on the next page.

2 Look at the *Observation checklist 2: What to look for in assessing attachment – one to five years* on page 31.

3 Make a worksheet like that on page 37 and list comments and/or observations from the case record that you feel will aid in assessing Danny's attachment to each of his parents. Consider his attachment to each parent individually. In assessing attachment it is important to determine the frequency and type of interactions initiated by each parent and child. In some cases there are many interactions but the child is responsible for initiating all or most of them.

4 After working on your list, look at page 38 where a sample analysis of the case appears and compare your worksheet with the sample.

Exercise 1
Identifying signs of attachment

Danny's case

Danny, age two and a half, the son of Carl and Tammy T., was born premature and with a cleft palate. He had a history of failure to thrive during infancy. He was hospitalised repeatedly for this condition and in the hospital he always gained weight. At six months he 'accidentally' broke his leg while his father was overseas. At present, Danny has been in foster care for several months. Reportedly, Carl abused Danny leading to a black eye and bruises on the buttocks. It was Tammy who called the social worker and reported the abuse, knowing her report would probably lead to admission to care.

The parents have not followed through with therapy as ordered by the court. They recently separated and are planning a divorce. The father, in particular, has asked for Danny's custody.

In her interview, Tammy reported that Danny is in care because 'my husband got mad and hit him'. She does not see Danny as a child who easily frustrates adults although she stated that she gets frustrated when he 'deliberately wets his pants'. She sees Danny as closely resembling his father. Tammy was unable to give any information about what Danny liked to play or how he kept himself occupied when he was at home. She stated that he is affectionate and 'easy going now'.

When the father was interviewed, he readily admitted spanking Danny excessively with a belt, but stated that the black eye occurred when Danny ran from him to avoid a spanking, slipped, and hit his eye on the corner of the bed. The discipline was taking place because Danny repeatedly got out of bed when put down for a nap. Tammy was napping at the time according to Carl and did not see what happened. Carl is able to give considerable information about Danny's likes and dislikes. He, too, sees Danny as resembling himself.

Tammy initially refused to visit with Danny in the nursery at the time of the evaluation because 'he is not interested in seeing me; he is more interested in the toys'. Carl played with Danny in the nursery while Tammy was being interviewed. Danny did not protest when his father left the nursery to go with the interviewer. The father reassured Danny that he would be back shortly and made a point of leaving his coat in the nursery as he told Danny that he would be back.

When we tried to test Danny, he protested about the separation and asked his father to go with him. On the way to the office, Danny imitated his father's walk with his thumbs in pocket. He crawled up into his father's lap in the office, took off his dad's glasses and put them on. His dad's comment as he took his glasses back was 'Oh, you remember our little game'. Carl was interested and pleased with Danny's performance levels during the testing. Although we had some difficulty understanding Danny's speech, Carl did not.

When Tammy came in mid-way during the testing, Danny interrupted his task and ran to her with arms up-raised. She picked him up, and her affect was appropriate. When his parents left, Danny indicated that he did not want them to. He clung to his mother and clearly said 'I want to go with you'. He cried momentarily and tried to follow when they left, but he was easily distracted following their departure.

Exercise 1:
Identifying signs of attachment

Worksheet

Danny and mother	*Danny and father*
Mother initiates – child responds	Father initiates – child responds
1	1
2	2
3	3
4	4
5	5
6	6
Child initiates – mother responds	Child initiates – father responds
1	1
2	2
3	3
4	4
5	5
6	6

Exercise 1:
Identifying signs of attachment

Worksheet

Danny and mother	*Danny and father*
Mother initiates – child responds	Father initiates – child responds
1 Mother picked up Danny and showed affection	1 Father knows Danny's likes and dislikes
2	2 Carl played with Danny in the nursery
3	3 Carl left coat in nursery so Danny knew he'd come back
4	4 Carl understood Danny's speech
5	5
6	6
Child initiates – mother responds	Child initiates – father responds
1 Danny runs to mother	1 Danny protested about separation from father
2 Danny did not want his mother to leave	2 Danny imitated father's walk
3	3 Danny crawled on his father's lap
4	4
5	5
6	6

4 Separation

Imagine yourself in a situation like this . . .
You are at home at night. You have put your three children to bed and have just gone to bed yourself. Your spouse is out for the evening and won't be home until later. Everything is quiet, and you are settling down to sleep. . .

Suddenly there is a knock on the door, quickly followed by heavy footsteps. Someone in uniform enters your bedroom and announces, 'You're coming with me'. He takes you and your children outside.

You all get into a car. You drive into a strange neighbourhood, far from your home. The car stops in front of a house. You are left in the car as one of the children is taken to the door of the house. The man in uniform knocks; someone answers the door; and your child is handed over to this person. The uniformed man returns to the car.

You drive further. The man takes your second child and leaves him at another strange house.

He drives further. He stops. You and your third child are taken to the door of a house. He knocks and when a person answers the uniformed man says, 'Here they are'. You are handed over to the person in this house and left there.

– How did you feel when the person came into the house?
– How did you feel when you left your neighbourhood?
– How did you feel as you were separated from your children?
– How did you feel as you were handed over to a stranger?
– What would you want to do?

A child coming into foster care may experience similar feelings.

Introduction
Most children who enter care, or move from one foster home to another, or move into an adoptive home experience separation from the person or persons to whom they are attached. One of the serious challenges in child care is helping children handle these traumatic separations.

In this section we first discuss children's reactions to separation and the things that affect those reactions. We then suggest ways that both workers and foster parents can help children deal with the separations that occur when they move from one family to another.

Reactions to separation

Children differ in the way they respond to being separated from their parents. This response varies from severe depression in children who are well-attached to their parents and then abruptly separated from them to almost no reaction in children who have been emotionally neglected and have virtually no attachment to their parents. The reactions of most children who come into care fall between these two extremes.

The child's reaction to separation from the parent can provide the worker with valuable information about the attachment between them. There are several important influences on the child's reaction to separation. These include:

- the nature of the child's attachment to the primary caretakers;
- the nature of the primary caretaker's bonding to the child;
- the experiences the child has had with separation in the past;
- the child's perceptions of the reasons for the separation;
- does the child view the separation as his or her fault? Children whose parents have been hostile or irritable and have threatened the child with separation seem to be particularly affected by it.
- the circumstances of the move itself; and whether the child has been prepared for the move or not, the attitudes of the people around him or her and the ability to express feelings and have them accepted all influence the child's reaction to separation.
- the environment from which the child is being moved;
- despite shortcomings that others may see in the child's environment, from the child's point of view the known is nearly always better than the unknown. However, if a child is actually fearful of his or her living environment, this may lessen the reaction to a separation.

All these factors influence a child's reaction to separation. In helping a child handle a separation, it is useful to know what a 'normal' reaction to separation is.

Bowlby[12] describes three stages that well-attached children go through when they are separated from the person to whom they are attached. These stages are most evident in the young child. They are:

1 the child protests vigorously and makes attempts to recover the mother, such as going to the door and trying to find her;
2 the child despairs of recovering the mother, but continues to be watchful. He or she appears to be preoccupied constantly and depressed. When a car drives up or there is a noise at the door, he or she becomes alert, hoping that the mother is returning; and
3 the child becomes emotionally detached and appears to lose interest in the mother.

What follows is a case example of a child who was well-attached and then separated.

Case example: John

At the time we saw John, he was four and had been in foster care for about three months. During his first six weeks in care, he was placed in an emergency foster home. During his stay in this home John was fussy and cried constantly.

In his second foster placement he was not so much fussy as withdrawn. He played for hours by himself, talking to himself in baby voices and making peculiar sounds. He had good eye contact with us when we examined him, but he seemed indiscriminately affectionate; he seemed to respond equally warmly to all adults. He was at his age level on developmental tests and was in good contact with reality.

The history revealed that John had lost his mother when he was 18 months old. His father became his primary caretaker. While he was moving and getting settled, he left John with an aunt. John had had almost no contact with the aunt before he was left there.

With the aunt he became very fussy. He regressed in toileting and smeared faeces. He alternated between being very depressed and having temper tantrums. The aunt had John placed in foster care.

When John was in the second foster placement, his father came for his first visit with the child. John's face 'lit up' when he first saw his father. He then looked apprehensive and acted ambivalent about getting close to his father. His father initiated many positive interactions with John. Eventually, John was able to say 'Don't ever leave me again, Daddy'.

John's history illustrates the stages that Bowlby describes as common in well-attached children who are separated. Because a history of strong attachment is rare in child care or because workers fail to recognise this sort of behaviour for what it is, there is a danger that children who have this kind of reaction may be classified as 'severely disturbed'.

It is not unusual for a child to act aggressively during separations from the parents and be very ambivalent toward them when visiting them or returning home. The child does not plan to act in this way but does so in response to unconscious stimuli. The function of this behaviour is to assist in the reunion process and to discourage the parents from leaving him or her again. Hence, this behaviour promotes rather than discourages bonding.

When this kind of behaviour occurs during visits between parents and child, all involved may tend to say that the visits are upsetting the child and should be stopped. Similarly, if this kind of behaviour occurs when the child is returned home to the parents, workers sometimes misinterpret the behaviour and assume the parents are doing something wrong. The parents may feel that way too. Actually, the child's negative behaviour stems from a healthy need. When a child returns home from foster care, workers need to make special efforts to support the parents and help them handle the child's anger over the past separation.

Reactions to threatened separation

Social workers also need to understand the relationship between fear and attachment. The primary function of attachment behaviour in the animal kingdom is protection from the aggression of predators. In human families, too, attachment behaviour is heightened when a family member is threatened. The function of both fear and attachment is protection. Sometimes the social worker who is considering removing a child from a family embodies a threat.

In such a situation, the child may cling to the parent and exhibit hostility or fear of the worker. This reaction is characterised by withdrawal from the feared object and movement towards a trusted person.

Sometimes there is conflict between the two aspects of this reaction. The diagrams opposite illustrate such a dilemma. Both diagrams portray a child, a dog and a parent. In both cases the child wants to get away from the dog and get close to the parents.

In figure 1 the child can get away from the dog and also get close to the parent. In figure 2, however, the child faces a dilemma. In moving from the feared object the child also moves further from the object to whom

Figure 1

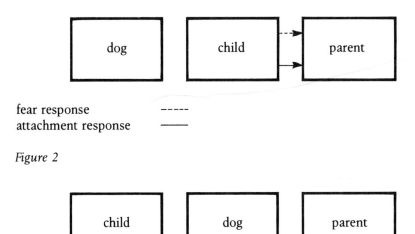

fear response   - - - - -
attachment response   ———

Figure 2

he or she is attached. Most attached children, up to an age where they can think well conceptually, will choose moving closer to the attachment object over withdrawing from the feared object.

Thus we can understand why an abused child may cling to an abusive parent when the social worker enters the home. The child may both fear and be attached to that parent. At the same time, the child fears and has no attachment to the social worker. The child chooses the parent.

The most frightening thing for a child is to be afraid and to be separated from the attachment object simultaneously. This is why moves are so frightening. All people's fears are more easily heightened when they are away from those to whom they are attached.

Making moves easier for a child: the worker's role
Most children's immediate reaction to an abrupt separation from their parents or to abandonment by them is intense anxiety. If the worker makes a comment like 'Most kids are really scared when they move into a new home', it frequently opens the door for the children to talk about their feelings.

This means that the social worker must deal with what happens when the door opens. It is important that workers be honest with children when they are moving from one home to another. They cannot gloss over the situation by telling the child that everything is going to be 'fine'. It also means that the worker may have to admit not knowing the answers to questions that the child asks.

If the child wants to know how long he or she will be in care and the placement is an emergency one, the worker may have to say that it will depend upon a court hearing the next day, or upon when the parents can be located, or whatever the truth is in each case. The child also needs to be assured that there will be frequent contact with the social worker early in the placement and that he or she will be informed about the plans made for their future.

The child then needs, first, permission to express feelings and second, acceptance of the feelings, no matter what they are. Social workers must avoid the tendency to minimise the child's feelings. Simply saying 'Don't be sad' or 'It's not your fault' is not helpful. The child's pain does not go away because the surrounding adults ignore it or are uncomfortable with it.

At the time of a move the child has very intense feelings, and is in a state of high arousal. It is a time when someone who helps the child cope with these feelings can build trust between them. This situation can be used to help build an attachment between the child and the adults who can accept these feelings. This makes use of the arousal-relaxation cycle described in Section 2.

The positive use of a painful and frightening situation for the child can occur only if the adults involved take on the job of helping the child deal with his or her feelings. Many children who come into care have already learned that it is not safe to let adults know how they feel, and there is a danger that this learning will be reinforced as the child moves into foster care. The child who doesn't express strong feelings may be easier to deal with in the short run but in the long run is likely to fare poorly. Expression of feelings can have therapeutic consequences for the child and lead to psychological growth; lack of such expression can lead to stagnation.

Most children who come into care are removed from their homes in an emergency situation . Usually the child has little advance warning and is not prepared to be separated from the family. After experiencing such a move, the child is likely to be more prone to suffering underlying anxiety about the unknowns in the future.

It is difficult to overcome the negative effects of this kind of traumatic initial separation. However, it is possible to use further moves or separations to teach the child that all moves do not lead to the same feelings or to the same outcome. Thus, the child should be prepared for a move whenever possible. Once the child is in care there are only very rare events, such as the death or emergency hospitalisation of a foster family member or abuse in the foster home, that justify moving a child without preparation for that move.

Making moves easier for the child: the foster family's role

Foster parents should play an important role in helping to prepare a child to move on leaving their home and in helping a child handle a move on entering their home. Traditionally, foster parents have not been helped or supported in this process which is painful for them as well as for the child. We will delineate briefly a few important things foster parents can do to help a child move. A more complete discussion of ways to minimise the trauma of the various moves associated with foster care is in Workbook 3, *Helping children when they must move.*

When the child leaves the foster home

We have said that when children move they experience very intense feelings. These feelings may range from fear, anger, uncertainty, helplessness, or resignation to relief. Foster parents can help a child who leaves their family to express these feelings. Some foster parents need a method to help them do this. One technique that has worked has been for the social worker to show the child a list of feelings and help him or her to identify their particular feelings. The social worker can then share this information with the foster parents.

Foster parents can also think about their own feelings about the move because often their own feelings are similar to the child's. It is particularly important at the time of the move for the child to know that the foster family cared about him or her. Letting the child know this is not to place a burden on the child, but rather to provide a lesson that relationships are important.

When children leave a home they also need to understand why they are moving. They need to be talked to straight about that. This helps make it unnecessary for them to do a lot of testing in the new family that they would otherwise do.

When a child enters the home

When a child moves into a new foster family, that family can use the fact that the child is in great discomfort to build an attachment between themselves and the child. If they help the child to express feelings, they alleviate some of the discomfort experienced by the child and increase his or her attachment to them.

Children need permission to miss their former family. If not given this kind of permission, some children may misbehave so they will be spanked so that they can cry for the family they have left. It helps, too, if children know that their former family wishes that they do well in their new home and hear that they are pleased when they do.

When a child is removed from the birth family, the most appropriate thing the foster family can do is to comfort the child physically, talk little, and accept the feelings from loss to anger that the child may have.

Fears, anxieties, nightmares, or night terrors are very common for children who are separated from their parents. Some children will withdraw more and will not want to talk. In these cases, foster parents can be physically close without insisting on talking. When a child is angry, foster parents can accept the anger and at the same time teach him or her appropriate ways of expressing it. Some children initially overeat when they are placed as though they were trying to fill a void in their lives. Others are too depressed or anxious to eat at all.

Foster parent observations during the first few weeks after placement are most helpful, not only in assessing the child's attachment to parents, but also in assessing the child's interpretation of the placement process and the reasons for placement. Often, when a child comes into care on an emergency basis, the parents have been abruptly lost. The feelings are similar to those that would occur had they been in a terrible accident and he or she does not know what will happen next.

Visits soon after placement are necessary to reassure the child that the parents are still alive and do still care about him or her. This is different from the traditional stance that the child needs an 'adjustment period'. Children in placement need pictures of both parents and siblings.

These visits are apt to tap further into both the child's and parents' strong feelings about separation. It is often much easier for the social workers and for the foster parents when there are fewer contacts between parent and child or if the child does not react to the visits that occur. However, once again, the child cannot deal with these feelings if they cannot be expressed. The long-term prognosis is worse for children who have few contacts with their parents and minimal reaction to these contacts.

Visits do often make things difficult for foster parents and they may need help in dealing with them. Ner Littner[13] has written an excellent article on this topic that should be shared with all foster parents. 'Only people cry', a story by Alice Winter[14], tells of a child's reactions to multiple moves from the child's perspective and is also a helpful article for foster parents to read.

When a child stays in a foster home

While a child is in a foster family, it is very helpful if the family puts together or contributes to a book about that child. This book can include pictures of important events in the child's life in that family and descriptions of how he or she felt during those events. Examples of things that should be included in such a book are:
– when the child had particular childhood diseases;
– what things the child was afraid of;
– what toys the child liked;
– what the child did on birthdays and at Christmas;
– what trips the child took with the foster family;
– who important members of the foster family's extended family were;
– what cute things the child did;
– what the child's nicknames were;
– what the child did when happy or excited.

A basic requirement is that the child have a picture of the foster family, their house and their pets. If photographs like this are kept in the case file of the family, they can be copied for each child as necessary. The book will be something the child can take on a future move, whether back to the biological family, to another foster home, or into adoption. It can ease such a transition by preserving the child's continuity with his or her past.

Exercise 2
Feelings at the time of moves

Directions:
Read the list below of feelings that children may experience at the time of moves. Then, in the left-hand column, list several children in your caseload, and on the right, identify the feelings that they may have had about moving. You will probably identify several feelings about each child.

Possible feelings:
Anxiety, fear, happiness, anger, sadness, loss, rejection, excitement, jealousy, guilt, resignation, helplessness, relief. You may think of other feelings.

Child	*Feelings*
1	
2	
3	
4	

---

5 Identifying and overcoming attachment problems

Case example: Richard

Richard, a particularly sensitive and perceptive nine-year-old, had spent much of his life in foster care. He was having problems with lying, stealing, getting his work done at school, and getting along with his peers.

During our first interview he asked, off-handedly, 'By the way, do you know what happens to kids who don't get enough loving when they are little?'

I responded, "Well, I think I know. But I'd like to hear what you think.'

'If kids don't get enough loving when they are three or four or five they become uncontrollable later,' he replied. 'Some foster kids who are eight, nine, and ten can't be controlled by their foster parents.'

I asked, 'What do you think can be done about that?'

'I don't know,' he said, 'but I know what you think. You think if they get extra loving later on it will make up for it.'

Introduction

Many children in foster care do not have normal, healthy attachments to their foster parents. The children's attachment problems frequently originate in their birth families. However, the instability of foster home placements and the series of moves that many foster children experience give them further problems in developing trust in others and a sense of age-appropriate autonomy.

The signs and symptoms of attachment problems that one may see in particular foster children are a result of the way their parents behaved towards them, their environment, and their own particular psychological traits. In general, children who have been severely neglected are the most apt to suffer from a true lack of attachment. Children who have experienced less severe neglect, intermittent physical abuse, or emotional abuse are more likely to exhibit signs of an imbalance in their needs for dependency and their needs for autonomy.

In this section, we outline specific kinds of problems that are frequently exhibited by children who have experienced faulty attachments to their parents. These problems are grouped into three categories: cognitive problems; psychological and behavioural problems; and delays in development. The checklist that follows outlines some of the specific problems that may be seen in each of these areas.

After discussing these problems, we consider ways to encourage attachment in children who are experiencing them. We believe the ability to help build an attachment between a child and the primary caretaker is critical.

Given the potential long-term effects that lack of attachment can have on a child, it is crucial that foster care responds in two ways. First, it should encourage attachment between the child and the present primary caretaker, whoever that may be. Even if it is planned to return a child in foster care to the biological family or to move him or her into an adoptive home, the development of an attachment to the foster parents should be encouraged.

The immediate need is for the child to learn trust. Further delay only makes this more difficult. A child who has experienced one healthy attachment will find it easier either to transfer this attachment to someone else or to form additional attachments.

Second, it is necessary to make timely permanent plans for children in care. This will limit the number of times children must move and experience the loss of the person to whom they are attached.

Effects of lack of attachment

Lack of attachment and its relationship to psychological and behavioural problems
Bowlby[15] has noted that unattached children have difficulties relating normally with others. For example, foster and adoptive parents of these children may feel that the children do not have a conscience, are manipulative, or are not genuine in their expression of affection. These parents may say 'I give and I give to this child, and it doesn't seem to matter'.

How do these kinds of symptoms relate to lack of attachment? Remember that a child's first relationship with the primary caretaker sets the stage for future relationships. In this first relationship the child learns what can and cannot be expected from others. Children who do not experience a healthy give and take in this relationship may not be able to experience it in others.

It is most difficult for the unattached child to grow socially. They have great difficulty learning to build and maintain relationships of any sort. They haven't learnt to care for others. Having received little love they have trouble giving it. They continue in their 'babyish' ways, self-centred and acting impulsively. They have difficulty incorporating rules or laws. Their first concern is 'What's in it for me?'

Because the children do not trust others, many of the kinds of behaviour seen in such children are aimed at keeping people at a distance. When one keeps this in mind, it is possible to see similarities in symptoms that would otherwise seem very different. Some of the behaviour patterns children exhibit to keep people at a distance are described overleaf.

Poor eye contact
In Section 2 on the 'Development of attachment between parent and child' we discussed the importance of eye contact to bonding between parent and child. It is not surprising that many children in foster care make little eye contact with others. Many are truly surprised that anyone wants to look at them.

In most abusive families, there is a struggle for control in the family. The parents in these disturbed families are very threatened when the children attempt to gain any control. If a child looks a parent in the eye, the disturbed parent may see that action as a challenge. Abused children tend to be very aware of what is going on around them. However, they tend to check things out by means of sidelong glances rather than direct eye contact.

Withdrawal
Many children with attachment problems withdraw from interactions with others. This withdrawal takes different forms. Some children withdraw physically. Others seem to put up a shield around them; they may be physically near but not close emotionally.

A third type of withdrawal resembles fear. As the parent reaches out to the child, the response is to cringe. If the parent hugs the child, the response is to pull away or tighten up. All children who withdraw from physical closeness this way have not been abused. Some may simply have learned about the effect their behaviour has on adults. Adults do

51

Observation checklist:
Long-range effects of lack of normal attachment

Psychological or behavioural problems

Conscience development
- May not show normal anxiety following aggressive or cruel behaviour.
- May not show guilt on breaking laws or rules.
- May project blame on others.

Impulse control
- Exhibits poor control; depends upon others to provide external controls on behaviour.
- Exhibits lack of foresight.
- Has a poor attention span.

Self-esteem
- Is unable to get satisfaction from tasks well done.
- Sees self as undeserving.
- Sees self as incapable of change.
- Has difficulty having fun.

Interpersonal interactions
- Lacks trust in others.
- Demands affection but lacks depth in relationships.
- Exhibits hostile dependency.
- Needs to be in control of all situations.
- Has impaired social maturity.

Emotions
- Has trouble recognising own feelings.
- Has difficulty expressing feelings appropriately; especially anger, sadness and frustration.
- Has difficulty recognising feelings in others.

Cognitive problems

- Has trouble with basic cause and effect.
- Experiences problems with logical thinking.
- Appears to have confused thought processes.
- Has difficulty thinking ahead.
- May have an impaired sense of time.
- Has difficulties with abstract thinking.

Developmental problems

- May have difficulty with auditory processing.
- May have difficulty expressing self well verbally.
- May have gross motor problems.
- May experience delays in fine-motor adaptive skills.
- May experience delays in personal-social development.
- May have inconsistent levels of skills in all of the above areas.

not want to scare children. Thus, eventually the child learns that cringing, fearful behaviour works to keep adults at a distance.

Chronic anxiety

When children are confident that a parent will be available when needed, they are less prone to anxiety that is intense or chronic. The most frightening situation for the children is one in which they need their parent and that parent is not available. This kind of anxiety is greater in children who have been moved without preparation or who have had other major changes in their lives occur abruptly. Children who experience chronic anxiety are also often very possessive and clinging.

Aggressive behaviour

Some keep adults at a distance by behaving aggressively. Adults who are hit, kicked, scratched or bitten every time they approach a child are likely to keep their distance. If children have tantrums whenever a demand is placed on them, many parents find it easier to stop making demands. Hyperactive behaviour also keeps adults away. It is difficult to get close to a child who is always on the move and easily distractable.

Case example: Eric

Eric is five years old. He has been in foster care for two years. During that time he has been in three different foster homes because he is 'uncontrollable'. Prior to entering foster care he had a history of extreme neglect and moderate abuse.

In his current foster home Eric has tantrums when he is asked either to do something or to stop doing something. When he has a tantrum he kicks at the walls, furniture, or people. One time he threw a toy car at the television set and broke the screen. Another time he made a big hole in his bedroom door. During these outbursts he screams, sometimes for an hour or more. Occasionally he scratches his face or hits himself on the head as well.

Indiscriminate affection

Although a normal child may be very talkative and sociable with strangers, the talk is rarely accompanied by physical overtures. On the other hand the child who is indiscriminately physically affectionate may go up, hug a virtual stranger, and say 'I love you'. He, or more commonly, she, will immediately climb up on the lap of the visitors to their home and start to hug and kiss them. These interactions frequently have a seductive quality about them.

If the child behaves this way towards many adults – or virtually all adults – the child is really saying 'No one is more important to me than others'. Since attachment means that a few people are more important than others, indiscriminate affection is a sign of attachment problems. It is difficult for foster or adoptive parents to feel close to a child who is acting close to everyone else. In addition, children who are willing to go with strangers pose real supervision problems for their parents.

Over-competency
Some children with attachment problems seem to be over-competent. They do not appear to need parents. They frequently insist on doing everything themselves. These are the pre-schoolers who never seem to need help with dressing or undressing. Some little girls who are excessively competent are at age five getting up, making their own beds, and tidying up their rooms without being asked. This may sound like desirable behaviour, but as anyone who has had a child will recognise, it is certainly unusual behaviour. When such children do need help they may grant the adult permission to help them, as in 'You may tie my shoes for me'.

Case example: Ronald
When we saw Ronald, he was four and a half years old and living with his father and step-mother. The history revealed that his parents divorced when he was one and a half years old. He lived with his mother for about a year after that until she decided she could no longer care for him financially. She and Ronald travelled several thousand miles by plane to the town where Ronald's father lived. Ronald was handed over to his father in a park.

Ronald didn't trust his step-mother, and he showed it in several ways. However, the behaviour she complained of most was his extreme over-competency. He refused to let her take care of him. For example, if she tried to help him dress, he would immediately thereafter totally undress himself and start again. He indicated that he had no need for her. This over-competency was evident in all aspects of his daily living situation.

Lack of self-awareness
Some abused children seem very aware of their environment but nearly unaware of their own bodies. They may overeat until their stomachs are distended, and they are at the point of vomiting. They may not react to pain and seem unaware of extremes of temperature. Many of these children are bedwetters. It is as if they never learned to pay attention to the signals from their own bodies or to what alleviates their own discomfort.

Such behaviour may develop in children whose parents are unresponsive to them in infancy. Some abusive parents take care of the child when they feel like it, rather than when the child needs it. Thus, the child does not learn to associate certain kinds of discomfort with certain kinds of relief.

Case example: John

When we first saw John he was six years old and had recently been adopted. He had a history of abuse and neglect and had lived with several families prior to his adoption. He had problems with overeating and with wetting both at night and during the day.

During one post-placement visit we made to the adoptive family, John complained of a stomach ache. He asked his mother if she thought he was hungry. She doubted that he was and suggested that maybe he needed to go to the bathroom. He said 'No', that he didn't think that was the problem.

After John moaned and groaned for several more minutes, his mother said, 'John, I want you to go upstairs to the bathroom. If that's not it, O.K., but I want you to try.' John went upstairs and returned with an obvious expression of relief on his face. This six-year-old child had not learned to distinguish between the empty feeling that accompanies hunger for food and the feeling of a full bladder.

Control battles
Both the lack of trust for others that poorly attached children have and the family power struggles that many abused children have witnessed contribute to problems such children have with control issues. Such children have trouble staying within clearly defined limits of behaviour. They appear to be constantly testing. Reasonable requests from parents lead to major confrontations.

Though outwardly these children seem to need to be in control of all situations, they actually feel that they have little control over their lives. This may come from being abused unpredictably, from being moved abruptly, or from experiencing other sudden major life changes.

The two or 20 syndrome

There are certain poorly attached children that appear 'too old for their ages' part of the time and immature at other times. They seem to receive little gratification from acting their chronological age.

Such children try to engage in activities usually preferred by older children. When they play with children their own age, they want to be in charge. They want few restrictions placed on their behaviour. In some ways, they act like an independent, twenty-year-old.

However, if someone sets limits on their behaviour or if they are frustrated, they revert to temper tantrums typical of two-year-olds. Teachers usually describe these children as immature because in a structured school situation their 'babyish' resistance to controls is more evident.

Delayed conscience development

Children with delayed conscience development tend to lie and steal. They may lie about very unimportant things even when there would be no negative consequences for telling the truth. It may also be difficult to tell when such children are lying.

The stealing they do may take the form of 'finding' things frequently at school, of taking money or other things from their family, or of stealing from stores. They often do not show signs of anxiety when they are caught. In fact, they may continue to deny their actions in the face of evidence of their misbehaviour.

Lack of attachment and its relationship to cognitive and developmental problems

Some of the symptoms exhibited by children who have had poor attachments are the same symptoms that are exhibited by children with what is called 'attention deficit disorder'. Children with attention deficit disorder may be hyperactive, easily distractable, impulsive, subject to extremes of emotions and have learning disabilities. They may, in other words, be children who seem to have a very short attention span, or who seem to 'always act before they think'.

They may also overreact to what is going on around them. For example, if a child gently brushes by a hyperactive child, the hyperactive child may perceive this as an open invitation to fight. Such children may have a very low tolerance for frustration. They may have difficulty moving from one task to another if they view the first task as incomplete.

A higher proportion of the children who come into care have attention deficit disorder than one would expect based on the proportion of children who have this problem in the population as a whole. One can speculate about whether these children were born with certain organic problems that made it difficult for them to form attachments, or whether the lack of attachment between the child and the parent precipitated certain organic problems.

There is increasing evidence of a strong genetic component in attention deficit disorder. Interestingly, it is possible that many of the parents of children in care experience attention deficit disorder themselves.

What kinds of adults do children with attention deficit disorder become? There have been some recent studies that indicate a high percentage of these individuals continue to have difficulties in adult life although hyperactivity *per se* usually diminishes during adolescent years. Many such individuals continue to be rigid in their thinking and expectations. They may remain emotionally unstable and unable to tolerate frustration. In addition, they may have a variety of other problems as a result of growing up in a school system that was not equipped to meet their needs. The literature affirms that many juvenile delinquents have a history of school problems and of learning disabilities.

Many of the parents of the children who come into care have problems like those outlined above. Thus, if we speculate that there is a higher incidence of attention deficit disorder among the parents of these children than in the population as a whole, from a genetic viewpoint, we would expect to see a higher incidence of it in children of this population.

However, in addition to genetic determinants of these problems, they seem to be affected by parent-child attachments as well. This should not be unexpected if we consider several well-known facts. Prior to birth the foetus possesses its full complement of neurons. If these neurons are damaged there will be virtually no regeneration. Thus, before the infant is born, his or her maximum intellectual potential is set. However, during the latter months of pregnancy and during infancy and early childhood, the task at hand is to get the neurons organised into patterns of responsiveness.

According to Gesell[16] during the first year of life the infant must learn how to learn. People learn new things throughout their lives, but they learn them in an established way. As their children mature, their perceptions become more discerning and they notice things not previously noticed. They incorporate these perceptions into their basic fund of knowledge.

It is through their relationship with their mother in the first year of life that children learn how to learn. The reciprocity in this relationship helps children sort out their perceptions of the world and teaches them what these perceptions mean. At birth, an infant does not recognise objects in the immediate environment or specific internal states of being. The infant does not know, for example, that a certain state of discomfort that we call 'hunger' is relieved by the intake of food. However, if the mother consistently identifies that discomfort with an empty stomach, the child learns to perceive that feeling as hunger for food. It is through this relationship with the primary caretaker that the child first learns cause and effect and thus learns how to learn.

Thus we could speculate that attention deficit disorder has two basic causes: it may occur for genetically determined structural or biochemical reasons. This kind of problem would not be affected by the adequacy and appropriateness of the mothering the child receives. It may occur in the child who has not experienced the mothering necessary to get a reasonably organised nervous system.

Practically speaking, by the time the child is old enough so that the nature of his or her perceptual problems can be identified, determining their underlying cause does not matter much. The important thing then is helping the child compensate for any perceptual deficits and providing stimulation to encourage further growth.

Children with attention deficit disorder frequently fail to perceive their surroundings accurately. Their misperceptions form a base from which they learn and incorporate new experiences. To help such children those around them must carefully observe them and identify the misperceptions and improve the way each child learns.

Children with attention deficit disorder find it more difficult than other children to handle changes in their environment and separation from those to whom they are attached. They are more prone to anxiety than other children. Their behaviour makes it difficult for their parents or foster parents to deal with them in a way that encourages bonding. This kind of response from the parents makes the child even more anxious, and what appears to be a never-ending cycle is created.

Identifying signs of lack of attachment

Instructions

Purpose:
To help you learn to identify signs of lack of attachment or faulty
attachment.

How to do it:

1 Read Roberta's case history below.

2 List comments and/or observations from the case record that you
feel indicate Roberta's lack of attachment or faulty attachment.

3 After working on your list, look at page 62 where a sample analysis
of the case appears and compare your list with the sample.

Roberta's case

*Roberta, who is now eight and a half years old, was abandoned by her
birth mother when she was one year old. At that time, she was
functioning at a six to eight-month-old developmental level. During the
following year in foster care she closed most of the gaps between her
chronological age and her developmental age. She was placed for
adoption at age two.*

*The adoption disrupted a year and a half ago because 'Roberta never
really got close' to her adopted parents. She has lived in three foster
homes since then. Her pattern in foster care has been to be superficially
compliant but after several months the foster parents describe her as
being 'sneaky' and 'there is just something about her'.*

*In her present foster home the history reveals that she sneaks food
and hides it in her room. This behaviour tends to make her foster
mother very angry. She occasionally sleepwalks and cries out in her
sleep. She is enuretic several times a week. She loves to help her foster
mother in the kitchen but 'forgets' her routine chores such as tidying up
her room and stripping her bed when it is wet.*

*Roberta has difficulty getting on with her foster siblings. She takes
the teen-aged daughter's make-up and then denies taking it. When she
plays games with the other pre-adolescents, she always disrupts the
game if she sees that she is not going to win. Roberta becomes totally*

enraged by events that lead to irritation or annoyance in most children.

At school she does well in reading, but hates maths. She does complete her papers but they are frequently so messy that they are unreadable. She is frequently out of her seat without permission, she talks out in class and is always either the first or the last in line.

The teacher reports that Roberta has difficulty getting along with peers. She has just started in the third form but she prefers to play with the first formers at recess. In the foster home, too, she plays best with a younger foster sibling whom she tries to boss.

The teacher comments that Roberta 'just seems to need more love'. Roberta frequently tells her how the foster parents prefer the other children to her. In fact the teacher bought her a pair of sandals after Roberta had complained that everyone else had got new sandals except her. Roberta clings to her teacher and wants to give her hugs and kisses every morning when she comes to school. Roberta behaves in a similar fashion with her social worker when she comes to the home.

When introduced to a female psychologist Roberta's first comment was 'Oh, I hope you are my new social worker: I just love to get new social workers'. When asked how she felt about mothers, her comment was 'Well, I don't like mothers too well. They always know what you are doing.'

Exercise 3:
Identifying signs of lack of attachment

Sample response

1 'Roberta never really got close' (adoptive parents)

2 'Sneaky' - 'something about her' (foster parents)

3 Night terrors

4 Enuretic (lack of self-awareness?)

5 Steals, doesn't do chores, lies (conscience development)

6 Over-reacts (e.g. when losing games)

7 Can't get on with kids her own age

8 Bossy with younger kids (over-competent?)

9 'Indiscriminate affection' (e.g. teachers, social workers)

10 Not in touch with feelings ('I just love to get new social workers')

11 Messy papers (fine motor developmental delay or lack of self esteem or doesn't want to mind?)

12

Promoting attachment in older children

When children have not experienced healthy attachments and are beyond infancy, how can someone help make up for it? We address this question briefly in the text and charts that follow.

In Section 2 on the 'Development of attachment between parent and child' we described two cycles related to bonding in infants. One of these cycles was called the 'arousal-relaxation cycle' and the other 'patterns of interactions between parent and child that result in bonding'. They are diagrammed below. These cycles can be adapted to older children as well.

The arousal-relaxation cycle

The cycle of positive interactions

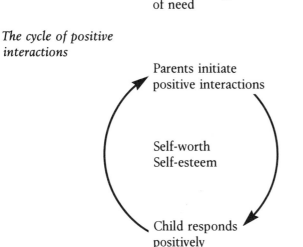

In analysing interactions that occur between an older child and a parent in terms of the arousal-relaxation cycle, it is important to be aware of several things. First, the child's needs that initiate the cycle may be either physical or psychological. The important thing is that these needs create intense feelings or states of high arousal in the child. The intense feelings may be negative, such as anxiety, fear, anger, rage or sadness, or positive, such as joy or excitement. The parent's role with these children might be not so much to satisfy the needs themselves but just to be with the children and encourage the expression of feelings until the body tension that accompanies intense feelings relaxes. At this time of relaxation children are most open to bonding.

Children in care are generally highly aroused at the time of moves. Social workers or new parents who allow and encourage children to express feelings are in reality encouraging bonding as well.

The positive interactions cycle works the same way for children who are beyond infancy as it does in infancy. Parents initiate positive things with the child, the child responds positively, and both parties are likely to continue. It is easiest for parents to begin initiating positive interactions with a child when he or she first moves in. This makes it less likely that parent and child will have to work to correct a cycle of negative interactions begetting negative interactions.

The other kind of behaviour that families can get involved in to promote attachment is 'claiming behaviour'. Claiming behaviour was discussed in Section 2 as well.

Social workers need to think of as many ways as possible to help families use these cycles to build attachment with children. The checklist that follows suggests some ways for families to get these positive patterns going.

Remember, both shared laughter and shared tears are powerful bonding tools.

Checklist:
Ways to encourage attachment

Responding to the arousal/relaxation cycle

- Using the child's tantrums to encourage attachment.
- Responding to the child when he or she is physically ill.
- Accompanying the child to doctor and dentist appointments.
- Helping the child express and cope with feelings of anger and frustration.
- Sharing the child's extreme excitement over achievements.
- Helping the child cope with feelings about moving.
- Helping the child cope with ambivalent feelings about the birth family.
- Helping the child learn more about his or her past.
- Responding to a child who is hurt or injured.
- Educating the child about sexual issues.
  others:

Initiating positive interactions

- Making affectionate overtures: hugs, kisses, physical closeness.
- Reading to the child.
- Sharing the child's life story book.
- Playing games.
- Going shopping together for clothes/toys for child.
- Going on special outings: circus, plays or the like.
- Supporting the child's outside activities by providing transport or being a group leader.
- Helping the child with homework when he or she needs it.
- Teaching the child to cook or bake.
- Saying 'I love you'.
- Teaching the child about extended family members through pictures and talk.
- Helping the child understand the family 'jokes' or sayings.
- Teaching the child to participate in family activities such as bowling, camping, or ski-ing.
- Helping the child meet expectations of the other parent.
  others:

Checklist:
Ways to encourage attachment

Claiming behaviour

- Encouraging the child to practise calling parents 'mum' and 'dad'.
- Adding a *middle* name to incorporate a name of family significance.
- Hanging pictures of child on wall.
- Involving the child in family reunions and similar activities.
- Involving the child in grandparent visits.
- Including the child in family rituals.
- Holding religious ceremonies or other ceremonies that incorporate the child into the family.
- Buying new clothes for the child as a way of becoming acquainted with child's size; colour preferences, style preferences, and the like.

- Making statements such as 'in our family do it this way' in supportive fashion.
- Sending out announcements of adoption.
  others:

Exercise 4:
Encouraging attachment

Instructions

Purpose:
To help you practise defining ways to encourage attachment.

How to do it:

1 Read Sharon's case history on the next page.

2 List as many ways as you can think of that the family might use in helping Sharon develop attachment to them.

3 After working on your list, look at the sample that one worker developed on page 69.

4 Now, pick a child in your caseload who has moved recently. First, summarise the case. Then, develop the same type of list for your own case as you did for Sharon (page 70).

Exercise 4:
Encouraging attachment

Sharon's case
Sharon is an eight-year-old girl who is being placed for adoption in a family with three older boys. Past history reveals that Sharon experienced considerable emotional and physical deprivation, rejection and physical abuse from her birth parents. She has had seven moves since she first entered care at age three.

Sharon has many fears including fear of the dark and fear of new situations. She is prone to nightmares. There is a history of both daytime and night-time wetting. She is a very demanding child who verbally pressures and manipulates adults. She gets little pleasure from being a child and prefers to 'pretend' that she is an adolescent going out on dates. She is very seductive in her relationships with males.

Sharon has many gaps in her basic fund of knowledge; she exhibits problems with logical thinking and basic cause and effect. Sharon has many problems with lying; she tends to 'forget' what she chooses not to hear. Her lying extends even to saying 'that is my favourite food' when in reality it is a food she dislikes. Other times her lying is aimed at keeping herself out of trouble.

She has marked difficulties with peer relationships. She does well in the self-help skills. She likes to help with household tasks. In school, she is reading above her age level but has some difficulty with maths. She shows appropriate responses and is an attractive girl who is quite outgoing. Her self-esteem is poor, as indicated by comments such as 'something is wrong with me', when she makes an error. She is able to talk about feelings and can tell of many ways that she and her present foster parents have fun together.

Exercise 4:

Encouraging attachment

Sample response

Arousal relaxation cycle

1 Parents could sit with Sharon, after her waking from nightmares

2 Help Sharon talk about her fears

3 Arrange a visit with previous foster parents

4 Help Sharon talk about past foster families

5 Develop a life story book

6 Confront Sharon about lies or stealing, help her to get better and support her afterwards

Positive interaction cycle

1 Doing household tasks with Sharon

2 Looking at life story book

3 Help Sharon with maths homework

4 Organise outings for Sharon and her new brothers

5 Mother give Sharon hugs, kisses, physical closeness

6 Give Sharon good choices

7 Get Sharon to join a group (e.g. Brownies)

8 Explain sex to Sharon

Claiming behaviour

1 Get a family portrait including Sharon

2 Have a family get-together to introduce her

3 Buy new clothes for her (will also positively reinforce her attractiveness)

4 Sharon is to practise calling her new parents 'Mum and Dad'

Exercise 4:
Encouraging attachment

Your own case

Case summary:

Arousal/relaxation cycle

Positive interaction cycle

Claiming behaviour

Exercise 5:
Case planning for attachment

Directions:
Which children in your caseload did you think of as you read through
this workbook? Identify three or four who have attachment/separation
problems and outline a specific plan for each child to encourage attachment, transfer attachment, or help child and family deal with separation
issues.

Child

Concerns

Plan

Exercise 5:
Case planning for attachment

Child

Concerns

Plan

References

1 Kennell J, Voos D and Klaus M 'Parent-Infant Bonding' in Helfer R and Kempe C H (eds) *Child abuse and neglect* Cambridge, Mass: Ballinger Publishing Co, 1976.

2 Fraiberg S *Every child's birthright: in defense of mothering* New York: Basic Books, 1977.

3 Desmond M M, Rudolph A J and Phitaksphraiwan P 'The transitional care nursery: a mechanism of a preventative medicine' *Paediatric Clinics of North America* 13, 1966.

4 Spitz R *The first year of life* New York: International Universities Press, 1965.

5 Wolff PH *The causes, controls and organization of behaviour in the neonate* New York: International Universities Press, 1966.

6 Yarrow L J 'Research in dimensions of early maternal care' *Merrill-Palmer Quarterly* 9, 1965.

7 Ainsworth M D and Boston M 'Psychodiagnostic assessments of a child after prolonged separation in early childhood' *Brit J Med Psychol.* 25, 1952.

8 Bowlby J 'Attachment and loss' in *Attachment* New York: Basic Books, 1970.

9 See 4 above.

10 Delacato H *The ultimate stranger* New York: Doubleday & Co Inc, 1974.

11 See 7 above.

12 See 8 above.

13 Littner N 'The importance of the natural parents to the child in placement' *Child Welfare* LIV 54, 1975.

14 Winter A 'Only people cry' *Women's Day Magazine* September, 1963.

15 See 8 above.

16 Gesell A et al *The first five years of life: a guide to the study of the pre-school years* New York: Harper and Row, 1940.

WORKBOOK TWO
Child development

CONTENTS

About this workbook

As children develop normally, they pass through a number of stages of development. At each of these stages, the child has to accomplish certain major developmental tasks. With each stage of development the child tends to exhibit certain physical, psychological, and emotional characteristics.

Although all children must accomplish the same developmental tasks, each individual child approaches them in a way that reflects his or her unique predispositions and experiences. The child's personality, physical abilities, and other individual attributes will certainly affect the way in which he or she exhibits the characteristics associated with a particular developmental stage. Nevertheless, there are significant common factors.

Ideally, families function to enable children to accomplish their developmental tasks. Within the family children learn to value themselves and to trust others. They learn about their own feelings and other people's. Within the family children learn how to talk and how to think.

Families provide safety and security, stimulation and encouragement, and reasonable expectations and limits. Children need support and reasonable external controls as they meet each developmental challenge and cope with inevitable frustration in this process. Children who do not receive support become bewildered, insecure, and without self-esteem.

Knowledge of the tasks and characteristics associated with each stage of development is a key to helping a child. Parents who understand developmental issues are less likely to be as upset by normal behaviour and more likely to support the child as he or she struggles with the basic tasks at each stage. They are more readily able to perceive what a child needs to help him or her grow. They are more likely to meet these needs and the child's undesirable, but normal, behaviour will be unlikely to persist into later stages of development.

The perceptions, abilities, and behaviour of all children change as they mature. At each stage of development, children face challenges and difficulties. As they strive to meet these challenges, almost all children exhibit some behaviour that is not seen as particularly desirable by the families with whom they live. The fact that undesirable behaviour reflects normal development does not mean that it can be ignored; on the other hand, it does not need to be treated as an incurable disease or a reason to move a child from a family. Workers must be able to help families help children meet the challenges of normal development.

In addition, many children in placement have lived or are living in environments that are not conducive to achievement of the developmental tasks and thus their behaviour may reflect unmet developmental needs.

Since the physical, emotional, and psychological aspects of a child's development are so entwined, delays in one often affect subsequent development in other areas as well. The earlier environmental deprivation occurs, the more severe will be the effects. Many children in care must struggle if they are to overcome these complex and long lasting developmental delays.

It is important that social workers be able to distinguish between normal behaviour for varying ages and those patterns of behaviour that indicate unmet developmental needs. Knowledge in this area prepares the social worker to do a better job of child and family assessment and case planning.

In this workbook we present material on child development in a manner that we hope will be helpful to social workers and others who deal with children in placement. As each stage of development is discussed, the major developmental tasks are outlined, and the changes in perceptions, abilities, and behaviour that children experience are highlighted. In addition, special developmental issues for children in placement at each stage are noted.

Throughout the book, we talk about the relationship between the child and the parents. We use the word 'parents' to mean primary caretakers who may be birth parents, foster parents, adoptive parents, or other relatives.

In addition, we often use the word 'mother' to replace primary caretaker. It is true that conditions are changing and that a growing number of fathers are taking on this primary caretaker role. However, the majority of primary caretakers still are mothers and most child development research done to date reflects this. Hence, for convenience we have sometimes used 'mother' to mean 'primary caretaker' in this text.

We hope that upon first reading you will gain information that will be of help to you in working with at least one or two current cases in your caseload. In addition, we hope that this workbook will also stand as a reference to which you can return in the future.

This workbook has six major sections. The first five sections describe normal development in the infant, toddler, pre-school child, child between six and ten, and adolescent. In each of these sections special issues of concern to the child in placement at that age are highlighted.

Although some comments are included in each of these sections as to ways to minimise the trauma of separation at various ages, more complete information and concrete suggestions are given in Workbook 3, *Helping children when they must move.*

A section on language development from birth to age five is included in the section on the pre-school age child. At the end of Section 3 there is a listing of the usual sequences for attaining developmental milestones in the sub areas of development: personal-social, fine motor adaptive, language, and gross motor.

Section 6 summarises several special developmental issues of which workers and parents should be aware. These issues include language development, conscience development and values incorporation, temper tantrums, fears and worries, and sexual development.

Case examples and exercises have been interspersed within the text so that the reader may apply the material presented to actual cases. The exercises may be used by an individual reader or as the basis for training sessions for social workers or parents.

Exercise 1 follows. Look it over and spend some time considering two cases from your caseload, following the instructions. When you have finished reading this workbook, come back and complete Exercise 1.

Exercise 1:
Identifying developmental levels

Instructions

Purpose:
To help you learn to recognise the developmental level of children in your caseload and to plan appropriate ways of meeting their needs.

How to do it:

1 Think of two different children in your caseload. Select one child whom you feel has developmental delays or is 'immature'. Select a second child who is functioning at age level.

2 Using the two worksheets that follow, write a brief summary of each case. Try to include all the information specified on the worksheets.

3 As you read this workbook, keep these two cases in mind and make notes or comments in the block marked 'Indicates developmental level'.

4 After you have finished reading this workbook, answer the questions in the 'conclusions' section on the second page of the worksheets.

Exercise 1:
Identifying developmental levels

Worksheet 1: 'Immature child'

Case summary:

Age at time of separation (from original primary caretakers):
Present age:

Observation notes:

Behaviour	Indicates developmental level	Normal or delayed?
1		
2		
3		
4		
5		

Exercise 1:
Identifying developmental levels

Worksheet 1: 'Immature child'

Observation notes:

Behaviour	Indicates developmental level	Normal or delayed?
6		
7		
8		
9		
10		

Conclusions:

At what age level(s) do you perceive this child is functioning?

What recommendations would you give the current parental figures for meeting this child's developmental needs?

Exercise 1:
Identifying developmental levels

Worksheet 2: 'Average child'

Case summary:

Age at time of separation (from original primary caretakers):
Present age:

Observation notes:

Behaviour	Indicates developmental level	Normal or delayed?
1		
2		
3		
4		
5		

Exercise 1:
Identifying developmental levels

Worksheet 2: 'Average child'

Observation notes:

Behaviour	Indicates developmental level	Normal or delayed?
6		
7		
8		
9		
10		

Conclusions

At what age level(s) do you perceive this child is functioning?

What recommendations would you give the current parental figures for meeting this child's developmental needs?

1 The first year of life

The primary task

During the first year of life, the primary task for the baby is to build a sense of safety and security and trust in other human beings. When a parent wonders, 'What should I do when . . .', the criteria for deciding should be, 'What will help my child trust me?' The infant develops a sense of security and trust from day-to-day experiences during the first year, not from occasional special or traumatic events. We know it is the quality of these daily interactions between parent and child that help the child develop physically and mentally.

Even during the first year of life it is not possible to separate a child's innate characteristics and behaviour from the effects of the way he or she is nurtured. We do know, however, that infants deprived of mothering will appear grossly retarded by the age of one. They may not be able to sit, stand, or walk. Their vocalisation and social interaction will be limited. They may develop 'failure to thrive' syndrome and be unable to grow physically. If their needs for security and affection are not met, they may not be able to give love or incorporate social values as they mature.

Normal development in the first year

Physical developments

During the first year of life the child makes tremendous gains in physical development. The rate of growth and development is so great that parents see changes in the infant's behaviour on nearly a daily basis. At no other time in an individual's life will developmental changes from month to month be so consistently noticeable.

The child's nervous system becomes organised during the first year of life. The rate and level of this organisation seems to be related to the quality of the relationships that the infant has with the parents. During the first year of life the child learns to recognise and understand many stimuli. Children learn how to learn during this first year.

In general the child gains control over the body in progression from head to foot and from the central part of the body out to the extremities. Thus the infant first gains voluntary control over the eye muscles. He or she is first able to focus on objects eight to nine inches (20 to 22.5 cm) from the eyes. From birth, the infant is interested in looking at the face of his or her human partner. Within the first month of life most infants learn to follow objects to the midline and within two months, 75 per cent are following beyond the midline.

The muscles of the lower part of the face are the next to come under voluntary control. Infants smile responsively prior to three months. Next comes control over the neck muscles so that the child learns to lift the head and neck up and gains control over the head when it is held upright.

The infant then acquires large muscle control in the upper extremities so that between three and four months he or she can put their hands together and can use their arms for support to raise their chest up when lying on their stomach. In fact, near that age the child learns to roll over, first from their stomach to back, and later from back to stomach. Shortly thereafter the child's head does not lag as he or she is pulled from a lying to a sitting position.

Between three and four months the child has enough control over the hand muscles to be able to grasp a rattle for a short period of time. By five months most children will reach for an object, and by six months will transfer objects from one hand to the other. Frequently they will put the object in their mouths in the process. At about this age the child learns to pick up small objects by use of a raking motion. Most children can use a thumb and finger grasp by the age of nine months.

By this time the child is gaining control over the large muscles in the lower extremities. He or she can pull themselves to a standing position and can stand alone with something to hold onto. Within the next month and a half most will learn to walk holding onto furniture and will learn to stand by themselves. The child learns to stoop and recover at about the same time as learning to walk alone. These developmental achievements usually occur at about one year of age.

By this time the child has learned to pick up small objects with a very neat, pincer-type grasp. The combination of this grasp and the mobility lead to a frustrating period for parents when the child sees and picks up every tiny thing on the floor and puts everything he or she has picked up into their mouth.

Language development

Language begins to emerge during the first year of life. The child *in utero* probably can hear; the newborn responds with distress to sharp sounds and prefers soft sounds. By the time the infant is three or four weeks old he or she turns towards sounds, and they respond most prominently to the voice of the primary caretaker (Wolff[1]). Vocalisations other than crying, such as coos, squeals and laughs, start during the first month of life but become more prominent in the succeeding two months.

Between six and nine months the child starts to imitate parents' speech sounds in a non-specific fashion. By this time he or she is getting control over the muscles associated with lips, tongue, and mouth. This physical fact, combined with the child's willingness to imitate, makes speech development prominent at this time. For a more complete outline of language development and material on language development, see Section 3 of this workbook.

Psychological and social development

As we mentioned in the introductory section, the primary psychological task to be accomplished during the first year of life is for the child to develop a sense of trust in others. The accomplishment of this psychological task, like all other psychological tasks, is primarily a reflection of day-to-day living rather than occasional isolated experiences.

When the infant experiences discomfort and cries, a parent usually identifies and remedies the state of discomfort, and the child experiences relief. Thus, a cycle is established that teaches the child that others will meet his or her needs. The repeated successful completion of this cycle is critical if the child is to develop a sense of trust and security and become attached to parental figures (see diagram overleaf).

At birth, the infant does not discriminate among the various states of discomfort he or she experiences, and react in a similar way when afraid, angry, or in pain. Gradually, as this cycle is successfully completed on different occasions, the child becomes able to discriminate among the varying states of discomfort and the forms of relief that alleviate the discomfort. Thus, the child begins to develop a sense of cause and effect. If the parent consistently identifies when the child is hungry and feeds him or her, eventually the child learns that that

particular state of discomfort is alleviated by food and that the cause of the discomfort is an empty stomach.

Awareness of the effects of this cycle helps us understand why so many children who come from abusive and neglectful homes have problems with lack of trust and with identifying and correctly remedying their own body discomforts. It is not uncommon to see five or six-year-old children who were abused or neglected during the first year of life who still have difficulty differentiating when they are hungry from when they need attention.

During the first year of life normally there are fluctuations in the child's emotional responses. During the first month of life the infant is getting accustomed to life outside the uterus and is often quite disorganised. Between four and six weeks the infant becomes more stable and tends to settle into a more scheduled existence. However, periods of emotional disequilibrium and increased fussiness re-emerge for short periods around two months and between four and five months. During these periods the child often fusses for no apparent reason, and little seems to be comforting.

By age four months the infant certainly distinguishes the parents from other people. There is no doubt that the child notices moves after this time. There is a growing body of evidence that infants of one to two months distinguish their primary caretakers to varying degrees and thus would react to a move. Although children prior to six months certainly do distinguish caretakers from others, most enjoy strangers as well and do not show signs of fear or discomfort when approached by strangers.

During the early months of life the infant responds most to the particular sensations that promote contact with others. They prefer looking at the human face and listening to the human voice. They prefer the feel of soft clothing and the sense of rhythmical movements that they experience as an adult partner holds them and moves with them. Infants are especially sensitive to developing attachment behaviours during the first six months of life.

At the age of six to nine months, as mentioned in Workbook 1, *Attachment and separation*, the child can consistently distinguish between family members and strangers, and begins to demonstrate fear or anxiety when approached by a stranger. The strength and frequency of these fear reactions increase as the child nears one year of age. This makes it increasingly difficult for the child to develop an attachment to a new primary caretaker during this period.

By the age of eight months, the child plays a more active part in trying to keep mother close by. The child obviously tries to catch the mother's attention. Since most children are somewhat mobile at this age, it becomes easier for them to achieve this aim. Such activities on the part of the child are a necessary part of forming an attachment and should not be discouraged. By the age of one year, the child and mother will have developed a unique pattern in terms of how they approach and respond to each other. This pattern tends to persist during the remainder of the pre-school years unless considerable effort is made to change it.

Often, we can see this pattern displayed. The baby's urge for closeness and attachment is so strong that if the mother doesn't stay close by, he or she behaves in a way that tends to draw her closer. Such infants are often clingy and whiney. If the parent rejects the child at these times, the clinging and whiney behaviour increases. In these cases, closeness to mother is maintained with primarily negative rather than positive interactions. If the mother shows the child that she is ready to remain close by, the child can relax and free energies for other activities.

During the child's first year, attachment between mother and child normally increases, but dependency decreases. Attachment and dependency are not synonymous terms. According to Ainsworth[2], as mentioned in Workbook 1, *Attachment and separation*, the anxious, insecure child may falsely appear more strongly attached to the mother than the secure child who can explore fairly freely in a strange situation using the mother as a secure base; who is not distressed by the appearance of a stranger; and who shows awareness of the mother's absence, greeting her on her return, and then resumes previous activities.

In contrast, the insecure child may not explore even when the mother is present; may become extremely alarmed by the appearance of a stranger; may seem helpless and in acute distress when the mother leaves; and on her return may seem either disinterested or in distress but in either case, incapable of making an organised attempt to reach her.

During the child's first year of life, he or she becomes more perceptive, takes a more active part in the relationship with the parents, and becomes less dependent upon them. This sets the stage for the primary tasks of the second year of life – beginning to become autonomous.

Minimising the trauma of separation

During the first year of life
When children change parental figures during the first year of life, it is difficult to minimise the trauma of the move as the child does not have the verbal or intellectual skills to be prepared ahead of time. Our only avenues for smoothing the way involve active transferring of the parenting from the former primary caretaker to the 'new' caretaker. This is especially difficult to accomplish when children come into care. Changes in basic daily routines should be kept to a minimum if possible. The new parental figures need to understand how and why the child's basic trust may be undermined by a move at this time, and be willing to focus on rebuilding trust for adults after the move.

Many children who come into care during the first year of life have not yet had the opportunity to learn to trust parental figures. In such cases the new parental figures will have this as their major task.

Effects of separation or loss during the first year of life
Even before children reach the age at which they are obviously anxious about strangers, they are affected by moves from one home to another. They no doubt are aware of changes in rhythm and routine that occur

with a move. The child reacts to the differences in temperature, noise, and visual stimulation that vary from household to household. He or she may lose their sense of being able to rely on the environment and the individuals within it.

Interruptions in parenting will interrupt the child's process of sorting out his or her perceptions of the world. Since precursors to logical thinking and basic cause and effect reasoning begin even at this young age, we may see disturbances in this area. Children who have been asked to adjust to varying routines and environments during infancy may have their sense of security upset enough that they may become less flexible in the future.

During the latter half of the first year the psychological tasks are to increase recognition and awareness, to differentiate primary caretakers from strangers, and to increase reciprocity and mutuality in terms of inter-personal relationships. Loss of parental figures during this stage of development is likely to lead to problems in terms of trusting caretakers and in terms of social interactions.

In Exercise 2 on the next page, you have an opportunity to identify a child's developmental levels and needs during infancy.

Exercise 2:
Identifying developmental needs in the infant

Instructions

Purpose:
To help you learn to identify developmental levels and needs of infants so that appropriate foster care placements may be selected.

How to do it:

1 Read Jason's case history.

2 Answer the questions on the next page and then compare your own answers with those of another social worker on the sample worksheet.

Jason's case
Jason is a 13-month-old who has just come into care. His mother is 18 years old. The father left the family when Jason was one month old. His mother frequently leaves Jason alone for several hours in the evening while she goes out with friends. During the day the mother spends most of her time watching television. She rarely holds Jason; she props his bottle. Little verbal or physical stimulation for Jason has come from his mother.

Jason is below the third percentile in height and weight and has poor muscle tone. He spends most of his time lying passively, rarely moving or vocalising. Jason does not yet drink from a cup. He can, but rarely does, roll over. He sits unsupported for just a minute or two and then topples forward. Jason will momentarily hold a rattle but shows no active interest in it. He rarely cries and never laughs or squeals.

Exercise 2:
Identifying developmental needs in the infant

Worksheet

---

1 At what developmental level(s) does Jason seem to be functioning?

---

2 What type of foster home would you select for Jason?

---

3 What type of advice would you give to the foster parents in terms of meeting Jason's developmental needs?

Exercise 2:
Identifying developmental needs in the infant

Sample worksheet

---

1 At what developmental level(s) does Jason seem to be functioning?

At about the level of a three- to four-month-old baby but his vocalisation is underdeveloped even for this age.

---

2 What type of foster home would you select for Jason?

Where there is a foster mother who likes and is experienced with babies, who has time to give a lot of attention to Jason, and who understands that some babies need special attention to help them catch up on their chronological age.

---

3 What type of advice would you give to the foster parents in terms of meeting Jason's developmental needs?

An explanation of the level at which he is functioning, of the need to treat him first as a very young baby, to help him develop security and trust but also to give him lots of stimulation, attention and physical contact to help him catch up.

---

2 The toddler years

The primary task
The overriding task for the child from one to three years is to separate psychologically from the mother and to begin to develop self confidence and self esteem. When faced with a 'What should I do when . . .?' question about a child of this age, the criteria for deciding should be, 'What will make my child feel more capable?' Although this urge for autonomy exists from the time the child is mobile, it becomes most evident between the ages of one year and two and a half.

Normal development
At about 12 months when the child stands and walks, his or her perspective on the world changes literally and figuratively. As the child begins to walk, he or she develops the capacity to pick up very small objects. As a result the child is eminently capable of 'getting into things' as he or she exploits these two newly acquired skills. The typical child at 12 months is very social. In a secure setting, he or she may even seem to be somewhat indiscriminate in giving affection as they smile and talk with everyone.

Although we speak of the 'terrible twos', the period we are referring to usually extends from 18 to 30 months. The toddler goes through a normal oppositional, stubborn, egocentric stage that is necessary to the development of his or her identity. In fact, it has been found that those children who do not go through the normal oppositional stage are more dependent later on in life.

During the second year of life the toddlers do not get on as well with others as they did previously. They do not seem to be in good emotional equilibrium. They are impulsive and have a short attention span. They become easily frustrated and are prone to temper tantrums.

At the age of 12 to 18 months, the child typically becomes apprehensive about being physically separated from the mother. Toddlers tend to be constantly underfoot as they cling to their parents. This relates to the fact that the developmental task for the toddler is psychological separation and individuation. When the mother is physically absent, the toddler feels out of control of the situation and becomes more anxious and apprehensive. As toddlers lose sight of the mother and then find her again, they are learning about themselves as individuals. They use the mother as a safe base from which to explore the world.

Prominent words in the vocabulary of an 18-month-old are 'me', 'mine', and 'no'. These words support the child's emerging autonomy. The child begins to distinguish between 'you' and 'me' and starts to separate his or her own identity from the mother's. Games such as 'Point to your nose: point to my mouth,' help him or her learn this type of differentiation.

18-month-old children are very egocentric. They do not yet perceive other people as individuals like themselves. Their defiance and resistance in this period are not so much aggressive as self-protective. They are trying to establish themselves in the world.

We can see toddlers begin to internalise the values of others during this period. As they approach an object the parents don't want them to touch, they say 'no' in a firm voice and may accompany this with a smack on the offending hand. Later, as the children approach this object they themselves say 'no, no' but cannot yet quite stop themselves from touching. They need the parent's reinforcing 'That's right; that is a no-no.' However, shortly thereafter children will reach out to touch this object saying 'no, no' and then quickly withdraw their own hand or will even give themselves a smack. This is the very beginning stage of incorporation of values and is, as such, a precursor to conscience development.

As toddlers reach two years of age, their ability to perceive things and to imitate behaviour has become more developed. They love to mimic their parents and to 'help' them with household tasks. They cooperate better with dressing themselves, although they can usually take off more garments than they can put on. Children of this age will play alone or play in a parallel fashion with other children. They are still 'selfish' and not ready to share.

Two-year-old toddlers still do not fully accept the mother as a separate individual. They alternate between being dependent and being self-contained. The resurgence of fear toward strangers that occurs at 18 months subsides.

They are capable of showing a wide variety of feelings – frustration, anger, sadness, fear, and affection. They also show signs of pity, sympathy, modesty, and shame. Two-year-olds can be most touching when they try to comfort an upset parent with 'poor mummy' or 'poor daddy'. Two-year-olds are aware of praise, and smile when they hear it. They may even praise themselves with statements such as 'good job'.

Between two and three years, children go through a period where extremes are the norm. They are either very dependent or very independent, and their mood changes from hour to hour. They are extremely aggressive or extremely withdrawn; very helpful or very stubborn. They are now steady on their feet; their vocabulary grows by leaps and bounds. Toilet training becomes feasible and, for most children, day-time training is completed by the third birthday.

Parents' role with toddlers
What kind of environment helps the child attain the psychological tasks at hand for these two years? The toddler needs parents who can give encouragement without pressure for the development of new skills, who help him or her feel 'big' and capable. In addition, it is the parents' responsibility to provide for the child's safety and wellbeing. Changes in the environment can do much to prevent accidents and to promote healthy parent-child relationships.

In order to protect the toddler, cleaning materials, medicines, and poisons must be kept in inaccessible places. Inaccessible places get harder to find during this period as the child learns to climb up on a chair to get desirable objects. Until the child learns to manage stairs, most parents use gates to block them off.

Late during this period the child learns to turn a door knob to open the door, so until then keeping certain rooms of the house closed off is a sensible safety precaution. After these kinds of practical changes are made in the environment, enough 'nos' invariably remain to provide the child with ample opposition for growth.

The child's short attention span and distractability are the parents' principal allies during this period. Substituting a safe toy for a forbidden one usually works. Reasoning does not. Although a quick tap on an offending hand or a single smack on the bottom may help to reinforce verbal requests, repeated harsh physical punishment does not help psychological development.

If the parents perceive the normal negativism of the toddler age as a personal attack and get into repeated win-lose battles, they may well be in for difficulties with the child later on. Through such conflicts children learn to behave as though their integrity as a person is in danger if they submit to even the smallest demands of another. Resistance and conflict, rather than mutuality, become the primary mode of interaction between such parents and children.

Children of this age are creatures of routine. Changes in routine or abrupt transitions usually result in a child who is more easily frustrated and upset than normal. All mothers have had the experience of disrupting their child's usual nap routine to take them for an afternoon appointment, and all mothers have learned that they 'pay' for this change in routine for the remainder of the day.

A special note should be made about the child's difficulty in following the mother until about the age of three. The toddler has difficulty in moving toward a *moving* object. This should not be interpreted as 'naughty' or resistant behaviour. Usually the mother must transport the child by buggy, grocery trolley, or in her arms. When mother and toddler are out for a pleasure walk, it is common to see the mother walk a short distance, remain stationary until her child catches up with her, and then repeat this sequence.

Toddlers in placement

In this section, three issues are highlighted because of the particular need for workers to be keyed into them. The first is the expression of assertion and anger during these stages. It is particularly important for workers to be able to help birth parents, foster parents, and others interpret the child's development in the expression of assertion and anger, for it is this behaviour that will concern all of them and will be brought to the attention of the worker. For similar reasons, toilet training is highlighted here. Finally, the developmental effects of separation are noted here so that workers can help avoid, identify, and work through these reactions.

Assertion and anger

As toddlers gain in independence, their anger is aroused chiefly by interference with their physical ability. By 21 months, frustration may also stem from their inadequate ability to express their wants and needs.

When 18-month-old children are angry, they are apt to have a tantrum, crying intensely and throwing themselves on the floor. They

98

may also hit, kick, and struggle if an adult tries to control them. Toddlers of this age tend to be rough with animals and with younger children. They are apt to pull hair and to hug too tightly.

Typically, two-year-olds are not as aggressive as one and a half-year-olds. However, they may hit, poke, or bite other children. They are into the ownership stage and will engage in a tug-of-war over toys and other objects. Although they may 'mess up' the house, generally they are not destructive.

By age two and a half they have become more destructive, and they are more aggressive both with other children and with adults. They attack other children with the intent to hurt, usually in disputes over toys.

Without warning they may walk up to and hit a stranger. They may, again, have kicking, hitting, and head-banging type tantrums.

Toilet training
Toilet training cannot occur until the child becomes aware of the sensations of a full bladder and a full bowel. Many mothers learn to identify the signals of an impending bowel movement and place the infant or toddler on the pot just in time; however, this is not true toilet training.

Commonly toddlers first become aware of wet or full pants immediately after they occur rather than before, much to the frustration of parents. However, this is a necessary stage, for until the child becomes aware of the discomfort *after* it occurs, he or she cannot become aware of the full sensation prior to urinating or defecating. Children who have a low sensitivity to skin sensations may be delayed in terms of toilet training.

It is also quite common for children to 'go' just after they get off the potty rather than while they are on it. Again, although this is very frustrating to parents it indicates that the child is beginning to relate the potty to going to the bathroom; he or she just has not yet mastered the proper sequence.

It is very difficult to toilet train a child who is wearing nappies. Switching to training pants is necessary to complete toilet training in regard to urination. Many children are quite regular in terms of the time of day that they have their bowel movements, and so it is easier for the parent to put the child on the potty at the appropriate time.

Since children at this age tend to be stubborn and messy, parents often attribute difficulties in toilet training to the child's stubbornness. However, with most children this is not true initially.

It is only if parents make a control issue out of toilet training or use harsh disciplinary techniques, that the stubbornness of this age may extend to toilet training as well. This is not likely to happen if the parents are relaxed but helpful about teaching toilet skills.

One of the most frustrating events for parents is when the child has a bowel movement during a nap or early in the morning and expresses his or her messiness by smearing and playing with the faeces. The child does not know that this is wrong. Rather, it fits with toddlers' strong urges to explore and mess with anything they can get their hands on.

Minimising the trauma of separation

The toddler years
It is important that toddlers be prepared for moves by adequate pre-placement preparation if at all possible. If the move gives the toddler the message that 'strangers may come and take you away from parents anytime and without parental permission', long-range, chronic worries and fears are likely, as well as lack of trust for parental figures to be able to keep children safe and secure.

The goal during the moving process should be to transfer attachment from the previous caretakers to the new caretakers as much as possible. This means that the two sets of parents need to have contact and that the 'old' parents need actively to transfer the day-to-day caretaking tasks to the 'new' parents, thus giving the toddler permission to take from the new parental figures. (See also Workbook 3, *Helping children when they must move.*)

Because memories of this age are later triggered by similar emotions or by events similar to those occurring near the time of a move, we must be very alert to noting *all* events surrounding the move on a permanent record which will accompany the child. Such records can be invaluable in helping both the child and subsequent parental figures understand the child's reaction to various events in his or her life.

Case example: Peter
Eight-year-old Peter had difficulty on trips to the grocery store with his adoptive mother. He seemed to 'fuzz out' at these times and be unaware of his surroundings. He would wander off in the store as though he were

in a daze. Such behaviour was not evident in other situations. The adoptive parents were very confused by Peter's behaviour and decided perhaps they just shouldn't take him to the stores. They mentioned this behaviour to their social worker, who, in looking through the record, learned that Peter had come into care at the age of two in rather unusual circumstances. His family had been well known to the child care staff and to the police because of frequent bouts of family violence.

Following one such episode, when the police and social worker went to the house, a relative threatened to harm them both. Peter's mother told them that if they left she would immediately bring Peter to them at the corner car park so that he could be admitted to care. The car park was that of a large grocery store.

Subsequent trips to the grocery store triggered memories of the first move on an unconscious basis and triggered Peter's feelings of loss and confusion that accompanied his initial separation from his birth family. Once Peter and his adoptive parents understood the root of his behaviour at the store, they could work together on helping him learn that grocery stores need not be associated with loss.

Post-placement contacts with previous caretakers are important to the toddler. If they do not occur, it is common that the child will, at the age of four to five, think that the previous parental figures are dead. Pictures of past families make it possible for subsequent work to be done on separation issues once the child is old enough verbally and cognitively to deal with these feelings. If a child moves during the toddler years, it is nearly certain that he or she will need help as they mature in understanding the reasons for the move.

Effects of separation or loss on the toddler
Separations at this stage of development tend strongly to affect the development of the child's autonomy. Children who experience losses at this age may have problems in developing an appropriate balance between dependency and autonomy.

Some children with separation or loss experiences will become very dependent and clingy. Such children are usually afraid to show age-appropriate autonomy. Since they do not trust that adults will be there when they need them, they insist on keeping adults constantly in sight by demanding or clinging.

Other children who have experienced separation from or loss of attachment figures at this age may go to the opposite extreme and become too autonomous. Such children are apt to parent themselves. They withhold affection and may seem stubborn and resistant.

Such developmental reactions to separation and losses are not necessarily of short duration. Frequently, if not recognised and remedied, these reactions persist for years. It is not uncommon to see nine, ten, and eleven-year-old children in foster care who are still constantly clinging in spite of numerous attempts to break them of this habit. Other children show the effects of extreme autonomy through secondary school years and adolescence.

Underlying both these reactions is a lack of trust for others. The first is a 'I can't count on you wanting to stay close so I will have to keep an eye on you' response; the second is 'I can't count on you being close when I need you, so I will have to count on myself'.

Since these problems are frequent for children in care, social workers and foster parents need to be aware of the conflict between dependency and independency that characterises this age period. If there have been interruptions in the child's caretaking during this period, then his or her later experiences must provide opportunities for increasing trust and for increasing age appropriate autonomy. It must be recognised that the effort of children to control their environment is a healthy coping mechanism that must be kept in proportion so that it works for the children instead of against them. Exercise 3 asks you to explore these issues.

Exercise 3:
Identifying unmet dependency needs and dealing with the behavioural regression in such cases

Instructions

Purpose:
To help you learn to identify a child's unmet dependency needs and to plan to meet them.

How to do it:

1 Read Joshua's case history.

2 Answer the questions on the next page and then compare your own answers with those of another social worker on the sample worksheet.

Joshua's case
Joshua is five. He has been in and out of foster care since he was two because of repeated episodes of neglect by his mother and physical abuse by several of her boyfriends. In the foster home there is an infant and two toddlers. Occasionally, the foster mum finds Joshua sitting under the desk, rocking and sucking on a baby bottle he has taken from a younger child.

At bedtime Joshua rocks himself in the bed until he falls asleep. He continually grabs the toddlers' toys from them and seems to prefer playing with such toys rather that with toys more appropriate to his age. Sometimes he speaks very clearly; at other times he uses 'baby talk'.

Exercise 3:

Identifying unmet dependency needs and dealing with the behavioural regression in such cases

Worksheet

---

1 What unmet dependency needs does Joshua appear to have?

---

2 How would you explain his problems from a developmental standpoint to the foster parents?

---

3 What suggestions do you have for the foster parents to meet Joshua's unmet needs so that they will not persist later in his life?

Exercise 3:
Identifying unmet dependency needs and dealing with the behavioural regression in such cases

Sample worksheet

---

1 What unmet dependency needs does Joshua appear to have?

He has not been given consistency and
reliability or been able to develop a
sense of trust because of the repeated
separations and neglect.

---

2 How would you explain his problems from a developmental standpoint to the foster parents?

He has not been able to go through the
normal toddler stages of alternating
between dependency and becoming more
autonomous, and he has not developed
a sense of trust.

---

3 What suggestions do you have for the foster parents to meet Joshua's unmet needs so that they will not persist later in his life?

They need to allow him to be dependent and
to develop trust by explaining absences and
separations, showing affection—especially at bedtime—and giving him a lot of individual attention.
At the same time they need to praise and encourage
him for any new achievements. They should talk to
him about his past and be aware of what
triggers off feelings of loss and confusion.

---

3 The pre-school years

The primary tasks
The pre-school years are when proficiency in self care within the home setting is attained: this is the period of questions; the time of play and continuing individuation and independence for the child.

Normal development
By age three the child's need to be physically near the mother is no longer so urgent. Three-year-olds can feel secure away from the mother in a strange place if they are with people that they got to know while in her presence. Sensitivity to this is a very important consideration when moving children into foster or adoptive placements.

In general three-year-olds seem to be in good equilibrium. They are usually happy and contented; they enjoy play by themselves, they seem to have achieved some measure of emotional and physical self control. They are generally friendly and helpful. They have learned to help dress and undress themselves and, although they may have occasional accidents, they usually do not need nappies in the daytime.

The readiness of three-year-olds to conform to the spoken word is one of their outstanding characteristics. It is possible to bargain with three-year-olds – 'You do this, and I'll do that for you.' They have this capacity because they each realise that they are a separate person from others. While bargaining works, reasoning does not yet. Reasoning requires more conceptual skills than three-year-olds usually have. Distraction is still a useful disciplinary technique.

In general, three-year-olds are less rebellious than they were at two. When they do resist, they use language rather than biting, scratching, or kicking. They enjoy gross and fine motor activities. Three-year-olds begin to take turns – the first kind of sharing.

Three-year-olds frequently ask questions to which they know the answers. This behaviour is, in part, an effort to find out which information is consistent and which inconsistent. From the child's point of view, the world is a very confusing place. Some perceptions seem consistent; others do not. For example, what is acceptable behaviour at one time may not be acceptable at a different time or in another setting. Loud, boisterous play may be all right at certain times of the day, but not when parents are trying to sleep or a baby is napping.

Three-year-olds are capable of prolonged anxiety and jealousy. Their greatest fear is one of abandonment. As a child turns four, some of the two-year-old stubbornness re-emerges; however, this stubbornness seems 'softer' and frequently has a playful quality about it. The four-year-old enjoys silly talk, silly names, silly rhyming, silly showing off.

Four-year-olds tend to be afraid of the dark. Often a night-light solves many bedtime problems. They may fear strange noises. Four-year-olds enjoy being somewhat scared by adults in play; they will run and scream and then ask the adult to 'do it again'.

The typical four-year-old is likely to return some physical aggression while continuing to be verbally aggressive. He or she engages in name calling and bragging; plays in a group and may aggressively exclude others from it.

They are talkative and give long explanations in answer to parental questions. When they misbehave, they are prone to blame others or deny their involvement. They may behave badly on purpose in order to get a reaction. Four-year-olds are able to focus on similarities and differences. Their questions reflect their efforts to conceptualise and to order their experiences rather than just a hunger for information. Most of their questions are of the 'how?' and 'why?' type.

Four-year-olds love dramatic, imaginative play. Although they are able to dress and undress themselves with little assistance, they frequently enjoy help as a form of nurturing. They begin to have a sense of past and a sense of future. When told 'in a little while' or 'in half an hour' they want to know how long that is.

Children at five seem to be in a good state of equilibrium; their perceptions and their abilities seem to mesh. Five is an age of self containment and independence. In general five-year-olds are more serious and realistic than they were earlier or will become later. They are orientated to the here and now.

Their childish way of speaking disappears. Five-year-olds are curious and eager for information; however, their questions are fewer and more relevant. Their ability to have a genuine exchange of ideas is limited. They have trouble suppressing themselves even momentarily and will interrupt frequently.

Five-year-olds enjoy brief separations from their home and their mother. They are friendly and talk to everyone. This is not to be confused with indiscriminate affection, which involves more than talk. A vein of politeness and tact is emerging. There is also an emerging sense of shame and a sense of status.

Five-year-olds are aware of being different from others, and of differences in others. They become increasingly aware of differences between the sexes.

When children of five paint or draw, the idea precedes the production, rather than the reverse as occurred when they were four. Their drawings and dramatic play are more realistic.

Five-year-olds are not as fearful as four-year-olds. Their fear of imaginary things slackens because they are so reality-oriented. However, they may be fearful of being far from their parents in the dark.

Bargaining continues to work as a disciplinary technique. If five-year-olds feel stress, they increase their activity level. Since they frequently become hyperactive under stress, some form of 'time out' procedure may help them regain their equilibrium. Distraction does not work as well as at earlier ages.

Minimising the trauma of moves

The pre-school years
Because of the prominence of magical thinking and continued egocentricity, it is very important that everyone involved in moving the pre-school age child be on the alert for the child's misperceptions as to the reasons for the move and for his or her particular brand of magical thinking.

Because the pre-school child tends to act out concerns through play, parental figures need to pay close attention to the child's verbalisations during play as this frequently gives clues as to misperceptions. Parental figures, both before and after the move, should note down any odd or peculiar statements that the child makes and share them with the social worker. Such statements, if looked at carefully, frequently give clues as to the child's particular piece of magical thinking. We cannot correct the child's misperceptions and/or magical thinking unless we first identify them. Further suggestions on minimising the trauma of moves at this age are given in Workbook 3, *Helping children when they must move.*

The pre-school child in placement

Again, a few developmental issues are highlighted here that are particularly important for social workers and parents of children in placement.

Because delays in language development are the most common developmental delay seen in the abused and/or neglected child, (Elmer and Gregg[3]) we are including a brief synopsis of normal language development during the first five years, so that those involved with children can identify those children with speech delays at an early age.

Assertion and anger in the pre-school child are highlighted here to help workers and parents separate disturbing but normal behaviour from that which may indicate a more serious problem. Similarly, normal development in relation to dependency and autonomy is discussed so that behaviour on this dimension can be more intelligently interpreted by worker and parent.

This section also includes a discussion of the pre-school child's propensity for magical thinking, and his or her need to resolve oedipal issues. Both of these areas may pose problems for the child who is separated from the parents in the pre-school years.

Following Exercise 4 at the end of this section there is a series of charts which outline the normal progression of development from birth to the age of five. These charts include personal-social; fine-motor adaptive; gross motor and language development.

Language development

Language delays are common among children in placement. This section contains a brief synopsis of normal language development during the first five years so that those involved with children can identify those children with speech delays at an early age.

Language development is essential because it makes possible the higher mental processes that allow humans to attain self-control and to delay gratification of urges. It gives children a way to express their feelings other than by acting them out. It also makes memory possible. Children's memories of the time before they could speak are scanty and are usually stored either as visual images or as feelings.

At infancy

From birth on, infants react adversely to loud sharp sounds. At about three weeks they start to respond positively to soft sounds, especially

109

the human voice. Even before they are four months old, infants make a variety of sounds; they babble, coo, chuckle, gurgle, and laugh. Even early in infancy, children are very responsive to the human voice and their vocalisations increase when someone talks or plays with them.

Midway through the first year of life, infants begin to make vowel and consonant sounds and even put some sounds together into syllables. Within another month or so they begin to imitate speech sounds.

By age one most children are using 'mama' and 'dada' and have two or three other words in their vocabularies. They jabber a lot. They respond to their own names, to 'no, no' and to 'give it to me'. By 18 months most children have a vocabulary of about ten words (Gesell *et al*[4]). They can say 'no' and may use the pronouns 'me' and 'mine'. They are using words to replace or accompany gestures.

At two most children combine words into phrases or short sentences. Their jargon has almost disappeared. They use nouns more than other parts of speech. The vocabulary of the average two-year-old is about 300 words (Gesell *et al*[4]). Most can name some animals, objects, and parts of the body. They will usually try to imitate any single words said to them. Pronouns come into use during the period between 18 and 30 months, usually emerging in this order: 'mine', 'me', 'you', and 'I'. At two most children are still prone to calling themselves by their given names – 'Billy wants a cookie.' The rhythm of the typical two-year-old's voice is sing-song, and he or she may often echo what others say.

Between the ages of two and three, children begin to add 's' to words to make plurals. They learn to use the words they acquired earlier in sentences. They use nouns, pronouns, verbs, and some adjectives. They begin to understand prepositions although they can't use them. Their vocabulary increases to over 1,000 words (Gesell *et al*[5]). They use words to resist and to ask questions.

At four
At four children use questions to order their experiences and to begin to conceptualise and group things. 'Why' and 'how' introduce their frequent questions. They can count by rote. They learn to use prepositions . As adverbs become evident in their language, they have mastered all parts of speech. Conversation no longer interferes with their eating. They have learned the names of colours.

By age five, children's language is essentially complete in structure and form. They lose their infant articulation; they sound grown up now. Usually by five, the melody and rhythm of their speech are smooth as well. The most common articulation errors at this age are substituting an 'f' or 'd' for 'th'; softening 'r' until it sounds like 'w'; and substituting 'w' for 'l'.

Five-year-olds have acquired an ear for detail; they are able to ask the meaning of single words, rather than asking what an entire sentence means. They have difficulty suppressing their own views even temporarily; thus genuine interchange of ideas remains limited. In 'show and tell' type activities, they are interested in doing the show and telling rather than the listening.

Assertion and anger

By age three pre-school children have gained increased self-control and exhibit less aggression. Increased use of language allows them to express their wants and desires so that they are not so easily frustrated, and vocalisation may be used to express anger and frustration when it occurs. Anger is now aroused less by interference with physical activity and more by interference with their possessions or with their plans. They commonly use verbal threats to assert themselves and express anger.

Age four with its return of stubbornness is accompanied by a return to physically aggressive behaviour. Biting, hitting, kicking, and throwing things are not uncommon in the four-year-old. In addition, four-year-olds are verbally aggressive and may use name calling, bragging and boasting to assert themselves. They tend to be rough and careless with toys and may aggressively exclude others from the group.

Five, as mentioned earlier, tends to be an age of equilibrium which means that children are exposed to less frustration and we see less aggression. When angry, they may stamp their feet or slam the door. 'I hate you' or 'I wish you were dead' are common verbal expressions of anger for both the four and five-year-olds.

Dependency and autonomy

Three, four and five-year-olds use intellectual powers and imaginative skills as they play. Through play they continue to work on the balance between dependency and autonomy. Thus we see two recurring themes in play (Hymes[6]).

On the one hand pre-school children love to play at being baby. They may choose to take on the role of the weak, helpless, and defenceless. This occurs when they take the role of the baby while playing house, or the sick person while playing doctor, or the prisoner when playing cops and robbers, or cowboys and indians. When they take on this helpless babyish role, they may want to rock, suck from a bottle, or get into a cot. They are likely to want to play under tables or to construct a cosy corner or 'tent' for this type of play.

The second kind of play involves being big, strong, and bossy. When children engage in play this way, they want to be the mother or father, the teacher, the doctor, or the policeman. When they take on these roles, they are likely to be very bossy, even tyrannical.

Their play reflects their feelings and their thoughts, not their experiences. Foster parents and social workers sometimes assume that children playing out a 'big' role are reflecting the type of parenting they have experienced in the past rather than expressing a developmental need to feel 'big' and in control of things.

Magical thinking
As part of ego development each individual must come to grips with integrating the 'good' and the 'bad' in him or herself. One of the ways that a child does this is by developing imaginary friends. The imaginary playmates are frequently blamed for anything that the child does wrong. All the 'bad' in the child is attributed to the imaginary friend. Or, sometimes the imaginary friend becomes the personalisation of the scared, dependent, little aspect of the child. Thus, a pre-school child may say '*I'm* not afraid of the dark but Sammie is. You'd better leave on the light or he may be scared and cry, and then *I* couldn't sleep.'

Case example: Johnnie
Johnnie is a four-year-old who was placed for adoption when he was nearly three. In spite of firm recommendations to the contrary, his adoptive parents changed his name from Gerald to Johnnie. In the six months he was in adoption placement, Johnnie developed a series of behavioural problems and did not measure up to the adoptive parents' expectations. He was reprimanded each time he referred to himself as Gerald.

The adoption disrupted, and Johnnie was placed in foster care. He was adamant that his name was Johnnie. He was upset when his foster parents tried to use his original name of Gerald, although Johnnie had been his name for only an eighth of his lifetime. In foster care Johnnie was 'too good'. He seemed very apprehensive about making any mistakes, or any messes, or about asserting his autonomy in any way.

In an attempt to determine the nature of his conflict about the name Johnnie's social worker compiled a life story book. She showed him pictures of himself as an infant, and identified those pictures as Gerald. When she got to the part about the adoptive placement, she talked of the name change to Johnnie. She then talked about Johnnie's experience in the adoptive home and his return to foster care. She explained that Gerald and Johnnie are really one person. At this point Johnnie became agitated and repeatedly said, 'Gerry is a bad boy; he's naughty; I'm Johnnie.'

It was clear that Johnnie was going through the normal 'good boy' versus 'bad boy' conflict that each pre-school child has to resolve. However, for Johnnie the name change became associated with the split between good and bad. To this little boy, Gerry signified the 'bad child' who had to move from the foster home to an adoptive home and who did not measure up. Johnnie was the 'good child'; however, he had not done a 'good enough' job of being Johnnie in the adoptive home and thus had to leave. Back in foster care he was doing his best to be the 'good' Johnnie so he would not have to move again.

Pre-school children are egocentric and prone to 'magical thinking'. Magical thinking includes the idea that 'wishes come true'. Many pre-school children feel guilty about their thoughts, wishes or desires. Most gradually find out that their wishes do not make things come true. However, the wishes that all pre-school children have sometimes such as 'I don't like you and I wish you weren't my mummy any more'; or 'I want to have a new family instead of you'; or 'I wish you were dead'; have 'come true' for children who have been moved into placement. If this happens, then the magical thinking is reinforced and is apt to persist long beyond the common age for it to subside.

Children who lose a parent through any means – death, divorce, or placement in care – tend to blame themselves for the events in their life. They feel this way both because of their egocentricity and because of magical thinking. If parents are sensitive about magical thinking, they may help children understand what they are doing and keep their behaviour from continuing beyond the age at which it is appropriate.

Case example: Suzanna

Suzanna was a child of six whose mother had died after a long lingering illness when Suzanna was four. During the course of her mother's illness, Suzanna was frequently separated from her; she became angry about these separations and, on occasion, wished that her mother would die.

After her birth mother's death, Suzanna's father remarried. She and her step-mother had many difficulties in their relationship. The behaviour that upset the step-mother most was what she called 'the look'. She had learned that when the day stared out with 'the look', it rapidly progressed to one negative interaction after the other. The step-mother felt that on those days nothing she did mattered. She was quite certain that if, in the course of therapy, we could get rid of 'the look' many of their problems would disappear.

Initially I was quite sceptical of the mother's perceptions in this case. However, in the course of therapy, one day Suzanna became very upset with me, and she gave the 'the look'. Once I saw it, I recognised it as an attempted spell. As a result of her experiences when she was four, Suzanna feared that her wishes made things come true. From her perception it had happened once, and it might happen again. If she and her step-mother got off to a bad start in the morning, Suzanna would put a 'spell' on her before she left home. She then, of course lived in fear all day that it might come true. Being preoccupied with that mixed wish-fear, she would have a bad day at school and a bad day with her step-mother when she came home.

Suzanna's greatest fear was that she might be a witch. This fear was heightened by the consistency with which a bad day followed 'the look', and her step-mother's fear of it.

Oedipal issues

During this same age span the child is going through the Oedipal stage. During the Oedipal stage the child competes with the parent of the same sex for the attention of the parent of the opposite sex. It is not uncommon for the pre-school age boy to say 'When I grow up I am going to marry mummy' or for the girl to make a similar declaration with regard to her dad.

However, the child soon starts to realise that to get the exclusive attention of the parent of the opposite sex something must first happen to the parent of the same sex. The pre-school child is faced with a dilemma. The parent he or she wants 'to get rid of' is also an important love object. To win means that they will lose as well. There is also guilt associated with these thoughts of getting rid of the parent of the same sex.

In addition, the magical thinking that is so prominent at this age increases the child's fears that something may happen to the parent of the same sex because the child has wished to eliminate that parent. The child may 'act out' in order to be punished. If the punishment occurs at the hands of the parent of the same sex and is extreme, the child's fears of retaliation for his or her 'bad' thoughts are reinforced. If the discipline is appropriate and fair, then the child's guilts and fears will more likely subside. If through death, or foster care placement, the child loses the parent of the same sex, the child becomes increasingly frightened of his or her own omnipotence.

The child may also view loss of the parent of the opposite sex as punishment for 'bad' thoughts. The child may even think that the parent of the same sex was losing the battle and decides 'If I can't have him/her then no one can.' At any rate loss or separations from parents during this critical stage in development may lead to long-lasting problems with sexual identification or to the persistence of the magical thinking into later years.

Sometimes parents who do not have a satisfying marital relationship behave in ways that increase the Oedipal problems. For example, a mother who is not receiving much attention from her husband may become over involved with her young son and focus all of her attention on him. Or, a mother who is lonely may take her son to bed with her whenever dad is out of town or working nights. Such behaviour on the part of the parents may increase the child's fears of retaliation if the other parent finds out what is happening.

Again, because of magical thinking, children may inappropriately attribute cause and effect. Children are very likely to blame themselves for everything bad that happens to them or to their family. Such blame has frequently been reinforced by parental statements that imply that all the parent's problems are the child's fault. Such statements as 'He will be the death of me yet' or 'If you aren't good, you'll be sorry' all tend to reinforce the child's sense of responsibility for all that happens.

In Exercise 4 that follows, you have an opportunity to identify Merrilee's needs and to describe how you would create an environment in which a pre-school child could exert her urges for autonomy and still have her dependency needs met.

115

Exercise 4:

Identifying the needs of the pre-school child and creating an environment to meet the needs for appropriate autonomy

Instructions

Purpose:

To help identify ways in which children have had their urge for autonomy undermined by moves during this stage of development.

To outline ways that would be appropriate for the pre-school child to exert his or her urges for autonomy while at the same time meeting the child's dependency needs.

How to do it:

1 Read Merrilee's case history that begins on the following page. (See also Workbook 3, *Helping children when they must move.*)

2 Answer the questions on the worksheet and then compare your own answers with those of another social worker on the sample worksheet.

Merrilee's case

Merrilee lived with her birth mother until she was 16 months old. During Merrilee's first year, her mother had been reported for neglect. It was not too serious, and Merrilee remained in the home. When Merrilee was 14 months old, her mother gave birth to a baby boy and after that, began to neglect her more seriously. Merrilee came into care while her baby brother remained with the mother. Later he, too, came into care although in a different home.

When Merrilee came into foster care, the agency staff felt that it would be too confusing for her to see her birth mother. The worker recommended an 'adjustment period' for both mother and child with no visits. After this initial adjustment period, both Merrilee and her birth mother seemed to have 'adjusted' so well to the separation that both the mother and the worker were reluctant to initiate contact between the two. The mother relinquished her rights after six months, never having seen Merrilee again.

Merrilee was a bright and precocious child who became a valued member of the foster family. The foster family wanted to adopt Merrilee; however, the agency was reluctant to allow this. They opposed foster parent adoption in general. In addition, they were concerned about confidentiality because the foster parents knew who the birth mother was. However, the foster parents had had an application in for some time to adopt an infant. Soon after Merrilee's placement with the foster family, an infant boy became available for adoption through a private agency. This boy was placed for adoption with the foster parents, and another adoptive family was sought for Merrilee.

An adoptive family who lived 350 miles away was selected. The initial placement was that the adoptive family would come and pick up Merrilee at the social services department and take her for an all-day outing. They planned to return her to the social services department so that her worker could take her to her foster home for her last night there. The following day the foster mother was to bring her into the agency; the adoptive family would then take her to their home. There was no plan for the foster and adoptive parents to meet.

This first visit, an all-day outing, went very well, as first visits frequently do. The adoptive family asked Merrilee if she would like to spend the night with them and she said yes. They called the social worker who agreed with the change in plan. *The following morning, the adoptive parents brought Merrilee back to the agency to say her final good-bye to her foster mother. Her foster father who was at work and who knew that he would be upset by the separation, said his 'good-byes' to Merrilee over the phone. The worker took her from the room with her adoptive parents to a room down the hall. Her foster mother was waiting there to give Merrilee her belongings and to say good-bye. Merrilee then returned to the room where her adoptive parents were waiting.*

The adoptive parents changed Merrilee's name so that she could feel as if she were having a 'fresh start' in her new family. Merrilee had long, naturally curly hair. Her foster mother had frequently brushed Merrilee's hair. She did this as a way of being physically close to and nurturing Merrilee. She also used this as a way to raise Merrilee's self esteem by commenting what beautiful hair she had and how pretty she was. The adoptive mother didn't know this history and suggested that Merrilee have her hair cut, 'like your older sister's hair'. Merrilee agreed.

I met Merrilee when she was four and a half years old. At that time, she was constantly fighting control battles with her mother. For example, she was not to leave the garden without permission. Merrilee didn't sneak out of the garden; instead, she would sit perched on the fence until she was sure her mother was looking out of the kitchen window. Then, she would go over the fence. If she were asked to do something such as help set the table, it never quite got done.

In some respects she seemed overcompetent, never asking for help. Merrilee had trouble sitting in a comfortable fashion on her parents' laps. She couldn't cuddle. She was prone to many fears, but the most prominent one was her fear of strangers. Whenever the family had company, Merrilee would become alternately hyperactive and clingy, demanding a lot of attention.

118

Exercise 4:
Identifying the needs of the pre-school child and creating an environment to meet the needs for appropriate autonomy.

Worksheet

1 The adoptive parents have contacted you and asked advice about ways that they can handle Merrilee's problem behaviour. Using a developmental approach, how would you explain Merrilee's behaviour to the parents?

2 What recommendations would you make about how to help Merrilee exert her autonomy in more appropriate ways?

3 What recommendations would you make with regard to meeting Merrilee's dependency needs?

119

Exercise 4:
Identifying the needs of the pre-school child and creating an environment to meet the needs for appropriate autonomy.

Sample worksheet

1 The adoptive parents have contacted you and asked advice about ways that they can handle Merrilee's problem behaviour. Using a developmental approach, how would you explain Merrilee's behaviour to the parents?

Her behaviour is not 'bad' but is an attempt to deal with all that has happened to her in the past. Because important adults in her life (mother and foster mother) disappeared, her sense of trust has been broken and she cannot maintain an appropriate balance for her age between dependency and autonomy.

2 What recommendations would you make about how to help Merrilee exert her autonomy in more appropriate ways?

Find things she can do well and praise her for her achievements.

3 What recommendations would you make with regard to meeting Merrilee's dependency needs?

The parents need to make her feel loved and valued so that it's safe for her to be dependent. They should do things with her – e.g. shopping, outings, having fun together, making a life story book. They should promote attachment behaviour.

Developmental milestones: personal and social

Birth – 1 month

Looks at face transiently

Smiles selectively in response to mother's voice at 3 to 4 weeks

Quiets to human voice at about 3 weeks

Body tone improves

Capacity to stay awake grows

Basic body functions gradually stabilise

1 – 3 months

Smiles responsively to human face

Regards human face

Tracks human face beyond midline by 8 to 9 weeks

3 – 6 months

Orients more toward mother than anyone else

Uses vocalisation to interact socially

Probably smiles spontaneously

Waking periods become longer and better defined

Individual traits become more obvious

Attention span increases

Smiles at image in mirror

Uses head, eyes, and hands together well in reaching for toys and the human face

May like to play peek-a-boo

Smiles readily at most people

Plays alone with contentment

Takes solid food well

6 – 9 months

Begins to be afraid of strangers

Probably reaches for familiar persons

Shows desire to be picked up and held

Feeds self finger foods

Puts feet in mouth

Pats mirror image

Plays peek-a-boo

Starts drinking from a cup

Chews and bites on toys at play

Rarely lies down except when asleep

Has well established routines

Begins to respond to own name

Begins to respond to 'no, no'

Interacts differently with various family members

May hold own bottle

9 – 12 months

Repeats performances for attention

Acts socially with family; shy with strangers

Begins to develop a sense of identity

Is capable of varying emotions such as fear, anxiety, anger

Begins to develop a sense of humour

Actively seeks attention

Becomes aware of other's emotions

Plays pat-a-cake

May drink from cup by him/herself

12 – 15 months

Becomes more demanding, assertive, and independent

Has poor emotional equilibrium

Vocalises rather than cries for attention

Has a sense of me and mine

May use spoon, spilling a little

May imitate household tasks

Probably drinks from a cup unassisted

Reacts when mother leaves

15 – 18 months

Claims things as 'mine'

Begins to distinguish 'you' and 'me'

Maintains a concentrated, but wary, interest in strangers

Resists changes in routine or sudden transitions

Expresses autonomy as defiance

Reacts poorly to sharp discipline

Generally is not changed by scolding or verbal persuasion, as words are not yet important enough

Diversion and changing the environment are most useful disciplinary techniques

Does not yet perceive other persons as individuals like him/herself

Imitates and mimics others

Probably uses spoon well

May help in little household tasks

Probably can take off piece of clothing

Engages in solitary or parallel play

Shows or offers toy to examiner

18 months – 2 years

Continues solitary or parallel play with other children

Is more social with mother

Follows mother

Helps dress and undress self

Washes and dries hands

May indicate wet or soiled nappies

Probably can do simple household tasks

Pulls person to show things

Asks for food and drink

Understands and asks for 'another'

Mimics real life situtations during play

Is self-centred but does distinguish between self and others

Conscious of family group

Discriminates edible substances from inedible substances

2 – 3 years

Can put on clothing

Probably can dress self with supervision

Learns to separate from mother easily at about 3 years

Plays interactive games

Is toilet trained

Unzips and zips; unbuckles and buckles; unbuttons and buttons clothing

Has an identity in terms of name, sex, and place in family well entrenched by age 2½

Initiates own play activities

Dawdles

Likes praise

Alternates between dependency and self containment

Shows pity, sympathy, modesty and shame

Has good steering on push toys

Can carry a breakable object

Can pour from one container to another

Often is fearful of certain sounds and noises

Gets drink unassisted

Learns to avoid simple hazards (careful of stairs, stoves, etc.)

3 – 4 years

Conforms to the spoken word

Can make 'bargains'

Carries out little errands near home

Is capable of prolonged anxiety or fear

Understands taking turns

Starts to share

Is less rebellious than at 2 or 4

Uses language to resist

Toilets self during day

Plays with a group

May dress without supervision by age 4, except for back buttons and tying shoes

Fears loss of parents

Often is fearful of seeing certain objects

4 – 5 years

Is dogmatic and dramatic

Argues about parental requests

Control issues prominent for many children

Begins cooperative group play

Has a good imagination

Often has unreasonable fears

May have nightmares

Creates alibis to avoid trouble

Likes silly rhymes, silly sounds, silly names, etc.

Is physically aggressive

Probably dresses without assistance, except for back buttons and tying shoes

Washes face and brushes teeth

Is self sufficient in own home

Likes to dress up in grown-up clothes

Laces shoes

Can go on errands in the neighbourhood

Calls attention to own performance

Tends to be bossy and critical of others

Begins to sense time in terms of yesterday, tomorrow, and sense of how long an hour is etc.

Developmental milestones: fine motor adaptive

Birth – 1 month

Follows with eyes to midline

Mouth and eye muscles are the most active muscles

Has a sucking reflex

Makes seeking movements with mouth

Has a grasp reflex, but does not reach

Hands usually closed

1 – 3 months

Grasps rattle briefly

Follows dangling objects past midline

Puts hands together

3 – 6 months

Looks at small objects

May reach for objects frequently using both hands

Most follow for 180°

Sucks at hands or fingers

Regards hands

Reaches for objects with one hand

May transfer objects from one hand to the other

Looks for objects which leave visual field

Rakes pellet or raisin with hand

Inspects objects with hands, eyes, and mouth

6 – 9 months

Grasps an object in each hand simultaneously

Transfers objects from hand to hand

Probably has a thumb finger grasp

Develops tongue control

Begins to develop sense of twoness

Puts things in and out of container

Probably works for toy out of reach

9 – 12 months

Probably has neat pincer grasp

Bangs together objects held in each hand

Momentarily brings one object over another

Grasp release crude

12 – 15 months

Visually prefers circle over other shapes

Has a neat pincer grasp

Puts ball in box

Puts pellet or raisin in bottle

Builds a tower of two cubes

Probably scribbles spontaneously, grasping pen or pencil in the palm

15 – 18 months

Has an exaggerated grasp release

Turns pages several at a time

Knows where things are or belong

Starts to point

Frequently gives evidence of knowing that something has been completed, such as waves 'bye-bye' and reports of soiling

Holds spoon

Holds cup

Dumps pellet from bottle after demonstration

May copy vertical line

18 months – 2 years

Builds a tower of four cubes

May build tower of six cubes

Probably imitates a vertical line

Dumps pellet from bottle spontaneously

Strings beads or places rings on spindles

Matches colours frequently

Folds paper once imitatively

Turns pages singly

Can wiggle thumb

Can wiggle tongue

Tries to snip with scissors

Uses colour names incorrectly

Uses number words to accompany serial pointing, a precursor of true counting

Starts to imitate horizontal line

Imitates shape of train with blocks

2 – 3 years

Builds a tower of 8 cubes between 24 and 30 months

Holds pencil by fingers, instead of grasping in palm

Imitates horizontal line well

Draws continuous circles

Can unzip and zip things

Unbuckles after imitation

Adds chimney cube to train

Completes formboard

Likes crayons

Likes puzzle type toys

Folds paper lengthwise and crosswise but not diagonally (cannot yet imitate diagonal line with pencil either)

Builds a tower of 9-10 cubes between 30 and 36 months

Probably matches colours, but does not name them correctly

Imitates building of 3 cube bridge

Copies a circle

Buckles after demonstration

Points to simple geometric shapes when named

Completes formboard quickly and correctly

Understands big versus little

Begins to be able to unbutton

3 – 4 years

Copies cross

Has a smooth grasp release

Draws picture and names it after drawing

Understands longer versus shorter

Understands 'give me the heavy block'

Draws person with two parts

Can button

Can lace

4 – 5 years

Counts five objects correctly

Draws a person with three parts

May copy a square without demonstration

Probably copies a square after demonstration

Draws unmistakable person, but arms and legs may still come directly from the head

Copies a triangle

Copes linear figures (i.e. C, T, L) with rare reversals

May continue to have some problems with diagonals

Developmental milestones: gross motor

Birth – 1 month

Lifts head when on abdomen

Averts head to preferred side when on back; only momentarily to mid-position

Moves extremities equally

1 – 3 months

Lifts head up to 45° when on abdomen

Grasps rattle briefly

Holds head erect when held in sitting position

Bears fraction of weight when held in standing position

3 – 6 months

Holds head up to 90° when on abdomen

Holds head more frequently at midline

Correlates arm and hand movements in large part with position of head and eyes

Rolls from side to back

Rolls first from abdomen to back

Rolls from back to abdomen

Bears increasing amount of weight when held upright

Head does not lag when pulled to sitting

6 – 9 months

Sits without support

Is increasingly mobile

Stands holding on

Pushes self to sitting

Pulls self to standing at close to 9 months

Leans forward and can push self back to erect position

9 – 12 months

Crawls with left-right alternation

Walks with support

Stands momentarily

Takes a few unsteady steps

12 – 15 months

Stands well alone

Walks well

Stoops and recovers

Falls by collapse

15 – 18 months

Runs stiffly

Climbs up on furniture

Walks backward

Walks into ball in attempt to kick

18 months – 2 years

Kicks ball forward on demonstration

May throw ball overhand

Walks up steps holding on with one hand, marking time

Gets down stairs on abdomen or bottom

Runs fairly well

Pulls toy as walking

Squats in play

Kicks ball on verbal command by 2 years

2 – 3 years

Jumps in place with both feet

Probably throws ball overhand

Walks on tiptoe after demonstration (many walk on tiptoe spontaneously before)

Tries to pedal tricycle and sometimes succeeds by 2½ years

Tries to stand on one foot

Jumps from bottom step

Probably can pedal tricycle by 3 years

Probably can stand on one foot momentarily by 2½ – 3 years

May do broad jump by 2½ to 3 years

3 – 4 years

Probably can stand on one foot for 5 seconds

May hop on one foot

Probably can do broad jump

4 – 5 years

Probably can hop on one foot

Probably can skip, alternating feet

Probably can catch ball bounced to them

Probably can do forward heel-toe walk

May do backward heel-toe walk

Language: receptive and expressive

Birth – 1 month

Cries prior to sleep

Cries if uncomfortable or in state of tension. Cries are undifferentiated initially but gradually vary with cause

Responds to bell

Smiles selectively in response to mother's voice by 3 to 4 weeks

Quiets to human voice and soft sounds

Startles to loud sound

1 – 3 months

Babbles and coos increasingly

Most laugh out loud

Most squeal and gurgle

3 – 6 months

Crows and squeals

Spontaneously vocalises vowels, consonants, and a few syllables

Responds to tone of voice and inflection

6 – 9 months

Says mama and/or dada non-specifically

Begins to imitate speech sounds

Turns to voice

Many single syllable sounds – ma, da, ba

Spontaneously blows bubbles

9 – 12 months

Imitates speech sounds

Obeys 'give it to me'

Uses 'Dada' and/or 'Mama' specifically as names

Experiments with sounds

12 – 15 months

Increases use of jargon

Communicates by gesture

Vocalises more than cries for attention

Usually has 3-5 word vocabulary

Understands word 'no'

Shakes head to indicate 'no'

Points to picture of dog

15 – 18 months

Vocalises 'no'

Has a vocabulary of about 10 words

May point to parts of body

Uses words with gestures

Uses jargon fluently

Points to pictures of common objects and may name them as he/she points

18 months – 2 years

Uses words 'me' and 'mine'

Markedly increases vocabulary

Points consistently to body parts

Combines two to three words

Names pictures of common objects

Follows simple directions

Probably discards jargon during this period

Understands 'yours' versus 'my'

Starts to use word 'you'

Uses mostly nouns

2 – 3 years

May use plurals

Says first name

At 2 years has a vocabulary of 300 words

Calls self by given name

Uses word 'I' by 2½ years

Speaks with sing-song rhythm

Uses phrases and 3 to 4 word sentences

Probably uses plurals by 2½ to 3 years

May give first and last name by 2½ to 3 years

Uses verbs more often

Begins to use adjectives

Tells own sex by 3 years

By 3 years has a 1,000 word vocabulary

Learns to listen and listens to learn

Asks 'What's that?' often

Probably understands big versus little by 3 years

3 – 4 years

Uses words for ordering perceptions

Uses questions to learn language structure

Probably gives first and last name (not necessarily true for foster children, as last name is rarely stressed at this stage for foster children)

Tells age by holding up fingers usually

Probably answers simple comprehensive questions

Probably understands prepositions and starts to use them

Probably understands colour names

Probably understands longer versus shorter

Counts to 3

Repeats 3 to 4 digits

Repeats 3 to 4 nonsense syllables

Has 50 to 75% use of consonants

By age 4, has vocabulary of 1,500 words

4 – 5 years

Uses colour names

First understands, then uses adverbs

Uses prepositions

Defines words in terms of use

Understands opposite analogies

Asks lots of why and how questions

Counts out objects correctly to 5 at least, many can count out 8 to 10 objects

Names common coins

Uses consecutive rather than comparative thinking (big, bigger, biggest instead of big versus small)

Loves new words, especially 'funny sounding' words

Tends to talk constantly

Increasing use of imagination

Enjoys humour and self laughing

Probably can identify composition of common objects

Follows 2 to 3 stage command

Can make elaborate replies to questions

Has a vocabulary of 2,000 words or more

Uses all parts of speech correctly

By 5, most infantile articulation disappears

Uses consonants

Corrects own errors in learning to pronounce new words

4 The ages six to ten

The primary task

The primary task for children between six and ten is to master problems they encounter outside the family unit. They devote their energy to learning in school, to developing motor skills, and to social interactions primarily with peers of the same sex. The issue of 'fairness' or lack of it in life is important to children at this stage.

Normal development

At six

The outstanding characteristic of the six-year-old is poor ability to modulate feelings. The typical six-year-old is very active. He or she constantly wriggles; bites their nails; kicks tables, or falls off their chair. He or she is either dancing with delight or drooping in despair.

Sometimes as children approach age six, they again aspire to more than they can manage to accomplish easily. They become more frequently frustrated; they may scream and have temper tantrums. The insistence of six-year-olds on having their own way is a sign that they feel out of control of their life.

Six-year olds are good at starting things, but poor at completing them. They depend on positive direction and guidance from adults. A well-regulated schedule of consistent mealtimes, bedtimes, and other daily rituals is helpful at home. At primary school, they need a teacher who is in charge in the classroom, but who understands as well the child's need for physical activity and physical closeness.

Not infrequently six-year-olds go back to sucking their thumb, talking baby talk, and retrieving old favourite stuffed animals from the toy box. Children are usually as confused by this behaviour as parents are. Telling them that they are acting like a baby or making fun of them doesn't help. If parents comment that kids their age often use baby talk, but that they – the parents – like it better when they talk the way they usually do, it will often help. This gives children a chance to express themselves again, and the parents a chance to praise them for correct performance.

In general praise works better than discipline with six-year-olds, which means that parents need to look for behaviour they can praise and avoid focusing on negative behaviour. Frequently the creative parent can find behaviour to praise that interferes with undesirable behaviour. Praising a child for putting his or her hands down works better than reiterating, 'Don't pick your nose!' The focus needs to be on what the parent wants the child to *do* rather than on what he or she is *not* to do.

Although six-year-olds enjoy doing tasks *with* someone else, they do not do well when sent off to do a task *for* someone else. 'Let's clean your room together. I'll make your bed while you pick up your clothes and toys,' works much better than 'Go and clean your room'. Repeated reminders seem to be necessary for children of this age.

Many six-year-olds take things that belong to others and then lie about their actions. It is not uncommon for children who have just started school to come home with pockets full of small toys and pencils that they 'found'. Having a child return them to the owner or turn them in to the 'lost and found' is more positive than forcing him or her to apologise for having taken them.

At seven

Children calm down as they reach seven. They do not like interruptions and become very absorbed in whatever they are doing. It is not uncommon for a seven-year-old to lie on the floor watching TV or playing before dinner while a parent calls several times for him or her to come and set the table. The child does not respond, and the parent is convinced that he or she is being 'ignored'.

However, the child may be concentrating. This is the age at which children learn to screen our distractions and focus on one thing. Children who are not able to do this have serious learning difficulties in school. In fact, it is the inability to focus on one stimulus and screen out others that poses so many problems for the brain-damaged child. If a child seems to have difficulty concentrating, it is a good idea to check and be sure that he or she isn't suffering from some kind of minimal brain dysfunction. If a parent touches a child who is so busy concentrating that he or she cannot hear, they will usually startle, but even then be able to 'hear' the parent.

Seven-year-olds, like six-year-olds, like physical closeness and occasional quick touching from the teacher. Children at seven still depend on reminders and guidance from adults. When they're upset, they become sullen and withdrawn. It's at this age that children frequently stamp off and slam doors. Seven-year-olds need reassurance from adults that it is okay to make mistakes, and they need help correcting those mistakes. They don't respond well to lectures or scoldings.

Many children in the first or second classes at school have high expectations of themselves. Such children may be frequently disappointed and frustrated by their own performances. They may act out or start crying, feel embarrassed, and then feel even more frustrated. If this sequence of events occurs at school, they may still have a lot of uncomfortable feelings when they return home. It is quite common in these circumstances for children to pick a fight with a parent so that they can release their pent-up feelings. This doesn't mean children plan this kind of event; it just happens because they are not yet very good at handling strong feelings.

Adults often wish children would just talk about their feelings. However, children of this age still have difficulties talking instead of acting out when they feel things strongly. They may be able to talk about the feelings in retrospect. The goal of supportive parents in this situation is to help children learn more appropriate ways of expressing frustration while, at the same time, not making them feel that they are 'wrong' or 'bad'.

Seven-year-olds have not learned to lose. Frequently if they see that they are going to lose, the game never quite gets finished. The playing board gets upset, or the child provokes the parent to say, 'If the game isn't going to be fun, just put it away'. Children of this age still frequently cheat in order to win. They have little sense of humour and cannot be handled with humour. They tend to think that people are laughing at them. They are becoming aware of 'fairness' and 'luck' and a frequent comment from seven on, for several years, is 'It's not fair'.

Reasoning can be used with the child who constantly bombards the parent with cries of 'It's not fair!' One such approach is to say to the child, 'Now let me get this straight. You want me to treat you just the same as your brother?' The child usually agrees. 'So the next time Johnny needs a spanking, you want a spanking too?' 'Well, I don't know about that.' About that time fairness seems to lose its powers – at least for the moment.

Of course, true fairness in dealing with children is not always equalising everything, but rather giving to each according to his or her needs. Some children need more attention than others; some need more discipline than others. In fact equalising everything for siblings poses many more problems than it solves. It implies that the child is in no way special or unique and that, in and of itself, does irreparable harm to the child's self-esteem.

Most seven-year-olds can tell time and can recite the months of the year, although it is common that in such a recitation they may accidently omit one or two months. They have an understanding of the order in which seasons occur. Their internal sense of time is also emerging.

At eight

Eight is an expansive age. Eight-year-olds tend to be selfish at times and demand considerable attention; at other times they are bright and cheerful. Eight-year-olds are impatient with themselves and with others. They may be pert in their talk with family members. They are very curious about what others are doing so they may seem nosey as well. Verbally they are often out of bounds. They boast, exaggerate, and may share private family information with virtual strangers.

Eight-year-olds are improving their gross muscle skills, but accidents are common as they misjudge what they can do. They are just beginning to be capable of sustained group activity and are learning to lose at games. They are very sensitive about receiving criticism, especially in front of others.

They are also interested in their past history; eight-year-olds love to drag out the baby books and family albums, and love to hear about their own escapades as a younger child. They are also very interested in the future and what it will hold for them. They may be sure that they will become an Olympic medallist or a movie star. It is best that parents treat these boasts as possible long-range goals. Time will put a child's true potential into perspective – who knows, this child may be a future gold medallist!

Eight-year-olds express a deepening interest in life and life processes. They are better observers than they were at seven. They begin to see conclusions, contexts, and implications that they didn't see before.

Eight-year-olds begin to have a sense of humour. Eight is the age of the riddle. Nothing infuriates eight-year-olds more than having their riddle ruined when their sibling pops up with the answer.

At *nine*

Although typical nine-year-olds do experience quick extreme emotional shifts, they are short-lived and thus they appear to be more stable. Children of this age are becoming more independent. They are more responsible, cooperative, and dependable. They are capable of concentrating for several hours. This is the optimum age for children to perfect their proficiency in basic subjects at school. In fact, if they cannot read, use basic maths concepts, and write by now, it is unlikely that they will acquire these skills without considerable special effort on the part of both the child and the school.

Nine-year-olds like to plan ahead. They may appear absent-minded, but they are usually just busy thinking. They like to classify, identify, and order information. Frequently nine-year-olds take up a collecting type hobby.

They are beginning to learn to function within a group and to subordinate their own interests to those of the group. In fact, at school the teacher becomes more of a facilitator, and peer pressures become increasingly important.

Nine-year-olds work hard and play hard. They become interested in competitive sports and although they may not like to lose, they learn to lose. In fact, a nine-year-old's interest in sports is primarily related to the social aspects of the game – an attitude that frustrates more competitive parents.

At *ten*

Age ten, like age five, is a nodal stage when the child's perceptions and abilities seem to coincide. Ten-year-olds seem relaxed and casual. They can participate in discussions of social and world problems. In fact, it is a good time for parents to share their values on these matters with their children.

Friends are coming into direct competition with the family for the ten-year-old's time and for his or her esteem. It is not uncommon for a ten-year-old to believe something a friend has said rather than something the parent has said. Sharing secrets and pondering mysteries with friends delight children of this age.

Ten-year-olds enjoy family activities as long as they don't interfere with activities with friends. Peer influence is important so ten-year-olds do not like to be singled out in front of friends. A wise parent or teacher knows it is more effective at this age to criticise, correct, and praise the child in private rather than in front of a class or even other family members.

Minimising the trauma of moves

Ages six to ten
Because the child this age usually has reasonably good verbal skills and has developed some internalised sense of time, the preparation process for forthcoming moves is accomplished more easily than in the pre-school age child. However, adults need still to be listening for signs of magical thinking or misperceptions. The clues and cues to these usually are easier to identify in the child this age than in the younger child.

Adequate pre-placement preparation can go a long way in helping children of these ages understand forthcoming moves and resolve feelings about them. When pre-placement preparation is impossible because of an emergency move, we still can help the child understand what has happened in retrospect.

A major focus in helping children deal with moves is to help them identify their underlying feelings and deal with them. A second major focus for children this age should be on their being an active part of the moving process. Although the child needs reassurance that the adults are ultimately responsible for the decision making about the move, they need to know that we can only do our job well if they share with us their feelings – worries, concerns, hopes, and dreams – about the move.

Children ages six to ten in placement
Those who work with children of this age group in placement need to be particularly keyed to two development issues. The first of these is the normal development of assertion and anger. This is critical because angry or assertive responses by children in placement may be normal, but very often set off serious repercussions such as another move or severing of a relationship.

The second key issue is the effects of separation and loss on development at this stage. These two issues are discussed in the remainder of this section.

Assertion and anger
Between five and a half and six, as the child enters the period of emotional disequilibrium, aggressiveness tends to return. Since the youngster is going through an age of increasing frustration, there tends to be a recurrence of temper tantrums. This is an ideal time to teach children more appropriate ways to express frustration since they have verbal and intellectual skills they did not previously possess. They may destroy things if sent to their room or they may refuse to remain in the room because of their increased aggressiveness. They are quite likely to call people names; these names are most likely to be bathroom words such as 'you are a big piece of poop'. They are likely to make verbal threats. Overall, they tend to contradict, argue, and resist. They may hit or kick at adults who confront them and may hit or kick at other children. Cruelty towards animals may also be present at this age.

Seven-year-olds are less aggressive and have fewer tantrums. They exhibit less resistance to requests. The most common objection children make at this age is 'It isn't fair'. If angry, they prefer to withdraw from their parents rather than stay and fight as they did at six.

Typical eight-year-olds show even less aggression overall. They respond to attack or criticism with hurt feelings, rather than aggression. When they are very angry, they may become aggressive verbally. Name calling may still be present.

By age nine the swearing shifts from a vocabulary related to elimination to a vocabulary with sexual words. Fighting and 'beating him up' are common talk among boys, but again the actual aggression is more likely to be verbal than physical. Nine-year-olds are critical of others and may object to what others say or do.

It is not uncommon for a child of ten to have one last physical tantrum when confronted by parents about something. It is as though the child is asking 'Can you still control me?' Following such an outburst the child is quite likely to be very embarrassed by his or her own behaviour. However, ten, with the associated overall emotional equilibrium, is not characteristically an angry age. Crying is a common response to anger at this age.

Reactions to separations or losses between ages six and ten
Again, child placement workers need to be particularly aware of the effects of separation and losses that occur as a child passes through the stages of development described here. Separations or losses during

these years are likely to be contaminated by magical thinking or misperceptions than are separations at earlier ages. However, even with the child's increased ability to understand and conceptualise, he or she cannot handle separations or losses without supportive help.

Helping children understand that they may have more than one feeling about a loss or separation, and that having mixed feelings is normal, can help. For example, a child of this age can identify that 'part of me feels sad and part of me feels mad'. However, because of the emphasis on fairness at this age, the child may get caught spending all of his or her energy on 'why me?' or 'it's not fair' and not move further in terms of resolution of the loss.

The child's ability to understand time is important in terms of adjustment to shorter separations. However, the child's fear of the unknown means that we must be as honest as possible with him or her about what is happening now, what we think will happen in the future, and when events will occur.

If the child of this age is spending his or her emotional energy coping with feelings about separations and losses, this may interfere with the ability to accomplish the primary developmental tasks of this age, including learning in school and developing friendships with other children of the same sex. Separations and losses during these ages may cause a temporary regression to earlier stages of thinking (i.e. a reversion to magical thinking) or less mature behaviour. They may also interrupt the normal progression of conscience development.

Another important aspect of development to keep in mind in terms of children in care is the need for children during the latency years to learn more about themselves as a baby and pre-school child and to incorporate this knowledge into their continually emerging self identity. Children in care who do not have access to information about their early years and about their birth parents have difficulty in terms of self identity issues.

It is important that parents who adopt children at younger ages be aware that their children will need to know more about their past as they reach the latency ages. Adoptive parents must understand that this need in no way reflects upon the child's attachment to the adoptive family, but rather relates to a healthy desire to increase knowledge about themselves and integrate it into their self identity.

Increasingly, social workers, foster parents, and adoptive parents are being asked to deal with latency age children who have been sexually abused in previous homes. These children, by a variety of behaviours, indicate underlying developmental needs. They particularly need parenting which clarifies for them alternate modes of parent-child interaction and allows them to experience physically nurturing non-sexual relationships.

Exercise 5:
Dealing with a sexually abused child using a developmental approach

Instructions

Purpose
To help you learn to deal with a sexually abused child using a developmental approach.

How to do it:

1 Read Rhonda's case history.

2 Answer the questions on the worksheet for Exercise 5. Then, compare your own answers with those of another social worker on the sample worksheet.

Rhonda's case
Rhonda is seven years old. Her mother died two years ago after a long illness during which she was repeatedly hospitalised. Prior to her death, Rhonda's mother had told her own mother (Rhonda's grandmother) that she thought that her husband had been sexually abusing Rhonda. She said she had confronted him and he had denied abusing Rhonda. Rhonda's mother was concerned about what would happen after she died and told her mother that she had told Rhonda to tell her grandmother if Daddy did anything 'naughty' to her.

Following her mother's death, Rhonda took over the mothering of her younger brother. The babysitter noticed this both before and after school when she had both children while Rhonda's dad worked. The babysitter also commented that when the father came to pick up the children after work, Rhonda would run and kiss him on the lips. She'd greet him with a comment such as 'Did you have a hard day at work, Daddy?'

Her teacher had noted that Rhonda was 'daydreaming constantly' and falling behind in school. She had few friends and isolated herself during playtime. Recently the grandmother made an unannounced visit to the home and found Rhonda's father lying on top of her with both his and her clothes partially off. The grandmother contacted the welfare agency. Rhonda and her brother were removed from the home and taken into care. Rhonda's father is awaiting trial on charges of sexual abuse.

Exercise 5:
Dealing with a sexually abused child using a developmental approach

Worksheet

1 From a developmental standpoint what are the issues involving Rhonda with regard to sexual development and sexual identification?

2 What behaviours might one expect to see in Rhonda in placement?

3 Knowing that Rhonda experienced the loss of her mother during the Oedipal stage and the stage of magical thinking, how do you think Rhonda perceived and coped with the loss of the mother?

Exercise 5:
Dealing with a sexually abused child using a developmental approach

Worksheet

4 What would you expect Rhonda's reaction to separation from the father to be? How might she perceive this reaction?

5 What type of foster home would you select for Rhonda?

6 How would you advise the foster parents in terms of meeting Rhonda's needs with regard to developmental issues in the area of sexual identification?

Exercise 5:
Dealing with a sexually abused child using a developmental approach

Sample worksheet

1 From a developmental standpoint what are the issues involving Rhonda with regard to sexual development and sexual identification?

She lost her mother during the 'Oedipal' stage when she needed to feel that her mother was not upset by her feelings for her father. She needed to be able to identify with her mother to resolve this stage.

2 What behaviours might one expect to see in Rhonda in placement?

She may be very sexually provocative with men. She may daydream a lot and may not concentrate. She may have a lot of fears, nightmares, etc. She may find it difficult to relate to a foster mother.

3 Knowing that Rhonda experienced the loss of her mother during the Oedipal stage and the stage of magical thinking, how do you think Rhonda perceived and coped with the loss of the mother?

She will blame herself and feel her 'magical thoughts' have come true. She will feel herself to be omnipotent and yet be frightened and guilty. She coped by trying to take her mother's place with her father and by being a mother to her younger brother.

Dealing with a sexually abused child using a developmental approach

Sample worksheet

---

4   What would you expect Rhonda's reaction to separation from the father to be? How might she perceive this reaction?

With both relief and a sense of loss. She will feel she is being punished, deservedly, for her 'bad thoughts' about her mother.

---

5   What type of foster home would you select for Rhonda?

Foster parents who are comfortable with sexual issues and with each other.

---

6   How would you advise the foster parents in terms of meeting Rhonda's needs with regard to developmental issues in the area of sexual identification?

They need to help Rhonda identify with a woman and accept her femininity, and to feel valued in a non-sexual relationship with a man. They need to be alert to correct her magical thinking.

---

5 Adolescence

The overall task

Although many people equate adolescence with the teenage years, the physical and emotional changes that mark adolescence start at age 11. This is especially true for girls who, on the whole, tend to mature physically two years ahead of boys. In this section, we will discuss ages 11 to 16 as the adolescent years. The chart below highlights the sequence of physical changes that mark adolescence.

Figure 1
Sequence of physical changes

Female
1 breast enlargement
2 development of straight pubic hair
3 maximum growth spurt
4 development of kinky pubic hair
5 onset of menstruation
6 development of axillary hair

Male
1 growth in size of testes
2 straight pubic hair
3 increased size of penis
4 beginnings of voice changes
5 first ejaculation
6 maximum growth spurt
7 axillary hair
8 marked voice change
9 development of beard

From Normal Adolescence: Group for Advancement of Psychiatry New York, Vol VI, Report 68, 1968

Normal development

Adolescents are moody. Normally they alternate between being unreliable and being dependable and responsible. As they separate from the family, they are likely to oppose family rules, values, and expectations. They seem to be preoccupied with complying with the peer group and opposing the family. At the same time they have a strong need to belong in the family and to be taken seriously.

Adolescents have both abundant sexual and aggressive impulses. It is important that adults help them separate these two issues and learn to deal with each in socially acceptable ways.

The psychological tasks to be accomplished in adolescence bear a marked similarity to those of the pre-school years. The task of pre-school children is to separate from family members, particularly their mother, and to become independent individuals within the family structure. During adolescence, individuals must find their place in the world at large just as during the pre-school years they needed to clarify their place within the family. To do this children frequently act in opposition to the family as a whole.

Adolescence is an age when control battles between parent and child emerge again and when frustration is a prominent part of the child's experience. Any issues that were poorly handled during the pre-school years may re-emerge during the adolescent years. Adolescence provides an opportunity for re-cycling and successfully solving unresolved developmental issues.

In general, during adolescence, young people experience a year of opening horizons with new difficulties followed by a year of consolidation of gains. In other words, both parents and children can expect a year filled with crises to be followed by a year with some measure of reprieve in which to repair relationships and enjoy each other before the next stage is reached.

At 11

Typical 11-year-olds show some similarities to both the early toddler stage and to the child of five and a half to six. They are again emotionally unstable, and are always in motion. They are assertive, curious, investigative, talkative, and sociable. They have a vast appetite both for food and for experience. They can fly into rage at short notice and burst out laughing with little provocation. They tire easily. They are in such a state of disequilibrium that even their temperature control is uneven; they always seem to be either too hot or too cold.

The child of this age is starting to see parents as individuals, not just as parents and is becoming critical of them. Frequently, adjusting at school comes easier than adjusting at home. In general their best behaviour is away from home.

At this age children hate to go to bed at night and hate to get up in the morning. Although they usually begin to take an interest in clothes, they usually don't take good care of them. 11-year-olds hate work and frequently spend more energy avoiding tasks than it would take to accomplish them.

This is the poorest age for getting along with siblings. 11-year-olds like school more for friends than for learning. They compete for grades and in athletics. 11 and 12 are the most fearful of the adolescent years. Fear of wild animals, snakes, bugs, and ghosts is common.

At 12

Typical 12-year-olds are less insistent, more reasonable, and more companionable. They try to win the approval of others. Although their peer group is increasingly important to them, they are less competitive within it than they were at 11. They are able to do more independent work at school and, in general, need less supervision. In fact school, at this age, is a source of great satisfaction for most children because of their capacity for prolonged periods of factual learning and because of their increase in conceptual ability. If children have problems in school, then one of their major chances for positive feedback is eliminated. 12-year-olds enjoy discussions and debates, but they are calmer in their arguments than they were at 11 and don't resist just for the sake of doing so.

This is normally a period that favours integration of the personality. Parents often describe 12-year-olds as likeable. Children of this age have a great enthusiasm for things they like and hatred for the things they dislike. They are able to deal with others, and can be dealt with, through humour.

There is a wide range of difference noted in the rate of physical growth among 12-year-old boys. 12-year-olds show an increasing interest in the opposite sex. Yet because of the wide difference in the rate of development between girls and boys there are resulting variations in their interest in the opposite sex.

At 13

13-year-olds show a certain resemblance to seven-year-olds. Compared to 12-year-olds they are less outgoing and inquisitive and may sometimes seem withdrawn and moody. They use their withdrawal from the family as a chance to mull over and incorporate experiences; the withdrawal is not an indication of retreat from reality. 13-year-olds are reflective. They spend a lot of time in front of the mirror, as well as reflecting mentally. This is an age when most adolescents are going through marked physical changes and much of the time in front of mirrors is spent integrating the 'new' person with the old self-perceptions. The mirror fosters self discovery and self assurance.

13-year-olds are very sensitive to criticism. They may be critical of their parents, but usually this criticism concerns problems that they are trying to resolve themselves. This is a good age for parents to back off, because of the 13-year-olds' sensitivity to criticism.

13-year-olds are more likely to be annoyed or irritated than to have outbursts of anger. They are not as demonstrative. At the same time they are more aware of their own feelings.

Again, for good students, school is a source of satisfaction. Children of this age are better able to organise their time in school; their concentration is more sustained and their self control is more evident. They become selective about what they choose to compete in and usually choose things they are good at.

At 14

At 14 children typically become expansive and outgoing again. They are less withdrawn and seem happier. They seem to enjoy life. They are friendly both at home and away. Although they may be highly embarrassed by parental conduct, the relationships within the family are less tense. 14-year-olds and their family have more respect for each other and confidence in each other. 14-year-olds seem to be more objective and capable of self appraisal than they were at 13. They will look at both sides of an issue.

Girls at age 14 usually have the bodies of young women, while many boys have not yet matured physically. This is an age when further sex education is both needed and eagerly received. This is the peak age for telephone calls for girls. Since many of the girls phone boys, it may be a peak age for incoming calls for boys as well. The telephone not only allows the adolescent to spend more time with peers without ever leaving home, but it also allows the adolescent to talk about sex and relate to members of the opposite sex without risk of it leading to immediate sexual encounters.

At 15

15-year-olds are frequently lazy or indifferent – they don't appear to expend much energy. In reality their energies are focused inwardly rather than outwardly. Although most children are not as intensely moody as they were at 13, there is a similarity in the way they withdraw from the family. This, as at 13, is related to pre-occupation with feelings.

15-year-olds are experiencing a growing awareness and perceptiveness, though they tend to cover up their feelings in front of others. They are trying to sort out their own potential and limitations. They seem to resist even reasonable restrictions imposed by others as a way of asserting independence.

At 16
16-year-olds seem self assured and self reliant. By now both adolescent and parents take his or her increased independence for granted. In general, there are fewer arguments between parents and adolescent. 16-year-olds have their emotions pretty well in hand and seem to be not so touchy or moody.

Minimising the trauma of separation

In adolescence
The adolescent is usually a very active participant in the moving process, both prior to the move, during the move, and during the post-placement period. The adjustment is likely to be smoother if the adolescent feels that his or her thoughts and desires are being fully considered in the moving process.

Contracting and getting firm verbal and/or written commitments from the adolescent about how he or she is willing to work at making the placement succeed are techniques that increase the likelihood of successful placements.

Because major issues for adolescence revolve around separation – individuation, control issues, and sexual issues – these should be addressed directly during the placement process. If adolescents think that adults are trying to make all decisions for them or are trying to control them, they are likely to rebel more in a behavioural manner. If they think that they have been part of the entire decision-making process, such rebellion is both less likely and more easily confronted if it does occur. Statements such as, 'I'm confused; before moving you said that you thought the rules in this group home were reasonable; now you seem to be bent on breaking them' can be used if rebellion does occur. This opens the door for adolescents both to talk about how they feel and to take responsibility for their own behaviour.

Adolescents in placement

In this section, the information that is highlighted has special relevance to work with adolescents in placement. First, normal assertion and anger during adolescence is discussed. Again, this aspect of development is highlighted because normal expression of assertion and anger by adolescents in placement is much too often misconstrued and perhaps the cause of over-reaction. Understanding normal development can help sort out a particular adolescent's behaviour. In addition, this section highlights the effects of separation and loss on children in adolescence and some of the problems posed by trying to integrate the adolescent into a new family.

Assertion and anger in adolescence

It is important to remember that control issues emerge again in adolescence because the child is again working on making a psychological separation from the family. Children at age 11 get angry more often than they did at ten. It is common for children this age to yell, hit, and slam doors. Rather violent verbal retorts are common. It is the poorest age for getting along with younger siblings.

12-year-olds may still strike out physically or throw things when they are angry. However, this is the last age at which an immediate physical response to anger is usually seen. Verbal responses become more and more frequent. 12-year-olds often assert themselves by 'talking-back' to parents. At 13, the most common response to anger is leaving the room. Sulking is common and there may be tears in the eyes in response to anger.

14-year-olds do not anger especially easily. Physical responses and crying are much less common than they were previously. Swearing, name calling, and sarcasm are sometimes used; however, an even more important aspect of this is raised by adolescents who have lost parental figures earlier in life and who do not have sufficient memories for the separation and identification process. It is common for adolescents to need further information about their birth parents at this time and to come to further resolution about the separation and loss of these parental figures if the psychological tasks of adolescence are to be accomplished. Adolescents in placement, whether it be foster or adoptive placement, use both the parental figures with whom they are living and the memories or information about the birth parents during their struggle for independence.

Placing an adolescent into a new home poses special problems, particularly if it is an adoptive home. It is difficult to encourage attachment and bonding between parent and child when the primary developmental task is for the adolescent to find his or her place in the world, separate from other family members. Such placement may work best if the adolescent makes a firm commitment to the new relationship and if the new parents understand the difficulties they may face in building bonds with a child at this age. The parents must be firmly committed to helping the adolescent achieve a balance between attachment and independence. Because the oppositional drives seem strongest in early adolescence adoptive placements undertaken between the ages of 12 and 14 seem to face more difficulties than those undertaken later in adolescence at ages 15-16 (Jewett[7]).

When adolescents are placed in foster homes or in adoptive homes, parental figures must be cognisant of the adolescent sexual issues, so that they can be supportive in helping the child resolve such issues at the same time as they form non-sexual relationships with the adolescent.

With the increasing incidence of sexual abuse, even of the young child, all social workers and alternative parents must learn to become more comfortable dealing with the sexual issues which are emerging in such a large proportion of cases in child care.

Exercise 6 that follows deals with identifying unmet developmental needs in the older child.

Exercise 6:
Identifying unmet needs in the older child and creating an environment to meet these needs

Instructions

Purpose:
To help you learn to identify unmet developmental needs in the older child and to plan to meet these needs.

How to do it:

1 Read Tracy's case history.

2 Answer the questions on the worksheet for Exercise 6. Then, compare your own answers with those of another social worker on the sample worksheet.

Tracy's case

Tracy is 12. She was recently placed for adoption. Her birth family had a wide variety of problems. Her father is an alcoholic and frequently was gone from home for extended periods of time. Her mother had periods of depression. She was sexually promiscuous between her depressive episodes. Although Tracy had been visually exposed to many adult sexual encounters, there was no history of direct sexual abuse. There had, however, been some episodes of physical abuse by both the birth mother and the mother's various boyfriends.

Following one episode of physical abuse when she was eight, Tracy was placed in care. Attempts at intervention in terms of helping the family to be better able to meet Tracy's needs were unsuccessful because her birth parents did not follow through on any of the recommendations. Their parental rights were terminated when Tracy was 11.

In her adoptive home Tracy is the middle of three children; the other two are boys. The adoptive parents complain that Tracy is always underfoot and never gives them a moment of privacy. She constantly hangs on to one or the other of them. She even 'hangs on' to the boys. She constantly interrupts adult conversations. When her parents' friends come to visit, she hangs on to them and asks very personal questions that show no sign of tact.

When Tracy doesn't get her own way, she tends to pout, whine, and may retreat, crying, to her room. Although she likes to help her adoptive mother, her mother gets tired of having her underfoot. Frequently she asks Tracy to clean up her room or to dust in another part of the house. Such requests are usually met with passive non-compliance. Tracy will go to her room, but she will not complete the job.

Tracy does not do very well in terms of self-care skills. She takes baths or showers only when reminded. Frequently she comes to the table with dirty hands and face and unkempt hair unless specifically reminded to clean up for dinner. She hates to wash her hair. She likes her mother to wash her hair and is especially pleased if her mother curls her hair.

At school Tracy is behind academically. In spite of receiving extra help she gets poor marks. The teacher complains that she is very immature, that the other girls her age call her 'baby' and avoid her. Tracy is prone to nightmares. She is afraid of the dark and is afraid of thunder at night.

Identifying unmet needs in the older child and creating an environment to meet these needs

Worksheet

1 At what overall developmental level does Tracy seem to be functioning?

2 What advice would you give to her adoptive parents about the following behaviour:

– her hanging on behaviour:

– her constant interrupting:

– her whining and pouting:

– her poor self-help skills:

– her desire to help but refusal to do a good job when left on her own:

– her fears:

Exercise 6:
Identifying unmet needs in the older child and creating an environment to meet these needs

Sample worksheet

---

1 At what overall developmental level does Tracy seem to be functioning?

Somewhere between a toddler and a five-to six-year-old.

---

2 What advice would you give to her adoptive parents about the following behaviour: Overall to help them understand the level she is functioning at · and the need to achieve a balance between attachment and independence.

– her hanging on behaviour:

Be patient. Find ways of encouraging attachment and positive interaction.

– her constant interrupting:

Ask her to wait her turn but give her lots of opportunities for conversation.

– her whining and pouting:

Praise her if she can deal positively with a situation - look for positive ways out of situations rather than battles she has to lose.

– her poor self-help skills:

Help her to get into a routine by patient reminders, praise for remembering and looking nice, and doing the things she likes - e.g. curling her hair.

– her desire to help but refusal to do a good job when left on her own:

Do things with her at first and praise her for her achievements.

– her fears:

Establish comfortable bed-time rituals - e.g. talking, reading, playing a game together. Leave a night light.

---

6 Special developmental issues

In this final section we highlight four special developmental issues: fears and worries, temper tantrums, conscience development, and sexual issues. These issues were selected because of their particular relevance to children in placement. Some of these issues, such as temper tantrums, are likely to be of particular concern to the biological, foster, and adoptive parents involved with a particular child. Others, like fears and worries, are included because they are often problematic for the child in placement and those problems need to be detected.

Fears and worries
There are common, normal fears and worries that accompany each stage of child development. The parents' job is to help the child cope with and overcome these fears. Parents should *not* belittle the child or make him or her feel inadequate because of their fears – this cannot possibly help the child learn to feel brave and capable. Nor must they reassure the child excessively or try to remove all possibilities for fear as this is an impossible task.

The child has enough fears to cope with so that parental figures should not add to the fears by use of threats. A child's fears of abandonment are exacerbated by threats of leaving him or her in the event of a temper tantrum in the grocery store. A child who has a fear of going to the doctor is not helped by a threat of 'If you don't stop crying, I will tell the doctor to give you an injection.' If a child is going through a stage of many fears with regard to strange noises, the parents should not make loud, scary sounds to teach the child to get over the fear.

Acknowledging that the child is afraid while providing some comfort, will give the child more strength to overcome the fear. The parent may ask the verbal child if there is any way that the parent can help him or her with the fear.

During the first year of life infants usually startle in response to fear-producing sensations. Loud or unexpected noises are frequently frightening to them. Sudden movements may stimulate fear. Threats of falling, or being dropped, as well as threats of bodily harm or pain lead to fear reactions.

During the first half of the second year, children become afraid of separations from the mother and may cry vigorously when they see her leave. The sounds of mechanical gadgets, particularly those that move, such as vacuum cleaners and certain mechanical toys, provoke fear during this period.

Two-year-olds are afraid of noises such as trains, thunder, animal sounds, or flushing toilets. They may have fears of going down the drain. Separation from mother, particularly at bedtime, may still scare them.

During the second half of the second year children are also prone to spatial fears. They may fear being moved rapidly, and they may also react to having objects in their environment moved from their usual place. They notice and object to being taken by a different car route to a known place. They are fearful of large objects approaching them.

Visual fears predominate in three-year-olds. Children at this age are frequently fearful of masks, costumes, strange appearing objects, the dark, and animals. The fear of being left alone at night is still present, and three-year-olds may react adversely to separation from the parents at night-time while accepting daytime separations with a measure of grace.

Since children's imagination emerges between the ages of three and a half and four, they become prone to fearful thoughts and to fearful dreams. Four-year-olds are fearful of a wide variety of stimuli. Sirens and other loud sharp noises provoke fear. It is not uncommon for four-year-olds to be frightened of people who look 'different'. This may include people with physical disabilities, the elderly, or people of a different race from those they are accustomed to seeing. A fear of animals is frequently still present and many four-year-olds are very afraid of bugs. Fear of the dark is the single most common fear of four-year-olds. Children may want a night light or may want the parent to precede them into the room at bedtime before the light is turned on. If the parent agrees to such simple measures, it will help the child learn to trust that he or she has good ideas about how to overcome their own fears.

Sometimes children are afraid that something may be hiding under the bed. If the child wishes to look under the bed while the parent is there, that is fine. However, if the parent joins in the search for hidden fearful objects, this may imply that the parent, too, believes that something might be present.

Children this age use the word 'afraid' or 'scared' and may even enjoy being mildly frightened by an adult in play if, in general, adults in their life have been trustworthy. Since four-year-olds are able to imagine things, they are commonly fearful of 'monsters', or 'bogeymen'. This fear is frequently associated with their fear of the dark. Overall, their fears seem unreasonable to the adults in their life.

One of pre-school children's greatest fears is that their parents will not be available when they need them. Threats of separation or abandonment should *never* be used with the pre-school age child.

A common fear seen in children in foster care is fear of the water. This may be very extreme and may relate to any form of bathing or swimming, particularly if it involves getting the face and head wet. Frequently adults assume that the child has been threatened with drowning or has been held under water. Although this has happened in some rare child care cases, most of the time this extreme fear is not based on real events. It more likely relates to an overall lack of trust that others will not protect the child and keep him or her safe.

In general, five is not a particularly fearful age until the child reaches the disequilibrium that usually occurs between ages five and a half and six. Most of the fears of the early five-year-old are concrete down-to-earth fears, such as fear of bodily harm, fear of falling, or fear of being bitten by a dog. Thunder or sirens at night might be fear-arousing. The fear that mother will not be available when needed is still present and demonstrates itself in terms of fears that mother will be lost or will not be home when the child returns from school.

It is common for six-year-olds to be afraid of thunder, lightning, and fire. They also have a fear of deformities and a fear that mother may die. They are very fearful of even slight injuries to themselves and they respond out of all proportion to the extent of the injury. Every parent has had the experience of hearing their six-year-old scream that he or she is bleeding. The parent goes running, expecting that a trip to the hospital for stitches is imminent, and finds the child immobilised by a small scratch on the finger. Rather than ridicule the child or minimise his or her fears, it is best to wash it, plaster it, give the child an extra squeeze, and reassure them that it will heal quickly because they have a fine healthy body. This fear seems related to the child's emerging awareness combined with his or her lack of awareness of what the long-term effects of their own minor injuries may be.

Seven-year-olds fear the unknown and are quite likely to be fearful when they find themselves in a new or unfamiliar situation. However, they are beginning to learn ways to cope with their own fears, and they are no longer so dependent upon adults to help with them. Frequently they are ashamed of fears and may be embarrassed if they are seen crying.

By age eight, the child's fears are decreasing although they may fear not being liked. Eight-year-olds love to frighten others with snakes and bugs and scary stories.

Nine-year-olds do not have as many fears, but they have worries. They are upset by their own mistakes and worried about school failure. They enjoy frightening others and being frightened themselves. They are, in fact, proud of being 'frightened to death', but living through it. Nine-year-olds are not afraid if mother is not home after school so long as they know what to expect.

Ten overall is a less fearful age than the next two years. Fears of being killed or kidnapped may be present.

11 and 12 are the most fearful of the adolescent years. Children of these ages tend to worry about things they fear. Wild animals, snakes, and being alone in the dark are common fears. The fear of the dark is frequently related to lights shining in from outside a house causing shadows. Sounds that are not understood at night lead to fears of intruders. Worries usually centre on school and social concerns.

During the remaining adolescent years, fears become less prominent. Worries about personal appearance, social acceptance, popularity, grades, performing in public, applying for a job, and their personal future increase during adolescence as fears decrease. Some adolescents even worry about not worrying enough.

Temper tantrums

Understanding the causes of temper tantrums makes their occurrence more predictable. Ways to manage them also become apparent. Temper tantrums occur when three conditions are present simultaneously:

1 The child has a great need or desire.
2 He or she has an inability to achieve this need or desire.
3 He or she does not know how to express the frustration in an appropriate way.

161

Temper tantrums are most common between the ages of one and three. Children have a great need during this time to become independent and to feel 'big', yet frequently fail to achieve this. They run into opposition from others, and they face their own physical limitations. It is not realistic to expect toddlers to be able to express their frustrations 'appropriately' by adult standards. Of course, children differ in their ability to tolerate frustration and thus in their propensity to temper tantrums.

During the toddler years, some children do best if they are ignored during the tantrum, while others need to be physically close to an adult. If children become so out of control that they start to hurt themselves or others, then parents should physically control them. Allowing children to feel out of control is very threatening to them. They recognise they cannot stop their own behaviour and if no one else will stop them, they are at the mercy of all their internal impulses.

At any rate, during a temper tantrum, the children are uncomfortable. When the temper tantrum is over and the discomfort alleviated, they are very open to nurturance and acceptance by an adult. At the *end* of the temper tantrum, it is possible to build attachment between a child and an adult. This is when a child needs reassurance that the adult understands that he or she was frustrated, not 'bad', and that they are still loved. For the toddler all this can be communicated by physical comforting and closeness.

Four-year-olds frequently have a recurrence of temper tantrums with their increased stubbornness and resistance. Children between five and a half and six whose abilities have not yet caught up with their perceptions are again prone to temper tantrums. This is a common age for great frustration stemming from children's own perceived limitations rather than from parental opposition or restriction. This is confusing to parents, and they become frustrated themselves with children at this age.

When children between ages four and six have tantrums, the parents' goal should be to help teach the child how to express frustration appropriately rather than to alleviate the frustration. At this age most children cannot relieve their frustration by words alone; they need a physical outlet as well.

Again, at the end of the temper tantrum, discussing the cause of the frustration, reassuring the child that everyone gets frustrated, and being physically close to the child promotes bonding. The parents' modelling the way they themselves cope with frustration is very important. Parents who abuse their child or others when he or she is frustrated have not yet learned to handle their own frustration appropriately and are poorly equipped to help the child handle his or her feelings.

Hopefully, by the time children reach early adolescence, they will have learned the appropriate ways to express their frustration, since this is normally a time of increased frustration and impulsivity. Because of aggressive impulses and their increased physical size adolescents themselves are fearful of their own reaction to anger and frustration and they may seek to be alone – even by running away – as an attempt to deal with these feelings in a non-harmful way.

Conscience development and values incorporation

What is conscience? According to Selma Fraiberg[8], 'Conscience consists of a set of standards and prohibitions which have been taken over by the personality and which govern behaviour from within.'

Attachment is related to conscience development. Children must fear the loss of the love of someone they are attached to and trust if they are to develop a conscience. This does not mean that adults need to threaten children with loss of love. The fear is already there; it is overwhelming to children to be threatened directly. Threats of abandonment or loss of love undermine a child's sense of trust for an adult.

The greatest inherent fear of three-year-old children is that their mother may abandon them. If this occurs repeatedly, children do not learn to trust and to feel secure in the presence of others. There is no foundation for conscience development.

Conscience development takes a number of years to be completed; it doesn't occur in a matter of days, weeks, or months. Most children are nine or ten before their conscience is ingrained enough so that they feel guilty when they are quite sure they won't be caught. Until that stage, children feel best if they are receiving adequate supervision from adults so they don't have to struggle to maintain self control that is beyond their abilities. Conscience development continues throughout the primary and secondary years and is not complete until the adolescent is completely independent of his or her parents. Values continue to change during adult years as well.

Unfortunately, the word 'guilt' has received a bad reputation in the past few years. Much is said and written about the dangers of too much guilt, but guilt needs to be kept in balance. Too much guilt is paralysing; however, too little guilt is dangerous. Adolescents and adults with no conscience may steal, assault, and murder without guilt.

Conscience development in toddlers

As toddlers, children only experience guilt when they receive or anticipate disapproval from the outside. They stop themselves from touching a desirable object only when they know that it will incur their parents' disapproval and/or discipline. It is very important that parents give very clear messages about which behaviour they approve and which they disapprove. These do not need to be lengthy explanations; in fact, such explanations may be detrimental in the long run. Initially the disapproval can be expressed by the word 'no' said in a no-nonsense tone.

Approval can be conveyed by the single word 'good' spoken in a soft, approving tone and accompanied by a caress. When the child is speaking in short sentences around age three, short sentences can be used to express the approval or disapproval; for example, 'I really like it when you do this,' or 'I don't like that behaviour at all.' As the child approaches school age simple explanations of the reasons for disapproving of his or her behaviour should be given. Messages starting with the word 'I' are more helpful than those starting with 'you'. 'You' messages too often become a form of name calling.

Conscience development in pre-school children

Four and five-year-olds are at one and the same time the most truthful and untruthful of creatures. Basically they are very honest, often to the embarrassment of their parents, because they lack 'tact'. At the same time, they certainly are not above projecting blame onto another, even an imaginary friend at a pinch. Adults generally demand that their children always tell the truth. However, frequently this is not what they truly want the children to do.

'I remember being in a lift with my four-and-a-half year old daughter and a man who was a stranger to us. My daughter carefully scrutinised him and then offered, "You know, you would look better without a beard." Although she was merely expressing her honest opinion, I certainly was embarrassed!'

Frequently when children say something bluntly truthful, either about an adult or another child, parents reply, 'You don't really mean that.' This is especially common when the four or five-year-old honestly expresses his or her feelings about a sibling with 'I hate him.' Parents consistently try to talk the child out of being honest. The brutally honest way that children of this age express strong feelings seems to make adults feel very uncomfortable. Adults seem to forget the transitory nature of feelings.

Parents must reassess their own values when they are dealing with pre-school-age children. Frequently parents hold two values that are at times incompatible. Take for example 'honesty' and 'respect for your elders'. When these two values conflict, which value is the child to choose? Parents need to clarify and even rank their own values if it is important to them to transmit them to their child.

Usually we want children to be honest about their own behaviour; hopefully, we can accept their honesty about their own strong feelings.

When it comes to comments about others, we want them to be honest as long as they have something positive to say, but otherwise to keep quiet! This children learn as they acquire a sense of tact.

The years between four and six are crucial for conscience development. Most children do a number of things that their parents don't like during this period. Most of the time they are under the supervision of their parents or another adult, which is an important requirement for conscience development.

It is rarely necessary and usually dangerous to begin an exchange with a pre-school child with a phrase like 'Who took the cookies?' or whatever. At this age it is common to see the trail of cookie crumbs leading directly to the culprit who still has the remains around his or her mouth. If the parent asks 'Who took the cookies?' he or she is sure to get 'Not me' in response despite the evidence to the contrary. If the parent moves to 'Don't lie to me; I know you did it,' then the child feels deceived since the parent's implied message in 'Who took the cookies?' is that the parent doesn't already know the answer.

The parent who understands conscience development and wants to aid in its development says 'I see you took the cookies; you know that I don't like that. Now you just sit down here until you can tell me about it.' The implied message in this is 'I know what is going on so there is no advantage to lying; in fact the advantage is in telling the truth.'

If the parents are trying to encourage honesty about misbehaviour, then they should not punish children after they tell the truth. The implied message in this is 'You get into trouble telling the truth; learn to be a better liar.' If the rule infraction is one that needs more direct discipline then it's not the time to work on honesty, but 'I know that you did so and so, and this is what is going to happen because of it.'

The most useful adjuncts to the development of conscience at this age are parents' 'Big eyes and ears' that keep track of the child's activities. That is why children commonly think parents have eyes in the back of their heads – a useful misperception in terms of conscience development. Mother's big eyes and ears should not be limited to use in negative situations. She can make positive comments like 'It certainly sounded as though you were having fun playing in your room.' The important thing is for children to feel that their parents already know what is going on with them and that they might as well be truthful.

Since this is such a necessary stage of normal conscience development, it becomes apparent why it is difficult to aid conscience development when it is delayed and children are old enough to be out of parents' supervision much of the time.

The next step is noticing when children stop themselves from misbehaving and positively reinforcing this. An example will serve to clarify this.

Case example

I was seeing an eight-year-old in counselling with his parents. He had been moved several times before being placed in his adoptive home at age seven and did not have much trust in adults. Understandably, he had delayed conscience development.

His dishonesty was of great concern to his parents. Much of the counselling was aimed at helping the parents help the child develop a conscience. One day when the mother happened to glance out of the upstairs window, she saw the boy start to do something he had repeatedly been reprimanded about, then glance up at the window, and stop himself. Though she was beyond his sight, just the thought that she might be there enabled him to stop himself. Later his mother commented, 'I noticed you stopped yourself from doing so and so today; that's really good.' This told the child two things; first, 'I still know what is going on, and I would have stopped you if you hadn't stopped yourself,' and second, 'I like it when you can control yourself, and I don't have to.'

Conscience development in older children

By the time the child is six, parents can usually learn to tell the special way that each child has of expressing his or her anxiety when being untruthful. For one it is avoiding eye contact; for another it may be frequent licking of the lips, gulping or rapid clenching and releasing of the fists. Once the parents have learned to identify these 'give-aways' with certainty they should share their knowledge with the child. For example they should say 'Your mouth is telling me one thing, but your eyes are telling me something else. I have learned to believe your eyes in this situation.'

Many parents are reluctant to do this. However, a 'guilty' conscience occurs when children feel uncomfortable internally on doing something 'wrong', even when they do not fear being caught and punished by another. This internalised guilty feeling is usually associated with a feeling of anxiety. Helping children to recognise these feelings and their own behaviour demonstrates to them that they are capable of telling the truth themselves. A parent can say to a child, 'Pay attention to your eyes; what are they saying?' This method starts to hook the eyes and the mouth up to give a congruent message. It also helps the child to recognise his or her own discomfort and correct their own behaviour.

It is usually during these years between six and ten that children begin to confront their parents about discrepancies between their actions and words. At this stage of development a child might ask 'How come you say "always be honest", but you told me to tell the salesman you weren't home?'

In the past children were not exposed to as many different value systems as they now confront. Communities and neighbourhoods were more homogeneous. Children's friends, neighbours, teachers and schoolmates were more likely to hold values not too different from those they learned at home.

In more recent years communities and neighbourhoods are comprised of families with varying values. Children, even in their early school years, may be exposed to values in sharp contrast to those held by the parents. In addition the influence of television in terms of value judgements is considerable.

Wise parents will make sure that their children have contact with other families who have similar values. This becomes very important during the adolescent years. At this time young people are more open to learning values outside the home than in the home environment. It is usual for adolescents to use an adult other than their own parents to confide in. This confidant may be the parent of a friend or it may be a young adult. Parents should try to ensure that their adolescent has opportunities to confide in other adults who hold values similar to their own.

It is not uncommon for an adolescent to come home with 'news' that so and so believes such and such. Frequently this is the same value that the parents think they have been stressing themselves. However, it is best if they take an approach of interest and acceptance, rather than exclaiming 'What do you think I've been trying to teach you!'

With older children parents should teach values at times when the children are not under pressure. When children do not feel that a message is aimed at changing them, they are more likely to hear it and accept it. The larger part of value teaching takes place prior to adolescence. Yet many parents think that they can wait until those crucial years and then make their impact. Age ten is an ideal time for value teaching. Children at ten are old enough to understand, yet young enough to accept parental values more readily.

Adolescents frequently go through a period in which they reject their parents' values. Some of this seems to be necessary for them to separate from the family. The parents must manage to assert that their values have worked well for them without getting into control battles over them. Parents who achieve this are quite likely to find that the adolescent chooses to accept most of his or her parents' values as they reach adulthood. This acceptance comes because the adolescent chooses the values rather than bending to pressure.

Unfortunately many parents try to make control issues of values. This is rarely successful. The statement 'You may not ever smoke pot' is impossible to enforce unless the parents keep the adolescent under their eyes all of the time. 'You may not smoke pot in our house' is certainly easier to enforce. If parents make clear statements about what they approve or disapprove of, it is not the same as making a control issue out of a particular value. Again, they should take care to start their declarations with 'I think . . .' or 'I believe . . .' rather than 'You may not . . .'.

Exercise 7 that follows gives you an opportunity to consider conscience development issues that face the adoptive parents of a youngster in placement.

Exercise 7:
Working with delayed conscience development
In Workbook 1, *Attachment and separation*, we considered Sharon's case focussing on ways to encourage attachment; now we will re-examine it from a developmental viewpoint.

Instructions

Purpose:
To help you learn about children with delayed conscience development and think about strategies for working with them.

How to do it:

1 Read Sharon's case history.

2 Answer the questions on the worksheet for Exercise 7. Then compare your own answers with those of another social worker on the sample worksheet.

Sharon's case

Sharon is an eight-year-old girl who is being placed for adoption in a family with three older boys. Past history reveals that Sharon experienced considerable emotional and physical deprivation, rejection, and physical abuse from her birth parents. She has had seven moves since she first entered care at age three.

Sharon has many fears including fear of the dark and fear of new situations. She is prone to nightmares. There is a history of both daytime and night-time wetting. She is a very demanding child who verbally pressures and manipulates adults. She gets little pleasure from being a child and prefers to 'pretend' that she is an adolescent going out on dates. She is very seductive in her relationships with males.

Sharon has many gaps in her basic fund of knowledge; she exhibits problems with logical thinking and basic cause and effect. Sharon has many problems with lying; she tends to 'forget' what she chooses not to hear. Her lying extends even to saying 'that is may favourite food' when in reality it is a food she dislikes. At other times her lying is aimed at keeping herself out of trouble.

She has marked difficulties with peer relationships. She does well in the self-help skills. She likes to help with household tasks. In school, she is reading above her age level but has some difficulty with maths. She shows appropriate responses and is an attractive girl who is quite outgoing. Her self-esteem is poor, as indicated by comments such as 'something is wrong with me' when she makes an error. She is able to talk about feelings and can tell of many ways that she and her present foster parents have fun together.

Sharon picks up money from around the house and denies it. Frequently she comes home from school with pencils, small amounts of money, and other small objects that she claims to have 'found'. She sometimes lies about unimportant, inconsequential things that she would not be punished for doing. It has been noted that when she lies, Sharon's eyes become very large and her gaze is very direct. She frequently says 'and that's the truth' at this time. Sharon's adoptive mother teaches at the school that Sharon attends.

Exercise 7:
Working with delayed conscience development

Worksheet

1 At what age level does Sharon seem to be functioning in terms of conscience development?

2 What specific advice would you give to the adoptive parents about dealing with Sharon's various types of lying?

3 What would be your advice about the 'found' objects?

4 You may choose also to give suggestions about her fears and her preference to 'pretend' that she is an adolescent.

Exercise 7:
Working with delayed conscience development

Sample worksheet

---

1 At what age level does Sharon seem to be functioning in terms of conscience development?

She is functioning at a 'pre-school' level in terms of conscience development.

---

2 What specific advice would you give to the adoptive parents about dealing with Sharon's various types of lying?

Make it clear that they know when she is lying - her eyes give her away. Encourage her to be honest about misbehaviour. Keep track of her activities so that she feels they know what's going on and she might as well be truthful; and praise her.

3 What would be your advice about the 'found' objects?

Check with the school and return anything that had not been 'found'.

---

4 You may choose to give suggestions about her fears and her preference to 'pretend' that she is an adolescent.

Help the parents recognise these as the fears and behaviour of a younger child. Develop bedtime rituals and encourage attachment behaviour. Give her more sex education, help her become attached to her new mother and identify with her. Let her see that she can gain her new father's affection without being sexually provocative.

172

Sexual development

From a very early age the child's pleasurable sexual feelings are inhibited by parents. For instance, the mouth which is a source of pleasure to babies, becomes 'off limits' for anything except food. Even fingers and thumbs are frequently prohibited.

Children learn early on that there are certain other parts of the body, which to them seem associated with elimination, that they are not to touch. The confusing thing for children is that these are precisely the areas of the body that are the most pleasant to touch. Gradually, most pre-school children learn that while they cannot touch their sexual organs in public, they may do it in private. However, they are likely to feel guilty if they do so. At the same time they learn that although they may touch many parts of their parents' bodies, other parts are 'off limits'.

By age two and a half children's sense of identity is strongly associated with their sex and position in the family. For each family there are different expectations for the oldest girl, oldest boy, youngest child, and so on. The family's expectations and the degree to which children achieve them become part of children's sense of themselves and affect their self esteem.

Young children get good feelings about themselves if they perceive that their sexuality is valued by both parents. If either parent does not value a child's sexuality, then the child is likely to develop problems with self esteem and have difficulty feeling comfortable with his or her own sexual identity.

The Oedipal stage occurs between the ages of four and six and is characterised by the child competing with the parent of the same sex for the attention of the parent of the opposite sex.

As a result of children's tendency for magical thinking at this age, if they have occasional fantasies about harm coming to the parent of the same sex, they are likely to be afraid these fantasies will come true. A child may act out in the presence of the parent of the same sex so that the parent will get angry and punish him or her. This alleviates some of their guilt for their 'bad' thoughts.

It is best if the parent of the same sex as the child takes an active part in handling any overt demonstrations of the Oedipal conflict in the child. The parent can reassure the child that he or she had these same feelings when they were a child; that they are normal; and that the parents understand these feelings and are not upset by them.

The usual mode of resolution of the Oedipal concerns is through identification with the parent of the same sex. The child of the latency age years tends to have friends of the same sex.

Youngsters at the Oedipal stage become aware of the fact that their parents have a 'private' life that occurs in their bedroom and is not shared with the child. The child's natural curiosity about sex should be satisfied by talking or reading books with the parents rather than by observing the parents undressed or engaged in sexual intercourse.

Young latency age children enjoy the book *Where did I come from?* (Mayle [9]); however, some parents do not like the pictures in this book or its explicit nature. This book is included in a list of publications on sex education recommended by the National Marriage Guidance Council. The Family Planning Association and Health Education Council also provide lists of recommended leaflets, many available free of charge.

As children enter adolescence, they may become aroused by demonstrations of affection from the parent of the opposite sex. The child may become very uncomfortable about such expressions of affection and think themselves 'weird' to be sexually aroused by their parents. The adolescent can usually accept spontaneous expressions of affection such as a quick hug or kiss on the cheek. Physical horseplay also sometimes leads to strong sexual feelings in the adolescent. Thus, it should be avoided between parents and children of the opposite sex or between siblings of the opposite sex.

It is helpful to adolescents if there have always been commonsense rules about privacy and some measure of modesty around the house. This protects the adolescent from feeling sexually aroused by parental or sibling figures. Most adolescents feel guilty if they are sexually aroused by a parent or sibling and yet during early adolescence sexual arousal can occur with quite minimal stimulation. Parents need to respect the privacy of their children as much as they expect the children to respect their privacy.

Adolescents use the parent of the same sex as a sex role model; they choose to be like the parent of the same sex in some ways and choose to be different in others. At the same time, young adolescents use the parent, or other parents, of the opposite sex to win both confirmation and approval of their own emerging sexuality. Older adolescents seek confirmation and approval of their sexuality from their peers.

Young people entering their teens want and need sex education.

Teenage living and loving[10] is a Family Doctor booklet which offers a straightforward and factual account of sexual terms and techniques for 13-year-olds and upwards.

Exercise 8 which follows gives an example of the problems seen in the sexually abused adolescent. You will have an opportunity to outline a plan for meeting the adolescent's developmental needs.

Exercise 8:
Identifying the developmental needs in a sexually abused adolescent

Instructions

Purpose:
To give you an opportunity to identify developmental needs in the adolescent who has been sexually abused and to develop a plan to meet those needs.

How to do it:

1 Read Debbie's case history.

2 Answer the questions on the worksheet for Exercise 8. Then, compare your own answers with those of another social worker on the sample worksheet.

Debbie's case

Debbie is 14. Her mother physically abused her, and her step-father started sexually abusing her when she was 11. Debbie reported the abuse to a school counsellor. When the police became involved because of the sexual abuse, Debbie's mother and step-father left the area, leaving Debbie with a neighbour.

Subsequently, the mother's parental rights were terminated. Debbie's birth father, who lives in another area, was contacted about having Debbie to live with him. He expressed some interest but didn't follow through. So his parental rights were also terminated.

Debbie has had three foster placements since she was 11 and a half. All of her foster parents have described her as a sexually provocative child. She is seen as wilful and disobedient with foster mothers, although she usually obeys the foster fathers. She is also viewed as a manipulator.

During the past two years her grades have dropped from primarily As and Bs to primarily Cs and Ds. She has peer problems; most of her friends are boys and girls who also have many problems. Most of them have been in trouble with the law.

Debbie says repeatedly that everything would be fine if she could live with her dad whom she hasn't seen for five years. She blames the judge and social workers for keeping them apart. She phones her father, and he always accepts her reverse charge calls. She tends to see her birth father as 'super', while she sees her birth mother as 'a rotten no good whore'.

Recently she ran away from her foster home after being punished for not coming home on time. The foster family has requested that she be moved.

A maternal aunt who lives about 100 miles away has expressed an interest in Debbie. There is also a local family who have expressed an interest in adopting an adolescent like Debbie.

Exercise 8:
Identifying the developmental needs in a sexually abused adolescent

Worksheet

---

1 What are the indications of separation – individuation problems? Develop a plan for helping to resolve these problems.

---

2 What are the indications of control issue problems? What advice would you give to parental figures about handling these isues.

---

3 What are the indications of problems in the sexual area? Outline a plan for meeting Debbie's developmental needs in this area.

Exercise 8:

Identifying the developmental needs in a sexually abused adolescent

Sample worksheet

1   What are the indications of separation – individuation problems?
Develop a plan for helping to resolve these problems.

Debbie opposes the foster family rules, values and expectations. She cannot resolve the separation and loss of her parents and seeing mother as all bad and father as all good. She should not be protected from her father's rejection – this should be brought out into the open. Her anger with the social worker should be verbalised. She needs more information about her birth mother and help to understand her problems.

2   What are the indications of control issue problems? What advice would you give to parental figures about handling these issues.

Involve Debbie in discussions about moves and other issues. Get verbal or written commitments about what she will work at to make a placement succeed. This can be referred back to in any conflict and will help her take responsibility for her own behaviour.

3   What are the indications of problems in the sexual areas? Outline a plan for meeting Debbie's developmental needs in this area.

She is sexually provocative; she obeys her foster fathers and is wilful and disobedient with foster mothers. She needs some good sex education and she needs some affectionate and non-sexual relationships with adults, particularly a woman with whom she can identify.

References

1 Wolff P H *The causes, controls and organisation of behaviour in the neonate* New York: International Universities Press, 1966.

2 Ainsworth M D and Boston M 'Psychodiagnostic assessments of a child after prolonged separation in early childhood' in *Brit J Med Psychol*, 25, 1952.

3 Elmer E and Gregg G 'Developmental characteristics of abused children' in *Paediatrics* 40 (4), 1967.

4 Gesell A *et al The first five years of life: the pre-school years* New York: Harper and Row, 1940.

5 Gesell A and Ilg F *The child from five to ten* New York: Harper and Row, 1946.

6 Hymes J L *The child under six* New Jersey: Prentice Hall, 1969.

7 Jewett C 'Adolescent adjustments', lecture given in Lakewood, Colorado, 1980.

8 Fraiberg S *The magic years* New York: Charles Scribner and Son, 1959.

9 Mayle P *Where did I come from?* Michael Joseph, 1974.

10 Hemming J *Teenage living and loving* (Family Doctor) British Medical Association, 1984.

WORKBOOK THREE

Helping chil
when they m

[handwritten note: Can you photocopy pages — 243-282 (and to.]

CONTENTS

About this workbook

This workbook is designed for use by those who help children when they move in or out of care. The content is based on the assumption that the bonds children develop to the people who care for them in their early years are critical to their development. Children who have come into care have too often been denied their chance to maintain and build attachments to others. The psychological, emotional and physical health of these children has been jeopardised as a result.

Helping children when they must move suggests ways to reduce the damage done to children in care. It highlights services that may be employed to avoid moving children into placement and describes techniques that will minimise the trauma of those moves that are necessary.

This workbook will be most useful when used in conjunction with Workbook 1, *Attachment and separation*, which contains material that provides the foundation for much of the guidance offered in this workbook.

There are four major sections in this workbook. The introduction highlights the themes that will recur. Three of these themes are the importance of permitting children to have and express feelings, the necessity of explaining what is happening to children and the need for workers to recognise their own feelings about what children are doing.

Section 2 covers preventing unnecessary moves into care and minimising trauma when such moves must occur. The third section is on the life story book, a tool that is useful in helping children understand and handle all the transitions that placement may involve.

Finally, Section 4 provides guidance in moving children into adoption or restoring them to the biological family.

We have had extensive experience in presenting this material to child welfare staff. They have taught us that it is easy to feel overwhelmed by the content and immobilised by guilt about past mistakes. It is our hope that the reader will use this material to think about new ways of dealing with children currently on a caseload rather than focusing on the past.

We hope that upon a first reading you will be able to identify a new technique or idea to use with a child who is facing an attachment and/or separation issue. In addition, we hope it will also stand as a reference to which one can return when faced with problems.

Exercises are interspersed in the text. Completing the exercises requires applying the material to case situations. These exercises may be used by an individual reader or they may be used as discussion material in staff meetings or training sessions.

Exercise 1, *Identifying underlying messages*, follows opposite. Completing this exercise will help sensitise you to the key issues involved in moving a child into care. You may wish to return to this exercise after you have completed the workbook to see if, and how, your perceptions have altered or expanded.

Exercise 1:
Identifying underlying messages

Instructions

Purpose

1 To help you learn to identify how children perceive underlying messages at the time of moves so that desired messages may be conveyed and undesirable ones avoided.

2 To help you learn to identify how children communicate their feelings through their behaviour.

How to do it:

1 Read Merrilee's case history which begins on the following page. (We have already met Merrilee, in *Child development*, where we examined her case from a developmental point of view. Here we re-examine it in placement.)

2 Using the blank Exercise 1, Worksheet 1, identify the possible underlying messages to Merrilee associated with the things that have happened to her in placement.

3 After completing your list, look at the opposite page for another person's comments.

4 Using Exercise 1, Worksheet 2, page 190, identify the possible underlying messages to the adoptive parents as they relate to Merrilee's behaviour.

5 After completing your list, look at page 191 for one observer's interpretations and comments about Merrilee's behaviour.

Exercise 1:
Identifying underlying messages at the time of moves

Merrilee's case

Merrilee lived with her mother until she was 16 months old. During Merrilee's first year, her mother had been reported for neglect. It was not too serious, and Merrilee remained in the home. When Merrilee was 14 months old, her mother gave birth to a baby boy and after that, began to neglect her more seriously. Merrilee came into care while her baby brother remained with the mother. Later he, too, came into care although in a different home.

When Merrilee came into care, the agency staff felt that it would be too confusing for her to see her birth mother. The worker recommended an 'adjustment period' for both mother and child with no visits. After this initial adjustment period, both Merrilee and her birth mother seemed to have 'adjusted' so well to the separation that both the mother and worker were reluctant to initiate contact between the two. The mother relinquished her rights after six months, never having seen Merrilee again.

Merrilee was a bright and precocious child who became a valued member of the foster family. The foster family wanted to adopt Merrilee; however the agency was reluctant to allow this. They opposed foster parent adoption in general. In addition, they were concerned about confidentiality because the foster parents knew who the birth mother was. However the foster parents had had an application in for some time to adopt an infant. Soon after Merrilee's placement with the foster family, an infant boy became available for adoption through a private agency. The boy was placed for adoption with the foster parents, and another adoptive family was sought for Merrilee.

An adoptive family who lived 350 miles away was selected. The initial placement was that the adoptive family would come and pick up Merrilee at the social services department and take her for an all-day outing. They planned to return her to the social services department so that her worker could take her back to her foster home for her last night there. The following day the foster mother was to bring her into the agency; the adoptive family would then take her to their home. There was no plan for the foster and adoptive parents to meet.

The first visit, an all-day outing, went very well, as first visits frequently do. The adoptive family asked Merrilee if she would like to spend the night with them and she said yes. They called the social worker who agreed with the change in plan. The following morning, the adoptive parents brought Merrilee back to the agency to say her final goodbye to her foster mother. Her foster father who was at work and who knew that he would be upset by the separation, said his 'good-byes' to Merrilee over the phone. The worker took her from the room with her adoptive parents to a room down the hall. Her foster mother was waiting there to give Merrilee her belongings and to say good-bye. Merrilee then returned to the room where her adoptive parents were waiting.

The adoptive parents changed Merrilee's name so that she could feel as if she were having a 'fresh start' in her new family. Merrilee had long, naturally curly hair. Her foster mother had frequently brushed Merrilee's hair. She did this as a way of being physically close to and nurturing Merrilee. She also used this as a way to raise Merrilee's self-esteem by commenting what beautiful hair she had and how pretty she was. The adoptive mother didn't know this history and suggested that Merrilee have her hair cut, 'like your older sister's hair'. Merrilee agreed.

I met Merrilee when she four and a half years old. At that time, she was constantly fighting control battles with her mother. For example, she was not to leave the garden without permission. Merrilee didn't sneak out of the garden; instead she would sit perched on the fence until she was sure her mother was looking out of the kitchen window. Then, she would go over the fence. If she were asked to do something such as to help set the table, it never quite got done.

In some respects she seemed overcompetent, never asking for help. Merrilee had trouble sitting in a comfortable fashion on her parents' laps. She couldn't cuddle. She was prone to many fears, but the most prominent one was her fear of strangers. Whenever the family had company, Merrilee would become alternately hyperactive and clingy, demanding a lot of attention.

Exercise 1:
Identifying underlying messages

Worksheet 1

Things that happened to Merrilee	*Possible underlying message to Merrilee*
1 Foster care placement soon after birth of brother	1
2 No contact with mother soon after placement or ever again	2
3 No contact with brother ever	3
4 Placement of a baby boy with foster parents soon after Merrilee's adoptive placement	4
5 Learned to trust and love foster parents and then had to move	5
6 The moving plan of one pre-placement visit	6
7 No return to foster home after initial visit	7
8 Lack of direct contact with foster father for good-byes	8
9 Lack of contact between foster and adoptive parents	9
10 Change of name at 2½	10
11 Cutting of hair	11
12 Lack of contact of any type (no pictures, letters or direct contact) with foster parents after move	12

Exercise 1:
Identifying underlying messages

Sample worksheet 1

Things that happened to Merrilee	Possible underlying message to Merrilee
1 Foster care placement soon after birth of brother	1 Her mum loves her brother better than her
2 No contact with mother soon after placement or ever again	2 Her mum disappeared or doesn't love her
3 No contact with brother ever	3 Brothers and sisters aren't important
4 Placement of a baby boy with foster parents soon after Merrilee's adoptive placement	4 When baby boys come along, Merrilee has to go
5 Learned to trust and love foster parents and then had to move	5 When you love and trust somebody, you lose them
6 The moving plan of one pre-placement visit	6 Her feelings for foster parents and fears of new people aren't important
7 No return to foster home after initial visit	7 People can disappear and strangers can kidnap you and keep you
8 Lack of direct contact with foster father for good-byes	8 Foster father didn't care and it's not okay to have feelings
9 Lack of contact between foster and adoptive parents	9 The foster parents and adoptive parents don't like each other
10 Change of name at 2½	10 'Merrilee' was a bad girl
11 Cutting of hair	11 The way Merrilee was close to her foster mum isn't okay with this new mum
12 Lack of contact of any type (no pictures, letters or direct contact) with foster parents after move	12 They disappeared

Exercise 1:
Identifying underlying messages

Worksheet 2

Merrilee's behaviour	*Possible underlying message to parents*
1 Going over fence	1
2 Making bed and tidying up room without being asked (age 4½)	2
3 Not taking notice when asked to help	3
4 Not being able to cuddle	4
5 Fear of strangers	5
6	6
7	7

190

Exercise 1:
Identifying underlying messages

Sample worksheet 2

Merrilee's behaviour	*Possible underlying message to parents*
1 Going over fence	1 She's testing limits.
2 Making bed and tidying up room without being asked (age 4½)	2 She doesn't need parents.
3 Not taking notice when asked to help	3 She's defiant.
4 Not being able to cuddle	4 She's cold, she doesn't have feelings, she doesn't love me.
5 Fear of strangers	5 She makes me look bad, as a parent, in front of others.
6	6
7	7

1 Introduction

One of the the functions of child care is to provide short-term substitute care for children whose parents are unable to care for them adequately. We strongly agree with the many child advocates who feel that children have been placed in substitute care too readily and for much too long. Improved and expanded services to prevent family breakup and supplement family resources are desperately needed. When children must be placed out of their own homes, the amount of time they spend in care and the number of moves that they make from foster home to foster home must be limited. Adoption must be viewed as the alternative choice for children who cannot remain with or return to their birth families.

We are concerned not only with limiting the number of moves from family to family that a child must make, but also with handling those moves that must occur in ways that damage the child's potential for health as little as possible. Managing moves in this way requires an understanding of the importance of attachment between parent and child and the impact that separation has on both of them. Workbook 1, *Attachment and separation*, deals with these concepts. We will review a few points in this introduction.

Most children who come into care, or move from one foster home to another, or move into an adoptive home, are separated in the process from the person or persons to whom they are attached. The way attachments between humans develop and function is not completely understood. However, we do believe that a strong and healthy bond between a child and parent allows that child to develop both trust in others and self-reliance.

The bond that a child develops to the person who cares for him or her in early years is the foundation of their future psychological, physical, and cognitive development and for their relationships with others.

Children in care are in danger of losing all the strengths that come from strong attachment. Children who come into care are often moved suddenly without preparation. Once in care, the child's traumatic separation from the birth family is allowed to drift into permanent estrangement. Worse yet, the maintenance of a bond between the child in care and the biological family is sometimes actively discouraged. The child's feelings of loss are ignored or glossed over. Visits between parents and child are limited or proscribed. The child's emotional reactions to visits with the birth family are misunderstood and misinterpreted.

Then, with a child's attachment to the birth family severed, he or she is too often provided with no substitute. Foster parents are discouraged from developing attachments to the children in their care. Until recently foster parents were often prohibited from adopting children who may have grown up in their care. Moving children from one foster home to another often takes place without adequate preparation of the child or the families involved. Efforts are not made to ensure that the child grows up in a permanent, caring family.

Finally, some children who do move into adoption are cut off from previous attachments in the process. Children are discouraged from seeing or even talking about foster or biological family members to whom they were strongly attached. A belief that a child's strong and healthy attachments are important to his or her development leads logically to certain convictions about the way the child care service should work if it is to serve children.

Preventing family break-up

First, those working in child care need to do all that is possible to ensure that a child has a stable family over a lifetime. This means that child care must do much more than it has in the past to prevent the break-up of biological families. Each social worker, administrator and policy maker should become an advocate for adequate in-home services. Services such as emergency caretakers and emergency homemakers will help children keep their homes. Adequate therapeutic day care and crisis nurseries may prevent cases of abuse from occurring or being serious enough that the child must come into care.

If the child cannot be maintained in the biological family and comes into care, the foster parents' role should be to help the child maintain attachments to the biological family. The foster parents must also help the child to develop healthy and strong new attachments to them, and then transfer those attachments to the permanent caretakers of the child who may be either the biological parents or adoptive parents. Moves from foster home to foster home should be limited to all but the most unavoidable situations. In these cases 'old' foster parents should work with 'new' foster parents to transfer attachments. Children must be prepared for these moves.

This way of thinking departs from the past in several key ways. First, it means that social workers need to work intensely with the biological families that are at risk of breaking up. It means that foster families and foster children need to develop bonds. It also means that foster parents and birth parents must work closely and co-operatively whenever possible; and if a foster child moves into a foster home, then the foster parents and adoptive parents must become partners. The social worker's job is first to limit, and then facilitate and orchestrate the necessary moves.

Learning how children perceive moves

One key to humanising the process of moving a child from one family to another is to become sensitive to the way that children perceive moves. No two moves are exactly alike. The personalities of the participants, the events necessitating the moves, and the child's past experience with moves all affect the way the child perceives the move and thus reacts to the move.

Many children perceive moves into or out of foster care as being 'taken away' from those to whom they are attached. They see themselves as having no control over the move. These children may feel as if they have been kidnapped or snatched. Children who feel they have been suddenly taken away are prone to experience fear and anxiety chronically. Some children may cope with their sense of lack of control over their own lives by withdrawing, rarely asserting themselves, and always trying to please others. Others do just the opposite and become children who are constantly asserting themselves and trying to be in control of everything. These children do not trust adults.

In other circumstances children perceive a move as being 'given away'. These children tend to feel that they have not measured up in some way. They hold themselves responsible for the events leading to the move and are likely to suffer loss of self esteem. They may also feel sad and depressed if they think they have been 'given away' by parental figures to whom they were well attached. Children who have worked hard to change their behaviour and measure up in a birth home, foster home or adoptive home and then still face a move, will probably be angry as well.

Other children feel neither given nor taken away but believe instead thay they are in charge of moves. They believe that they chose to move and consciously did something that led to the move. Children from the age of three and a half to five and a half years are particularly prone to this sort of 'magical thinking', as exemplified by Suzanna's case in *Child development*.

Although younger children often believe that they have caused moves when they have not, adolescents do consciously choose to set up a move. Sometimes such action is an indication that the adolescent has problems such as failure to accept age-appropriate limits. At other times, it is a sign that there is a reason for the adolescent's behaviour such as abuse in the home.

Minimising the trauma of moves
We have highlighted the kinds of perceptions children may have about moves. Most of these are destructive to the child. Fortunately, the negative perceptions may be ameliorated if the child is prepared for the move, if all participants in the move are as open and honest with the child as possible, and if careful attention is given to the child's reactions to separation from those to whom he or she is attached. The way to minimise the trauma of moves is the subject of this workbook. At this point we will mention briefly two major themes that will run throughout all the suggestions made in this book: giving children permission to have feelings and explaining what is happening to children when they are moved.

Giving children permission to have feelings
All those involved in the process of moving the child need to give the child permission to have feelings. Sometimes this can be done by talking about other children. 'Some children who have moved have said they were mostly sad; others said, mostly scared; others said, mostly mad. Do you have any of these feelings?' Children may even need to be taught about feelings. 'When I get nervous, my stomach feels like something is jumping around in it; some people say they have butterflies in their stomach.'

Social workers, birth parents, foster parents, and adoptive parents all need to learn to let children express feelings. Even when adults say they want children to express feelings what they often mean is that they want children to *talk* about their feelings. When children have feelings and cry, scream or act out anger, adults tell them to stop. Children frequently think this means to stop having those feelings.

When children show their strong feelings by means of unacceptable behaviour, adults can accept the feelings at the same time they interrupt the behaviour. They can teach the child a new and more acceptable way to express the feeling. For example, if a child is angry and hits a sibling, the adult might say 'I know that you are really mad and that is okay, but I will not allow you to hurt anyone when you are angry. When you are mad and feel like punching something, you can punch this Bozo the Clown.'

When a child moves from one home to another, adults should avoid isolating him or her as a means of discipline. Sending the child to his or her room implies 'when you're naughty I don't want to be around you'. Many children who have experienced moves perceive the moves as occurring because they were naughty or in some way did not measure up. Isolating the child as a means of discipline not only reinforces such misperceptions, but also taps into all the strong negative feelings that occurred at the time of a previous separation.

Although sending children to their room or isolating them in some other way is a useful disciplinary tool for children who have not experienced traumatic separations, it is not a very helpful technique when children feel a high risk from past separations. Figure 1 illustrates the negative cycle that can be established when naughty behaviour is followed by a disciplinary response of isolation.

Figure 1

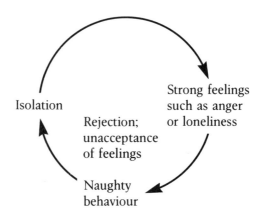

Isolation

Strong feelings such as anger or loneliness

Rejection; unacceptance of feelings

Naughty behaviour

Such a negative cycle can be ameliorated by having a child take a chair in the same room as the adult until the child has calmed down. This action gives the message, 'I will be close by until you are back in control of yourself; when you have strong feelings, you need to be close to people, not separated from them.'

Explaining what is happening to children
We believe that much too often children are not told about what is happening to them when they are moved. Foster care may seem familiar and logical to social workers but makes no sense to children. We have developed a method of explaining foster care to children. The idea is to explain the role of the various parents in their lives and to outline who is responsible for what. We draw three circles like those in Figure 2 and give the child an explanation of the different roles of each kind of parent.*

Figure 2

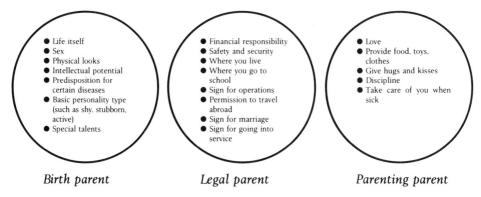

| Birth parent | Legal parent | Parenting parent |

*Based on an idea of Marietta Spencer of the Children's Home Society of Minnesota.

We say that every birth has parents. There can be no changes in birth parents. Each child has one birth mother and one birth father; no one can ever do anything to change this situation. All children in our society also have legal parents. The legal parent makes the major decisions in a child's life. The parenting parent is the person who is available on a day-to-day basis to meet the child's needs for nurture and discipline.

For many children, one set of parents are simultaneously the birth parents, the legal parents and the parenting parents. However, in foster care and adoption these different kinds of jobs are split up.

The child in care still has a set of birth parents. In the case of voluntary reception into care, the legal parent may still be the birth parent and the legal parenting role is shared by the birth parent and the agency. For example, the birth parent's signature might be required for an adolescent to join the Army while the agency may have the right to select the home in which the child lives and the school the child attends.

When parental rights have been terminated by the court, an agency or the court becomes the legal parent. When the child is fostered, the foster parents are the parenting parents. When there are disputes about who should be the legal parent and who should be the parenting parent, a court makes the decision.

When a child is returned to the birth home, but the agency continues to have legal custody, Figure 2 can help explain responsibilities. The birth parent then is the parenting parent and the birth parent, but aspects of the legal parent role are retained by the agency or the court.

If parental rights are terminated, the child continues to have the same birth parents; the agency or court is a legal parent and foster parents are the parenting parents. When we explain adoption to such a child, we tell him or her that termination means that no one set of parents will again fill all three parenting roles; however, adoption allows us to combine two aspects of parenting – the legal parent and the parenting parent – in one set of parents. The child learns that social workers or courts will no longer make decisions about him or her; but rather that the set of parents with whom they live will also be in charge of making the major decisions in their life.

In all cases this method of explanation accepts the fact that the child has a set of birth parents. The acceptance of birth parents and what they mean to a child's life is critical if we are to help children deal with their feelings about separation from birth parents.

A note on the social worker's feelings about moving a child

It is not uncommon for the social worker to be faced with the task of helping a child and family adapt to a move about which the worker has strong feelings. Perhaps the social worker has been working with a family to prevent out-of-home placement. If such a placement becomes necessary, the worker may have strong feelings about the move. The worker may feel guilty, 'Why wasn't I able to do enough to prevent placement?'; or frustrated, 'Why isn't the system providing *the* alternative service that might prevent placement?', or angry 'Why didn't the parent take my advice and follow through to prevent placement?'; or sad about what the child and family will face.

Other types of moves may involve other feelings. Workers may feel apprehensive or anxious; or excited and happy. They may feel a sense of loss when the move means that the child will get a new social worker. They may feel competitive with the new worker, thinking that they know the child and the background better that anyone else. They may experience a feeling of relief when some children move from their caseload.

When a social worker moves a child, the move may tap into unresolved issues in the worker's past. It is important that workers be aware of how their own feelings may make a move more difficult or easier.

Case example: Troy

Troy, aged six, was moving from a foster home to an adoptive home. Troy's social worker, Mrs Smith, had become close to Troy in her contacts with him. She had helped him with his life story book and had helped him deal with his feelings at the time of his relinquishment. She saw Troy as a very likeable child who would be easy to place for adoption. Mrs Smith had hoped Troy would be placed in the same community so that she could have continued contact with him since she knew him and his past so well. However, because so many people in the community knew Troy and his birth family, it was decided that Troy should be placed away from his birth community.

Troy's case history was sent to the local adoption exchange. Initially when studies for prospective families were sent to Mrs Smith, she seemed to find some flaw in each study and indicated that she 'wasn't certain' that the families would 'really understand' Troy and all that had happened to him. Mrs Smith's supervisor confronted her about the possibility that her own feelings for Troy were preventing her from being objective.

Subsequently an 'ideal' family was identified and selected. Mrs Smith had close contact with the family, the foster family, and Troy during the placement period. The adoptive parents and the foster parents felt that

199

Troy was ready to move after about two and a half weeks of pre-placement visits. However, Mrs Smith began to wonder if this was the 'right' family for Troy since he began to act out during and after the visits. He was also not relating to Mrs Smith in the same way as before.

Again, the supervisor pointed out that Mrs Smith's own feelings might be colouring the case decision. Mrs Smith recognised this; however, she also recognised that her empathy for Troy had been important in their developing the type of relationship that had been helpful and supportive to him during his foster placement. She was confused about what to do with all of her own feelings. She recognised that at the time of the final move she would probably be quite upset. Interestingly, on the day of the final move, Mrs Smith had an emergency come up in one of her other cases and her supervisor completed Troy's move.

It is important that social workers use their contacts with families in such a way that children and families are given permission to have feelings; are provided with modelling of appropriate expression of feelings; are given support to have individual feelings; and are encouraged to express feelings when they are denied. Exercise 2 that follows is intended to help you examine times when your own feelings have either helped or hindered your work with families.

Exercise 2 may be modified easily for use by foster parents. You would ask them to think of two children who have previously left their homes. In using this exercise with new social workers, new foster parents, or new adoptive parents, ask them to think about various types of separations they have experienced in their past. They might think about separation from siblings, parents or friends. These separations might have resulted from family moves, going to the hospital, leaving for college, or a first holiday alone without the family.

Exercise 2:
Social worker feelings at the time of moves

Instructions
___

Purpose:

1 To identify social worker feelings at the time of moves.

2 To demonstrate how social worker feelings at the time of moves can be either harmful or facilitating in the moving process.

How to do it:

1 Identify two case examples from your own caseload that involved moves of various types (such as into care; from one foster care situation to another; return to birth home; or a move into an adoptive home).

   You may include examples of cases that did not involve a physical move of the child but involved a movement into or out of your caseload, such as a transfer from foster care to adoption.

2 Close your eyes and try to remember where you were when the move took place. Where was the child? How were each of you dressed? What was the expression on your face? On the child's face? On the other adults' faces? What were *you* feeling? How did you express these feelings? To whom did you express them?

How did your own feelings interfere with or help you in recognising the feelings of the child and family members? Who was the identified client in this case? Did your feelings at the time of the move make you feel closer to or further away from, emotionally speaking, the client? How did your feelings at the time of the move affect your subsequent relationship with the client?

___

Notes:
On the next page is a list of feelings that people often have – not just at the times of moves. You may want to scan this list to help as you identify feelings in this exercise and others in this workbook.

Abandoned
Affectionate
Afraid
Ambivalent
Angry
Annoyed
Anxious
Apathetic
Assertive
Astounded
Awed

Bad
Betrayed
Bitter
Bold
Bored
Brave
Burdened

Calm
Challenged
Cheated
Cheerful
Clever
Competitive
Concerned
Condemned
Confident
Confused
Conspicuous
Contemptuous
Contented
Cruel
Crushed
Curious

Defeated
Defensive

Delighted
Depersonalised
Depressed
Deserted
Desolate
Despairing
Determined
Detesting
Devastated
Different
Disappointed
Disgusted
Distracted
Distressed
Disturbed
Divided
Dominated
Doubtful

Eager
Ecstatic
Embarrassed
Empathetic
Empty
Enraged
Envious
Exasperated
Excited
Exhausted
Exploited

Fascinated
Fearful
Flustered
Foolish
Fortunate
Frantic
Frightened
Frustrated

Furious

Glad
Good
Grateful
Grief

Happy
Hate
Helpful
Helpless
Homesick
Horrible
Hurt
Hysterical

Ignored
Imposed upon
Impressed
Incredulous
Indignant
Infatuated
Infuriated
Inspired
Insulted
Intimidated
Irritated
Isolated

Jealous
Joyous
Jumpy

Kind

Lazy
Left out
Lonely
Longing

Lost
Loving
Lovable
Low

Mad
Mean
Melancholy
Miserable

Naughty
Nervous
Nice
Numb

Obnoxious
Obsessed
Odd
Out of control
Outraged
Overjoyed
Overwhelmed

Pain
Panicked
Passive
Peaceful
Persecuted
Petrified
Pity
Pleasant
Pleased
Powerful
Powerless
Pressured
Proud
Puzzled

Quarrelsome

Queer

Reassured
Refreshed
Rejected
Relaxed
Relieved
Reluctant
Remorseful
Resigned
Resistant
Responsive
Restless
Ridiculous

Sad
Satisfied
Scared
Sceptical
Serious
Shocked
Silly
Sneaky
Solemn
Sorrowful
Spiteful
Startled
Stingy
Strange
Stupid
Stunned
Surprised
Sympathetic

Tempted
Tense
Terrible
Terrified
Threatened

Ticked-off
Tired
Thwarted
Trapped
Troubled

Unafraid
Uncomfortable
Uneasy
Unfortunate

Vulnerable
Vivacious

Weak
Wicked
Wonderful
Worried

2 Entering foster care

Can we prevent the move?

This workbook is intended to provide guidance to workers when they must help children move in and out of families; however, we feel that efforts to prevent these moves whenever possible are so important and often inadequate that we must spend a little time on prevention here. Many more services that may keep families together need to be developed and used. The kinds of services that may help are much more numerous and creative than many workers are aware.

In this section, some of these services are briefly described; we hope you are reminded of some that are or should be available in your community. We also offer a few aids for evaluating whether or not foster care is appropriate. It is easy to lose sight of what foster care can or cannot do for children and families. This section has been prepared for BAAF by Deborah Cameron, Child Abuse Review Officer, London Borough of Lewisham, and we are indebted to her for her help. (Examples of the American experience are listed as an Appendix, pages 282 to 287.)

Services which may help to prevent family break-ups

Although it is rare to find a whole range of services specifically aimed at preventing family break-ups in any one locality, it is possible with a little thought to mobilise a wide variety of resources to help a family to care for and enjoy their children. Similar services and agencies may have different names in different places, but it is always worth investigating the facilities offered by the following:

Community health services: Health Visiting and Clinical Medical Service.

Hospitals: Paediatric teams, social workers, occupational therapists, volunteer organisers.

Psychiatric services: Adult and child, community and hospital.

Education authority: Schools, Education Welfare Service, Educational psychologists, Home Tuition Service, school social workers and special projects.

Social services: community-based casework and groupwork, special projects, family centres (residential or otherwise), home care services, day care services.

Voluntary agencies and community organisations: these may be national or local, run by professional staff or volunteers, and can be geared to respond to vulnerable parents and children at risk, or to meet the needs of special groups, such as the deaf or children with cystic fibrosis, for example.

Probation and After-Care Service: including volunteer groups, special projects and groups, and the independent Prisoners' Wives Service.

General practitioners: an increasing number of group practices are starting befriending groups and patients' support groups, or may attempt to offer a more personalised ante-natal service.

The choice of services to be offered must depend as much on what is acceptable to the family concerned as on what may seem to be immediately appropriate, and an aptitude for lateral thinking on the part of the worker is a great asset. However, it may help to categorise the available facilities if they are sorted out into those agencies which provide immediate support in crises, those which offer a service to parent(s) and child within the home, services for parents and children to attend, and services which separate parents and children to some degree. Once agencies are listed under these categories in each local area, deficiencies can be identified and maybe even remedied, but since the combinations of services offered by the relevant organisations vary so much from place to place, the following notes simply indicate the type of facilities which may be provided by the different groups listed.

1. Community health services

The Health Visiting Service is available to every child under five. Children and parents are seen at home and at clinic. As well as advising on practical matters of health care and daily routine, the health visitors are often involved with mother-toddler groups, and can usually put parents in contact with other clubs and groups creches, perhaps helping to improve the network of social support available to them.

Clinical medical officers run health clinics with the health visitor and can monitor children's developmental progress regularly, compiling height-weight charts and advising parents on appropriate stimulation and care of their under-fives. Often potential problems can be nipped in the bud this way, but if necessary the clinical medical officers may be willing to offer appointments shortly before case conferences are due, or can arrange for the provision of special services, including speech therapy or occupational therapy, as well as referrals to medical consultants.

2 Hospitals

Paediatricians can arrange to monitor children on an out-patient basis, or to provide hospital beds for assessment, although they may not necessarily be prepared to pass on confidential information to other agencies. In many hospitals it is now possible for the parent(s) to stay in the hospital if children are admitted, and it is worth enquiring about this, as the service is not always immediately offered. The attitudes of nursing staff and the time they have available to offer parents may be different in each hospital, and this should be carefully considered if possible.

Consultant paediatricians are more often prepared to offer domiciliary visits than is generally realised, and in difficult cases this should be investigated.

Specialist clinics, like the Newcomen Clinic at Guy's Hospital, for example, can offer extensive developmental monitoring and advice to parents, but are most often based in large teaching hospitals.

Family units offering assessment and rehabilitation for vulnerable children and potentially abusing parents may also be based in hospitals, as in Newcastle and Oxford.

Occupational therapists are often trained in social skills work and have an interest in working with families to improve the level of parenting skills.

Speech therapists are also increasingly aware of the role of emotional deprivation in delaying language development and can offer a service to parents as well as direct work with children in some areas.

Social workers in hospitals can undertake crisis intervention work, advise on the available facilities, and help to ensure effective liaison with other hospital staff.

Volunteer organisers may sometimes be able to provide a befriending service for families under stress who are also hospital patients.

3 Psychiatric services

Adult psychiatric services are not necessarily equipped to respond to the needs of a patient's children, but can nevertheless provide very real support for some families. Consultant psychiatrists are generally ready to arrange home visits when appropriate and can sometimes arrange for a mother and child to be admitted to hospital together, although the quality of care which can be offered may need discussion unless the admission is to be to a special unit. Some psychiatric teams operate on crisis intervention and day care models, and take the needs of children into account by running supervised creches. Community psychiatric nurses can offer positive monitoring, support and advice to families if they are suitably experienced.

Child psychiatrists are also often prepared to undertake domiciliary visits or to advise social workers on a child's emotional needs, as well as to arrange in- or out-patient treatment, which is likely to include the whole family. Parent and child admissions are possible, and as well as the child guidance clinics, which may offer family therapy and psychotherapy, generally on the basis that a family can operate as a viable unit, day hospitals may provide the opportunity of less intensive but more frequent contact, including education, art therapy, speech therapy, as well as psychological, psychiatric and social work skills.

Clinical psychologists may also be involved in parent-child groups, or specialise in improving communication skills or helping parents and children to modify disruptive behaviour, for example.

4 Local education authority

Where children have an education problem, the *Education Welfare Service* can provide home visiting, and will also advise on what other education services are available to children. Volunteer support can also be laid on in some areas, either through the *Education Welfare Service* or through particular schools.

In addition to *nursery schools and classes*, which may help to stimulate vulnerable under-fives, most education authorities are able to provide special tuition for children, ranging from tutor groups, special classes and 'family' units – these may include volunteers and teacher's aides – through to day and boarding schools for delicate or maladjusted children, and home tuition. Handicapped children and their parents can be offered advice and support in connection with their particular educational needs, and children can, with their parents' permission, be referred to the educational psychologist for assessment. The psychologist may recommend any of the special educational services or simply monitor a child's progress and advise on appropriate steps to be taken.

Some schools go to great lengths to involve parents in their children's education. Teachers may also run 'latchkey' groups for children whose parents are working and support holiday play schemes, but much depends on the attitude of the local education authority.

School social workers and some school counsellors may offer counselling and group work support for vulnerable children who may be having difficulty with their family.

School nurses are attached to the community health services. Their records are independent of general school records and they can follow up work previously undertaken by health visitors and provide a tie-in with the school doctors from the clinical medical service.

5 Social services department

Home care sections, or their equivalent, may provide home helps for vulnerable families, and if advised about the home situation, may offer practical advice and relief child care as well as a housework and shopping service. In some areas senior home care staff are available outside normal office hours in emergencies and can provide night sitters to stay with families in order to avoid the children's reception into care, even if the parent(s) is (are) present. Many social services departments have specialist home-makers or family aides who will live in with families if necessary, or alternatively such staff can sometimes be specially recruited.

Day care staff are responsible for the full and part-time nursery places for vulnerable children, and there is a growing interest in encouraging parents to attend with their children. Transport may be available and there should be emphasis on stimulation and developmental monitoring, including loving attention, and regular clinical medical visits and speech therapy when necessary, as well as feeding and caring for the children.

Registered childminders are often the responsibility of the day care staff. A good minder can provide at least some of the love, stability and continuity of care that may be missing in a child's home, as well as individual attention for the child and sometimes support to parents, but minders are not normally council employees and can vary enormously. Day care advisers from the responsible section of the social services department will help a family's worker to decide on the most helpful form of day care for a particular child and his or her family, and it may be possible to involve parents fully in the discussion.

Family centre places are offered for parents and children together by some local authorities, either on a residential or day care basis. Such centres generally employ a multi-disciplinary staff team, who will assess the quality of parent-child interaction and offer practical and therapeutic support to the whole family, in order to try to improve their level of functioning and enjoyment of family life.

Social workers may offer group work support for parents and children or vulnerable children alone, as well as casework and perhaps family therapy. *Intermediate treatment* groups are also available to children as an alternative to care, and special schemes linked with or based on CSV's *Children in Care Scheme* can provide an intermediate stage between living in local authority care and being at home for older children. The emergency duty social worker operating outside office hours can give families a certain level of support and crisis intervention, especially if notified in advance about difficult sitiuations. Some fostering teams provide 'emergency carers' who will take children or a mother and child for up to 72 hours without a formal reception into care, and parents may also be given a break through holiday schemes, or supported family holidays funded by the social services department.

The *occupational therapists* working in local authority rehabilitation teams are, like hospital staff, often trained to help families with their social skills, parenting skills, and children's motor development through play and exercises.

Social services departments offer a range of specialist casework services for client groups with particular handicaps or special needs, such as the deaf, or mentally handicapped, for example and this may be very important for parents who have to cope with such problems.

6 Voluntary agencies

Casework. A variety of casework services is provided by such organisations as the NSPCC (which has a 24-hour emergency service), Family Welfare Association, Settlements and Social Action Centres, and so on, Agencies like ICAA, or those established to respond to even more specialised needs, may offer individual casework or detailed advice to worker and parents.

Family centres are run by NSPCC, Church of England Children's Society, Barnardo's, National Children's Home, and a number of other agencies. They may sometimes offer residential accommodation, though most offer day care for children and parents. The underlying philosophy of the centres may vary considerably, just as do different families' needs.

Mother and baby homes and other supportive residential accommodation are most often, but certainly not always, organised to meet the needs of the very young parent.

Playgroups and creches exist all over the country, run by all sorts of different organisations. Groups like Gingerbread or the National Childbirth Trust can provide a very high level of support for parents and children in some areas, while One o'Clock clubs and similar projects may be more low-key in their approach, but provide valuable social support for families, particularly those where non-working parents and their children feel isolated.

Parents groups can provide new parents, or those who have to cope with special disabilities, with considerable support, information and friendship. It is always worth contacting the specialist voluntary organisations for advice on the availability of parents' support groups.

Volunteers can often be more effective than professionals in averting child abuse, because of the intensity and commitment they can offer a family when properly supported. As well as the specialised groups, such as Parents' Anonymous or Parents' Linkline, which may provide a 24-hour telephone service, crisis intervention groups like the Samaritans may also help distressed parents who are feeling they may lose control. Volunteer groups may provide non-critical friendship to isolated parents over a period of years, or may be able to to provide practical assistance in emergencies but such befrienders will themselves need skilled back-up if they are to be able to cope with families in severe distress.

Holiday schemes. Many voluntary agencies run or are in contact with playschemes, some of which involve parents. Organisations like the Church Army can also offer holiday accommodation with a supportive, friendly atmosphere.

7 Probation and After-Care Service

The Probation Service has extensive experience of befriending and working with isolated, often aggressive people, and individual officers may well run group projects, perhaps for women offenders, which may help the parent who has a criminal record to modify his or her aggressive responses, or provide a lifeline for isolated parents. If parents are involved in a dispute over custody of their children, contact with the probation officer providing a welfare report is very important, and the service's extensive experience with voluntary befriending schemes may be invaluable in relevant cases.

8 General practitioners

Family doctors may sometimes be able to give extra time and attention to parents whose children are at risk, as well as occasionally offering the additional services mentioned above. This sort of preventive role is not always acknowledged, but may be extremely important to a desperate or anxious parent.

Of course, many other agencies can also provide crucial support to parents and children in critical family situations, but in most areas there are many gaps in the safety net, and it is doubly important to seek out and use all the help that may be available, if a parent feels it may be of help in his or her particular situation. The child is thereby given the chance of a better life at home.

Relative placements

If, despite all the efforts of the social worker, it becomes necessary to move a child, an important option to consider is placement with relatives. Throughout the world, children are placed with relatives during times of crisis within families. Such placements occur when a parent dies, is ill or incarcerated, or simply when a child has needs that are better met by other family members.

Placement with relatives should be considered whenever out-of-home placement is necessary. There are some definite advantages to relative placements. The child's trauma of separation may be reduced if the child is placed with known family members rather than with strangers. A sense of family and security may already exist between the child and the relatives. In addition, it may be easier for the child and birth parents to visit frequently if the child is staying with relatives.

Since relatives may be aware of the child's past, they have opportunities to help the child accept this past and feel a part of a worthwhile family group. A child may not have to deal with the 'good family' versus 'bad family' split that occurs in non relative placements. If children learn that other members of their family do not have the problems their parents have, it may help them realise they have more choices.

Although relative placements should always be considered when out-of-the-home placement is necessary, it is important that social workers be aware of some of the possible pitfalls. Many times the child who needs placement these days has been severely neglected or abused. Sometimes, the relatives themselves contacted the authorities that removed the child from the home. In these cases, parents may believe the relatives are conspiring with the social workers. Placing with relatives may cause further disruption in family support systems that will be needed when the child is returned to the home.

Placement with relatives may change other family relationships. For example, if the grandparents raise a grandchild and provide the long-term parenting for the child, the child's relationship with the birth parents and with aunts and uncles may become more like a sibling relationship. In general, grandparents in our society have a different role from that of parents. Grandparents frequently provide more acceptance and less discipline for grandchildren than parents do. They 'spoil' them. The parental role includes more discipline and less indulgence in general. If the grandparents serve as parents, they must keep these roles distinct and be willing to parent rather than grandparent the child.

Sometimes relative placements are not possible or useful because the parents were not nurtured in their own families of origin. In other cases, the relatives may be so highly critical of the parent who abuses or neglects the child that they do not support returning the child to the birth parents. Relatives may not accept a child because they do not accept the spouse of the relative.

Sometimes, a relative may make a home available only out of a sense of family obligation and not from real caring, concern, or understanding of the child's needs. A strong sense of family loyalty may effectively hide the real issues so that they are never resolved. At other times, family placement is so comfortable that the birth parents are not motivated to change so that the child can be reunited with them. Workers need to consider that the family dysfunction that necessitated placement may extend to the relative.

In summary, children should be able to have the assurance that if they are placed with relatives, their needs will be met and that if they are placed with strangers, it is because no relatives were willing and able to meet those needs.

Foster care placement

Finally, despite all efforts to provide services to children and families and to prevent moves, and to place children with relatives whenever possible, some children will be best served by foster placement. When making the decision to move a child into foster care, it is important to have a realistic picture of what problems foster care can and can't solve. Figure 3 overleaf summarises these strengths and limitations. The rest of this section deals with helping children move into foster care.

Helping a child move into a foster home

As we pointed out in the introduction to this workbook, the way children are prepared for a move can profoundly affect the way they perceive the move and the effect that move will have on them. Many abused or neglected children come into care on an emergency basis. In such situations the child is not prepared ahead of time for the move. Attempts to minimise the trauma must all take place after the fact.

If you complete the fantasy exercise on the next page you may get some idea of what this trauma is like. The trauma a child incurs when he or she is removed from the home when the parent is not there

Figure 3

Foster family care

Can	*Can't*
1 provide safety	1 solve family problems
2 provide shelter	2 provide security
3 provide respite for families	3 unlikely that it will provide stability and continuity
4 provide family while awaiting legal release or termination following abandonment	4 provide continuity in terms of schooling
5 provide an opportunity to assess the child without the family and vice versa	5 provide continuity in terms of medical care
6 *may* provide positive parenting experience	6 help parents deal with special needs of the child because not there
7 may provide for more adequate stimulation in cases of neglect	7 increase bonding to birth family

resembles the psychological trauma of kidnapping. If at all possible, it should be avoided.

Responding to the child's feelings
When children are moved without preparation they may either have very strong feelings or be so overcome that they are numb at first. In either case the child benefits from being physically close to someone who is caring. In many cases it is the foster parents who must fulfil this need of the child.

Fantasy exercise

Imagine yourself in a situation like this . . .

You and your spouse are at the dinner table. You are in the middle of a heated argument that has been going on for some time.
  Suddenly there is a knock at the door. A stranger walks in, looks at you, and says, 'You must come with me.'

—Imagine that your spouse does nothing.
  How do you feel?

—Imagine that your spouse cries and clings to you, saying 'Don't go . . . Don't let them take you.'
  How do you feel?

—Imagine that your spouse says 'Go ahead. Good riddance.'
  How do you feel?

—Imagine that your spouse fights for you.
  How do you feel?

This is a fantasy about being separated from the person to whom you are attached. Many foster children have lived through separation experiences like these.
  Foster parents must be helped to understand the types of feelings that children have when they come into care on an emergency basis and to learn ways to respond to these feelings. We have used the fantasy

exercise in foster parent training courses and have found that it helps foster parents experience and empathise with the feelings that may occur at the time of this move.

Another useful technique (Jewett[1]) has been to suggest to foster parents that they initially treat the child as if the child's parents had just been killed in a car accident. In such cases it is unlikely that adults would expect a child to be happy or relieved or comforted by verbal reassurance. Being close to the child and responding to his or her feelings would be natural responses.

Letting the child know about the foster family

With children who are old enough to talk, especially those who understood something about the process of coming into care, some other techniques can also be used to help minimise the trauma of the move. Such children are apt to be very concerned about where they are being taken. This is true whether or not the child has been in care before.

One agency that we know of has asked foster parents to prepare an album with pictures of their home, family and pets as well as some descriptive material about their family. These albums are kept at the agency. Thus, even in emergency placements, the worker can take the album and share it with the child en route to the home. This way the child has at least a visual image of where he or she is going before getting there.

Letting the child know about the birth parents

Children who come into care on an emergency basis should be able to see their birth parents as soon as possible. Many children who have been placed in foster care on an emergency basis have the fantasy that someone has harmed their parents or that therefore they can never be reunited. Such thinking is especially prominent in younger children.

Prompt visiting between a child and the birth family is essential to promote early return of the child to the home. If the child and parent are kept apart by agency policy, it becomes difficult for anyone to believe that the real goal of the agency is to reunite the family.

Children in foster care need pictures of their birth families and homes with them in the foster home. Such pictures give the message that foster parents view birth parents as important people and prevent the child from denying their existence. If the foster parents have difficulty allowing the birth parents to enter their home, even through photographs, the child is apt to be caught in the position of being disloyal to the birth parents if he or she accepts any closeness with the foster parents. On the other hand, if social workers and foster parents use the pictures of the birth parents as they discuss the child's feelings, they give the child the message that it is 'okay' to miss the birth parents. If no pictures of the birth parents are available, two pictures – one for the child and one for the parents – should be taken at the time of the first visit.

Maintaining a regular schedule of visits helps. The younger the child, the more important it is that the schedule be consistent. Young children have a poor sense of time but do develop a sense of rhythm for the events that occur on a regular basis. Overnight visits are confusing to the toddler and the young pre-schooler because they are apt to think that they are moving again without preparation. Day visits usually are not as confusing.

Ner Littner[2] has given an excellent description of the importance of the birth parents to the child in placement. As he points out, reactions to the visits in the older child usually indicate a need for more contact with birth parents, as well as a need on the child's part for additional help in recognising and dealing with strong feelings. These feelings are often an indication of attachment between parent and child. Yet many times foster parents and social workers consider these behavioural reactions to visits to be indicators of negative rather than positive relationships between birth parents and children.

Sometimes however, visits also provoke exceedingly strong reactions in very young children. If the child experiences serious withdrawal from reality or very extreme aggression during or following the visits, you might have to consider suspending the visits for a period of time.

Letting the child know about foster care
Children coming into care need to understand the role of the various 'parents' in their lives as well as the role of the social worker and the court. One way to explain this is to use the technique outlined in Section 1 on page 197.

The child's ecomap is a second tool for helping children understand the foster care system and what is happening to them at the time they enter it. It was developed by members of the Branch County Department of Social Services in Coldwater, Michigan, and is based on the family assessment tool called the ecomap developed by Ann Hartman[3]. The child's ecomap was originally designed as an initial interviewing tool to open communication between child and social worker. At the same time it assists the child in understanding his or her placement in foster care and the reasons for being removed from the birth home.

The ecomap also helps make the child aware of the social worker's job. The workers who developed this tool have found it to be most effective with children from ages five to 12. They recommend including the ecomap in the child's life story book described in Section 3 of this workbook. A blank ecomap and instructions on how to use it begin on the following page*.

The child should be advised of the treatment plan as soon as it is completed. The social worker needs to help the child understand what the child's job is while in foster care; what the parents need to accomplish to have the child returned to them; and what the social worker's job is in terms of facilitating this process. It is likely that further explanation will be called for as the treatment plan progresses. Even children as young as three or four need and deserve an explanation of what is happening to them and what the plan for their future is. Some agencies have the school-aged foster child read the case planning contract between agency and parent.

*The workers involved in developing this tool were Mrs Jean Felton, Mrs Doris Stagg, and Mrs Sharon Miller. They have given permission to incorporate this tool into this book.

1. Me

by _____

today is _____

I am _____ years old

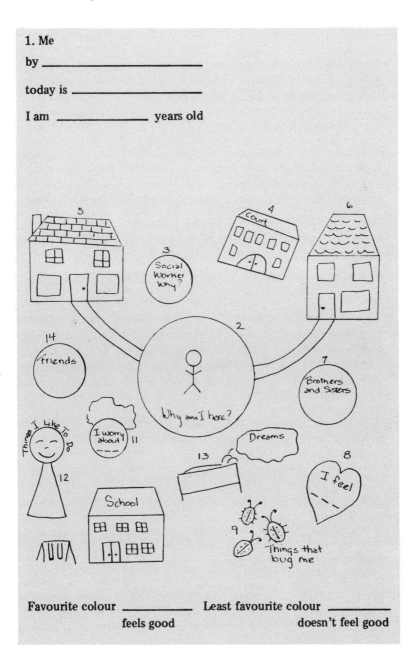

Favourite colour _____ Least favourite colour _____

feels good   doesn't feel good

Instructions for completing the child's ecomap

Give the child a copy of the ecomap and some crayons. As the various areas of the map are discussed, encourage the child to do the writing and colouring. Use the outline, adding questions as necessary.

1 Fill in the blanks.

2 *Why am I here?* Discuss this item to help the child come to terms with why he or she is in foster care. The child's misconceptions, especially those that may lead to guilty feelings, can be drawn out. Give the child a clear and realistic picture of why he or she is in care.

3 *Social worker:* Children are often confused about this new person in their life. Let the child know that your job is to work with him or her and the parents towards the return home.

4 *Court:* Briefly describe the hearing process and the role of the judge or magistrates.

5 *Homes:* The child can identify one of these homes as his or her home
6 and one as the foster home with pathways to both. If the parents are separated and there is contact with both parents, a third home can be added. Encourage the child to talk about similarities and differences in the two homes and parenting styles. Describe the role of the foster parents.

7 *Siblings:* A discussion of siblings, particularly if the child is separated from some or all of the siblings, can elicit the child's feelings about the siblings.

8 *I feel:* Encourage spontaneous verbalisation from the child.

9 *Things that bug me:* Let the child complete this. Younger children may respond to the visual cue by indicating that bugs bug them.

10 *School:* Give the child an opportunity to talk about previous school experiences and feelings he or she has about entering a new school while he or she is in foster care.

11 *I worry about:* Encourage spontaneous verbalisations from the child.

12 *Things I like to do:* Encourage the child to talk about things he or she

enjoys and things that others do that make them happy. This allows both you and the foster parents to know some of the child's interests and likes; and lets the child express his or her wishes.

13 *Dreams:* Encourage the child to talk about his or her dreams or nightmares.

14 *Friends:* Talk with the child about old friends and how he or she might go about making new friends in the new school.

Voluntary reception into care
Sometimes children can be prepared for the move from birth family and foster family. This is almost always true in voluntary placements. In addition, there is an opportunity to select the appropriate placement based on an assessment of the child's psychological needs and present functioning.

A thorough assessment should provide information about what type of environment would be therapeutic for the child. The ideal foster home would: (1) provide corrective learning experiences if the child has emotional problems or developmental delays; or (2) encourage continued psychological growth if the child has no delays or behavioural problems.

The social worker should discuss foster care with the child before he or she is placed. Figure 2 showing different aspects of parenting and the child's ecomap can help in this discussion. The child may need some help in recognising the goals others have for his or her behaviour in the foster home such as learning to take notice of adults or to have fun with a mother. The child should also be advised of the goals of the parents and how they will work on change while the child is out of the home.

The social worker can also outline what his or her role will be in terms of facilitating change. Children of school age need to be given clear information on what goals need to be achieved and by whom so that they may return to the birth home. When in care, they need to be advised of progress that is made towards these goals.

Foster family albums may be used to introduce the child to the prospective foster family. It is helpful if there can be a couple of visits between the child and the foster family prior to placement. When such visits occur, the worker is in a better position to help the child recognise his or her fears and worries about placement, as well as other feelings and to cope with these feelings.

Prior to placement a schedule and arrangements for visits between the child and the birth parents should be set up so that both the child and parent understand the expectations. Definite times, such as one month or three months, should be set up for re-evaluation of the plan of progress. These re-evaluations should include input by the foster parents as well as the birth parents. A child who is seven or older may be a part of the re-evaluation process.

Decisions made at the time of re-evaluation of the treatment plan need to be shared with the child as well as with all others involved. The social worker needs to share information about the birth parents' progress or lack of progress toward return of the child to their home with the child. Such re-evaluation should be conducted in cases placed on an emergency basis as well.

Children placed on a voluntary basis will have strong feelings about the placement even if they understand the reasons for it. They, like all other children in placement, need permission to have and to express these feelings. Again, pictures of the birth family are important to the child in placement.

Exercise 3 that follows gives you an opportunity to think of ways to minimise the trauma as a child comes into care. You will need to think about the messages you want to convey and strategies to accomplish your goal. After Exercise 3, the next part of Section 2 continues with a discussion of moving children from one foster home to another.

Exercise 3:
Ways to minimise the trauma for the child entering foster care

Instructions

Purpose:
To help you identify ways that might help minimise the trauma the child feels upon initial separation from the birth parents.

How to do it:

1 Reread the initial part of Merrilee's case history in Exercise 1 at the beginning of the workbook.

2 Review your responses to items 1 to 3 on Worksheet 1.

3 In the column on the left of the Exercise 3 Worksheet, identify the underlying messages you would like Merrilee to receive about her separation from her mother.

4 In the column on the right, identify ways you might get this message across to Merrilee, keeping in mind that she is two and a half years old.

5 On the lower half of the worksheet, assume that the circumstances are similar but that Merrilee is nine years old. Again, identify the messages you want Merrilee to receive about her separation from her mother and ways that you could convey these messages to Merrilee.

6 As you read this section, you might want to add additional messages and/or ways of conveying the messages to your worksheet.

7 After you complete this exercise, look at the sample answer sheet completed by one social worker.

Ways to minimise the trauma for the child entering foster care

Worksheet

Merrilee at 2½

Underlying messages you want to convey	Strategies for conveying the message

Merrilee at 9

Underlying messages you want to convey	Strategies for conveying the message

Exercise 3:
Ways to minimise the trauma for the child entering foster care

Sample worksheet

___

Merrilee at 2½

Underlying messages you want to convey	Strategies for conveying the message
It's okay for Merrilee to miss her mum and to miss home.	Comfort her when she's sad or angry; give her a picture of her mum; give her a toy or something from home.
Mother cares about Merrilee and loves her.	Continued contact with mum; mum can give comfort to Merrilee.
The foster mum doesn't replace Merrilee's birth mum.	Mum visits her in the foster home and cares for her there - e.g. feeds, bathes her.

Merrilee at 9

Underlying messages you want to convey	Strategies for conveying the message
It's okay to miss mum.	Talk about feelings she has; give her pictures of her mum.
Mum has problems.	Explain Mum's problems and why she has them.
Mum cares.	Encourage contact and Mum's involvement.
There is a plan for Merrilee.	Explain what's going on and what may happen. Use ecomap.

Moving a child from one foster home to another

Unfortunately, many children who come into care move from one home to another several times. It is not unusual for a child who has been in care for a period of three years or more to have made nine or ten moves. If we honestly believe that moves are traumatic for children, then one of the social worker's responsibilities is to minimise the number of moves that the child faces as well as to minimise the trauma of any moves that must occur by preparing the child ahead of time for the moves.

If a child is to be moved from one foster home to another or another type of child care facility, a full assessment of the child's psychological needs and the child's present functioning should be made so that a foster family or child care facility will be selected that can meet the child's needs.

The social worker must talk honestly with the child about the reasons for the move. The object of such a talk is not to place blame on anyone but to describe problems and unmet needs which the child or the family may have had. Children in care do understand that some children and some families have trouble getting along and that the same child may get along better with a different family.

It will always be necessary for the social worker to support the 'old' foster family as well as the child so that the foster family can help the child move from the home in the least traumatic way possible. Usually foster families have strong feelings when a child needs to move from their home. Sometimes the family feels guilty about not being able to meet the needs of the child; at other times the family may be angry at the agency for not preparing them for this particular child's behaviour. The foster family should be encouraged to express their feelings to the social worker; they may need much support in dealing with these feelings. If this is not done, the feelings are apt to be expressed inappropriately and to the child's detriment.

Procedures, such as sharing the child's life story book with the new caretakers, explained in detail in Section 4 of this workbook, might be considered in certain moves from one foster home to another. When a child moves from a foster home to a different type of child care facility such as a group home or residential treatment centre, then the child again needs to be told about the reasons for the move and the expectations others hold about the outcome of the placement. The child should be able to visit these facilities before placement.

When the child leaves a residential treatment centre to return to a foster or adoptive placement, it is also important to outline clearly who is going to be responsible for what aspects of preparing the child for the placement and for post-placement services. Sometimes the treatment centre staff will be actively involved in such visits and post-placement services; at other times they will not. Not only should the adults involved have a clear picture of who is responsible for what, but the child or adolescent should also be advised as to who is responsible for what decisions.

Exercise 4 gives you an opportunity to think about moving an injured child from a hospital to a foster home. It requires that you apply the suggestions for a successful move from one foster home to another to a slightly different situation.

Exercise 4:
Planning a move from a hospital setting to a foster home

Instructions

Purpose
To help the worker identify ways to prepare a child for a move from a hospital, following an abusive incident, to a foster home.

How to do it:

Some of the same principles for moving can be used when moving a child from a hospital or other institutional setting to a foster home.

1 Read Kenny's case history.

2 Outline a plan for introducing the foster parents to the child and for pre-placement visits.

3 Review the sample worksheet for comparison purposes.

Kenny's case
Kenny is three years old. He is in the hospital, following a severe head injury that resulted from abuse from his father. The head injury has left him with a partial paralysis on the right side. He also has some speech problems because of the injury. In the hospital he has become the favourite of the nurses. He is involved in both physical therapy and in speech therapy. He will soon move to a foster home.

Exercise 4:
Planning a move

Worksheet

Messages for Kenny	Strategies for conveying

Exercise 4:

Planning a move

Sample worksheet

Messages for Kenny	Strategies for conveying
The foster family are not strangers.	Visits in the hospital by foster parents and their children, if any.
The family knows about Kenny and how to take care of him.	Consultation for the foster parents with hospital staff and involvement and training in physical therapy programme.
The place Kenny will go to is familiar. The foster parents know that the unknown is scary.	Show Kenny pictures of the house, pets, school, etc.
This is an orderly and planned move.	Several visits and outings regularly scheduled and timed and a date to move.
It's okay to go with this family - especially this father.	Kenny's favourite nurses meet the foster parents and encourage Kenny to be with the dad - play with him, cuddle him, etc.

---

3 The life story book

Why use life story books?
We believe that a life story book should be started for each child at the time he or she first comes into care. The book is an account of the child's life conveyed in words and pictures. It should be developed throughout the child's time in care and should accompany him or her into permanent placement, whether that be back into the child's biological family or to an adoptive home. The book can be used as a tool to help the child understand his or her past, what is happening to their family and what it means to be in care.

One of the functions of the family is to provide continuous contact with a small number of people over a lifetime. The long-term relationships between family members allow each person an opportunity to clarify past events and re-interpret past events in terms of the present. Children in care are frequently denied these opportunities. They change families; they change workers; they may lose contact with birth family members.

When children come into care and move about, pieces of information about their life are lost. When children lose track of these pieces of the past, they often face stumbling blocks to their psychological development. We have known adolescents who grew up in care, who didn't know where they were born; who knew nothing about their birth parents; who do not know the names of their previous foster parents; and who have few recollections of previous moves.

It is difficult to grow up as a psychologically healthy adult if a child is denied access to his or her past. The very fact that adults hesitate to share information about the past with a child implies that this past is so bad the child won't be able to cope with it. Whatever the past was, the child lived through it and survived, and so can live with the truth. The truth can be presented in a harmful way that lowers the child's self-esteem or in a way that helps the child to understand and accept his or her past and thus raises their self-esteem. All individuals have a right to know about themselves. They have more of a right to this information than anyone else.

Case example: Russell
Russell was 55 years old, had been married for 32 years, and had a grown family. He and his wife were planning a long-awaited trip abroad. Russell needed his birth certificate in order to apply for his passport. He wrote for the birth certificate. When he received it, although his date of birth was correct, the names of the parents were not the names he expected. His parents were both dead. However, he contacted an aunt and cousin, both of whom told him that he had been adopted as an infant. Everyone in the family, except for Russell, his wife, and his children, knew that information.

The first line of defence against this kind of harm to the identities of children should be preventing family break-ups and making effective permanent plans for children, but the life story book can help children cope with the disruptions that do occur.

The life story book can also be a tool to use in preparing a child for a forthcoming move. As a social worker and child either complete the book together or review it and add to it, there is an opportunity to identify strong feelings about past events, to resolve issues, to correct misperceptions. The value of the life story book is summarised below.

The life story book can help:
1 to organise past events in a chronological schema;
2 to aid in ego development;
3 to increase self-esteem;
4 a child re-read at his or her own pace;
5 a child share in orderly fashion his or her past with selected others;
6 build a sense of trust for the worker who aids in compiling the book.
7 gain acceptance of all facets of the child's life and help the child accept his or her own past; and
8 facilitate bonding.

What goes into a life story book
Children like to have information about their own birth, including how much they weighed, how long they were, what day of the week they were born, and at which hospital. A baby picture should be included if one is available. If the child had any health problems at birth, those should be noted as well.

Photographs of the birth parents should be included when the child comes into care. Information about parents and siblings should be included as well. If a genogram has been completed as part of the assessment of the birth family, then a copy should be included in the book (Hartman[3]). Information about milestones in the child's development and behaviour in the home should be presented in words the child understands and should be accompanied by pictures.

Some social workers have told us that they have helped the abusive and neglectful parents compile their own life story books. This has been a tool that has helped the parents understand their own past. Many abusive and neglectful parents themselves have gaps in their knowledge. The worker who is willing to help them fill in these gaps will be trusted more than the worker who indicates the past is unimportant. Also if a parent has recognised the usefulness of a life story book, or of a genogram and ecomap, in helping them to understand themselves, they are more apt to help put together their child's life story book and to preserve and use it if the child returns from foster care.

Foster families should document the child's life in their home so that the material can be included in the life story book. Pictures of the foster family and the foster home should be included. One way to ensure having pictures available is for social workers to take pictures of foster homes every year or two as they are approved. The following list highlights the kind of information that foster parents might add to the life story book.

Information foster parents should compile includes:
1 developmental milestones
2 information about injuries, illnesses or hospitalisation
3 favourite activities
4 favourite birthday and other special occasion gifts
5 the ways the child celebrated special holidays
6 favourite friends
7 information about pets in the family
8 information about ways the child showed feelings
9 pictures of foster family and pets
10 pictures of the foster home
11 pictures of the child with the foster family
12 cute 'naughty' behaviour
13 ways the child liked to show affection

14 special trips or vacations with the foster family
15 information about reactions and frequency of visits with
    birth relatives
16 any special extended family members
17 names of teachers and school attended
18 report cards
19 special activities, such as scouting, clubs or camping
    experiences
20 church, Sunday school and other religious experiences

Most of the items are self-explanatory. A sentence or two about each
item, especially if accompanied by a picture, usually suffices.

The one item that needs some explanation is the one about 'cute,
naughty' behaviour. Most toddlers and pre-schoolers do some things
that upset their parents at the time but seem humorous in retrospect
and become the basis of family stories. Talking about such behaviour
gives the child a clear indication that he or she can and will change.
Even though there are frequently no pictures of these incidents, they
usually elicit strong visual images.

For example, one child as a toddler loved to sit on a sack of dogfood,
feeding dogfood first to the dog and then to himself. Another child
washed her hair in a mud puddle twice in one day as her mother tried to
get ready to go to a party.

If the child does have to move from foster home to foster home the
worker can review the life story book with him or her. This is a good
time to deal with old feelings and to clarify the past. The life story book
should go with the child when returning to the birth home. Taking a
Polaroid picture of the child and the family on the day of the return
home is a good idea. This picture can be added to the life story book
along with comments about the child's and family's feelings on that
day.

If the child is to be placed in an adoptive home, then pictures of the
child and the adoptive family should be added to the book. If the
adoptive parents have put together pictures or stories to introduce
themselves to the child, these can be added to the book.

If a child becomes legally free for adoption and if a life story book has
not been initiated by the foster care social worker, it falls to the
adoption worker to seek out information and pictures and to compile
the book with the child in preparation for adoption. For some children

who were placed in adoption without life story books, the building of such a book can sometimes ease problems in the adoptive home. It is never too late to do a life story book nor too early to start one!

If a life story book is not compiled until after relinquishment, social workers have had success in obtaining information and pictures by contacting the parents, even several years after termination of parental rights. The message to the birth parents in such cases has been: 'Suzie and her parents need more information about her past in order to help her understand what has happened to her.' Birth parents still have something to offer the child in this way even though they cannot parent the child. Requests from the adoptive parents for pictures or information reassures them about this. If the social worker makes such contacts, there are minimal problems with confidentiality.

More and more often parents are being asked to write letters or prepare tapes for children they are relinquishing. Such tapes and/or letters can be used repeatedly at various developmental stages to help the child understand what has happened in the past and to reassimilate this knowledge, in view of new developmental attainments. A sample of such a letter follows.

Dear Justin,

I'm sorry that I didn't write for so long. I know that you've been waiting for a letter from me but there were some important things that I had to think about and some decisions I had to make. You know how long it always takes me to decide things.

I hear that you've learned how to read now and can ride a bicycle too! Goodness, how you are growing! I hope you will be good at reading.

You know, Justin, everybody is good at some things but everybody finds out that there are some things that they can't do well, no matter how hard they try. Well, I am like most people. I can do some things pretty well, like driving a car and playing the piano. But some other things I can't do. Maybe I could do some of them if I tried but there's one thing I tried to do for six years and I don't think I can ever do right. That's being a good Mummy for you, Justin. I feel badly that I can't give you the kind of love and attention that you need. I've known for a long time that I wasn't able to. I know that things haven't been right between us. Even though we loved each other we weren't able to get along together. I hoped that we could but it just didn't work out for us.

So I had to go away and decide what would be best for us. I've decided that it would be best if I let you have a chance to have a Mum and Dad who could give you the kind of love and attention you need. I have asked Mrs Arnhem to find such a family.

I know that it will be hard for you to understand this. I suppose that you'll be really angry with me but I hope your new parents will help you learn to understand. I hope that you'll learn to love your new Mummy and Daddy and that you'll be happy with them. That's important to me. I'll never forget you.

I've given Mrs Arnhem some pictures of you when you were little and a picture of your Dad and I when we were happy together for you to keep. I kept the one of you learning to ride your first tricycle and the one of you and I at the zoo so I can always remember you.

I will always love you even though I can't be your Mum anymore.

Mummy Barbara

Adoptive children do not 'work through' their feelings once and for all about their separation from their birth parents or about what it means to be adopted. Just as the rest of us must periodically reassess what it means to be the only child, or the oldest child or whatever, so must adopted children re-incorporate this quality of their life into their gradually maturing sense of identity. Factual information helps.

The life story book or the information in it can be useful at several points in an adopted child's life. It has been our experience that most children initially bring up the subject of adoption, if it has not been raised by the parents prior to this time, when they are between five and a half and six and a half. Many children who are not adopted also question that possibility at that age. When children are between seven and nine, they usually achieve a noticeably higher level of cognitive ability and need to re-incorporate what adoption means into their perception of themselves.

In early adolescence, the task for all children is to begin to separate psychologically from their families. If a child is separated from the birth family for any reasons, the child faces not only the psychological separation from the family with whom he or she lives but also the psychological separation from the birth family carried within him or her by fantasy. Actual information about the birth family facilitates this important psychological task rather than hindering it. This does not mean that the child needs to have actual contact with the birth family to facilitate this process but, rather, that factual information helps.

When the individual becomes a young adult, again the relationship with family changes dramatically. It is a time when many individuals feel that direct contact with their birth family is necessary for the completion of the individuation process and for continued maturation. When adults face parenthood, the urge to know more about their own birth family again becomes important. Many adult adoptees undertake their own personal search for their birth parents at this time.

One question that has been raised about the use of a life story book in adoptive placements is 'What happens when a child with a life story book is placed in an adoptive family where other children don't have one? What will be the effect on these other children?' It is quite likely that the other adopted children will become anxious to have more information about their pasts. Their parents can help to obtain this information and may well become even more bonded to their previously adopted children by sharing in this search for further information about the past.

Many adoptive parents have become very active advocates of helping the children obtain information and pictures about their past. Workers have found that sharing in the gathering of information for life story books tends to help them in understanding their child clients and in feeling closer to them through the shared experiences. Adoptive parents can be helped to have an opportunity to gain further understanding and closeness with their previously adopted children by sharing in compiling their life story books.

Sample life story

This is a life story for a four and a half year old child. Since many of the important events in Sarah Ann's life occurred before the age of three, the social worker chose to write the story in the third person. For older children who take a more active part in compiling the life story, the first person is a good idea. In some cases the social worker may choose to use the second person for a young child who cannot yet read. The social worker and Sarah talked about what was being written and about the feelings that Sarah might have had at previous times in her life. This life story was written by the social worker as part of the preparation process for an adoptive placement.

The particular words used in a life story are often very important. The use of natural or real parents is avoided because of the connotation that adoptive, foster or step parents are either 'unnatural' or 'unreal'.

237

We also purposefully avoid the term 'forever' in describing adoptive homes. The term 'forever' is overwhelming in its implications both to parents and to children. The word 'keeping' implies the permanency that we are seeking for children when we plan adoptive placements without being overwhelming.

We use the words 'life story book' rather than 'scrapbook'. Although to many children the idea of a scrapbook is pleasurable, to the child in foster care who may have poor self-esteem, the term 'scrap' may have a negative connotation.

Sarah Ann Jensen's life story

Sarah Ann Jensen was born on Sunday, November 10, 1974 at Memorial Hospital in Denver, Colorado. She was a beautiful healthy baby who weighed 6lbs 3oz and was 19½ inches (47.5 cm) long. Her birth parents, Janet and Tom, were excited and proud of Sarah. However, soon after Sarah was born, her daddy lost his job. Sometimes her family didn't have enough to eat. Sometimes her family didn't have enough money to pay the rent.

Mummy Janet and Daddy Tom were worried. Sometimes when they were worried and Sarah cried, like all babies cry, Mummy Janet and Daddy Tom didn't know what to do. Sometimes when they worried about other things, they spanked Sarah too hard instead of picking her up and loving her.

Sarah's birth parents started having a lot of problems. They were angry with each other much of the time. Sometimes they got angry at Sarah even though, obviously, their problems weren't her fault. One day Mummy Janet got so cross that she spanked Sarah much harder than babies should ever be spanked. Afterwards she was sorry. Sarah's leg was badly hurt, and Sarah had to stay in the hospital for many days. This happened when she was nine months old.

At first in the hospital Sarah hurt and she was scared so she cried a lot. When Mummy and Daddy came to see her, she would cry like most babies do after they have been away from their mum and dad for a while. However, Mummy Janet and Daddy Tom didn't know that that was just how babies act. They thought that the crying meant that Sarah was angry with them. Pretty soon they stopped coming to visit.

When Sarah's leg was well enough so that she could leave hospital she was 11 months old. Sarah's Mummy Janet and Daddy Tom were still having a lot of problems. Sometimes when grownups are having lots of problems, they can't take care of babies. Sarah went to live in a foster home with Mr and Mrs Jones and their three children – Sam, who was nine; Virginia, seven; and Veronica, who was five.

Sarah learned to love Mummy and Daddy Jones and Sam, Virginia and Veronica. When she was about 16 months old, she learned to walk. She could already say about ten words. She used to have a favourite stuffed animal named Bunny that she took everywhere with her. Mummy Jones had brought Bunny as a present for Sarah the first time she came to visit her in the hospital. Sam loved to give Sarah piggy back rides; Virginia loved to read her stories; and Veronica, whom Sarah called 'Wonnie', taught her to turn somersaults.

When Sarah was two and a half her first mummy and daddy – Mummy Janet and Daddy Tom – thought they were ready to take care of her. While Sarah was living with the Jones family, her Mummy Janet and Daddy Tom had had a baby boy whom they named Jeffrey. They had also moved to a new apartment.

When Sarah started having visits with her Mummy Janet, Daddy Tom and baby Jeffrey, she was confused. She didn't remember her first mummy and daddy and she certainly didn't know Jeffrey. Nothing looked familiar. She didn't understand – two and a half-year-olds don't understand lots of things yet – why everyone said this was her 'real' mummy and daddy. She thought that Mummy and Daddy Jones were her 'real' parents because they took care of her the same way they took care of Sam, Virginia and Veronica.

At first she thought that Sam, Virginia, and 'Wonnie' would be moving with her, but she found out she was wrong. Sarah was confused. She was scared of moving to a 'new' house. She was sad about leaving the Jones' home. It also made her angry. She was so angry and sad that when she went to live with Mummy Janet and Daddy Tom, she cried and cried. She was so angry that she didn't want to take notice of them. Sometimes she felt scared too. When she especially missed the Jones family, she would sometimes hit Jeffrey. Maybe she thought that then Mummy Janet and Daddy Tom would send her back to the Jones' home; maybe she just didn't know what to do with all those feelings.

Mummy Janet and Daddy Tom didn't know what to do when Sarah cried. They didn't understand that Sarah was scared, lonely, sad and angry, and needed extra loving. They sent her to her room whenever she cried, but that just made Sarah feel more lonely and scared. She cried harder and harder. That made Mummy Janet and Daddy Tom really angry, and they started to spank her much too hard again and sometimes they told her she was a bad girl. Sarah believed them, but they were wrong; she wasn't 'bad'; she was scared, lonely, and sad.

One day Mummy Janet called Mr Dunlap the social worker, and said it wasn't working out with Sarah at home and that she would have to go back into care. Mummy Janet and Daddy Tom packed up all of Sarah's clothes, and Mr Dunlap came and got her. Sarah had been 'home' for two months. She still missed the Jones family; but Mr Dunlap didn't take her back to the Jones family. This time he took her to the Robinson home. Sarah was still confused and sad. She missed Mummy and Daddy Jones and their children.

The Robinsons had a baby boy named James and two big foster boys, Richard and Ronnie. Sarah didn't know how Ronnie could be a boy when in the Jones home 'Wonnie' was a girl. Every time Sarah saw Ronnie she thought of 'Wonnie' and missed her. She didn't like Ronnie and sometimes she would sneak his toys and hide them when he was at school. Baby James reminded her of baby Jeffrey and she would remember Mummy Janet calling her a 'bad' girl.

Sometimes Sarah wished that she was a baby again. Sometimes she would take Jamie's bottle and suck on it. That made Mrs Robinson cross and she would spank Sarah. She didn't understand how confused Sarah was. Sarah wouldn't call Mr and Mrs Robinson 'Daddy' and 'Mummy'. She would pull away from them. She was a very unhappy girl.

Mr Dunlap saw how unhappy Sarah was. He tried to explain to Mrs Robinson how Sarah felt, but she had trouble understanding. Finally, just before Sarah's third birthday, Mr Dunlap decided that Sarah was just too sad at the Robinson home so he moved her. This time she went back to the Jones' home.

At first she was happy to be there, but part of her kept being mad and scared that she might have to move again. Also there was another foster girl there. Heather was four and a half. She and Veronica played together lots of the time so sometimes Sarah felt left out.

Sarah had a special clown cake for her third birthday, and got her very own tricycle. It was a fun day. Mama Jones decorated the house with balloons. The other kids gave her books and clay. She was happy and felt very loved that day. She kept saying 'I love you mummy; I'm going to have all my birthdays at your house.' Mummy Jones told Sarah that she loved her too. Sarah asked, 'Can I have all my birthdays here?' Mummy Jones told her that Mr Dunlap would decide how many birthdays she would have with the Jones family.

Whenever Mr Dunlap came to visit, Sarah was careful to be extra specially good hoping that Mr Dunlap would let her stay with the Jones family. Mr Dunlap was working with Mummy Janet and Daddy Tom to help them understand how Sarah felt. When Sarah was three years and four months old, she started having visits every week with Mummy Janet and Daddy Tom. Sometimes they went to the park for a picnic or to the zoo. Sarah would have a good time on those days. But sometimes they went 'home' for visits. When that happened all the old, scared, sad and angry feelings would come back, and Sarah would cry and would have a hard time responding to them.

Mummy Janet and Daddy Tom wanted things to work out well for them all but it seemed no matter how hard they tried, Sarah and they didn't feel loving toward each other. Finally Mummy Janet and Daddy Tom decided that maybe it would never work out well for them and Sarah. Sarah stopped having visits. She wasn't sure why the visits stopped.

Part of her was glad she didn't have to go 'home' any more; but part of her was sad about it. She really didn't understand the mixed up feelings so she decided it would be easiest to 'forget' about Mummy Janet, Daddy Tom, and baby Jeffrey. Whenever anybody asked about her family she would only talk about the Jones family. If anyone talked aboutMummy Janet and Daddy Tom she wouldn't listen. She would just think her own private thoughts and wouldn't talk.

Sarah was still with the Jones family for her fourth birthday. She got a new dolly, whom she named Melody. She had a special ice cream cake that looked like a doll and her best friend, Tammy, came for her birthday dinner. Even Oscar the dog enjoyed some cake.

Soon after her fourth birthday, Mr Dunlap, Mummy Janet and Daddy Tom went and talked to the judge. They all decided together that Sarah would not ever ever go back to live with Mummy Janet and Daddy Tom. They decided that she should get a new set of keeping parents with whom she would grow up. Sarah said she already had a family – the Jones family. However, Mummy and Daddy Jones and Mr Dunlap explained that the Jones family is a foster family. Children live with foster families until they can either go back to their birth families or until they get a keeping family that is an adoptive family.

Sarah got a new social worker. Her name is Mrs Small. Her job will be to find Sarah's keeping family. Sarah still doesn't like the idea of moving to a new family. She wants to stay with the Jones family. When she thinks of moving, she gets sad and angry. Sometimes then she does naughty things. Mummy Jones doesn't like the naughty things but she understands how Sarah feels and tells her that when she is sad or scared, she should come and be close to her. Mummy and Daddy Jones will miss Sarah because they love her. Sam, Virginia, Veronica and Heather will miss her too. However, Mummy and Daddy Jones are happy too because Sarah will be getting a keeping family and won't have to keep moving. Even big people sometimes feel sad and happy at the same time.

Mrs Small talked to Sarah's first mummy and daddy and got pictures of Sarah when she was a baby. Sarah will keep those pictures as well as lots of pictures of the Jones family. She has pictures of every birthday since all of her birthdays were with the Jones family. Birthdays are special days. Mrs Small even got a picture of the Robinson family to put in Sarah's book, but Sarah doesn't care much about that picture she says. Sometimes Sarah likes to look at all the pictures; sometimes she doesn't.

At bedtime Sarah and Melody, her special doll, talk to each other about what kind of keeping family they dream of. Mrs Small has told Sarah and Melody that they will have a chance to meet the keeping family before Mrs Small decides for sure if it is the right family for Sarah and Melody. Mrs Small says that lots of families want keeping children and lots of children need keeping families and that her job is to help the right family and the right child get together. She says that she will be sure to tell Sarah's keeping family about how much Sarah loves Mummy and Daddy Jones and Sam, Virginia, Ronnie and Heather.

Mrs Small will tell them that sometimes when Sarah gets sad, angry, or lonely she forgets and does naughty things instead of remembering to come and be close to a mummy and daddy and talk about her feelings. Sarah's keeping family will help her with that. When Melody gets lonely, or if she is naughty, Sarah says she will be sure to hug her because she knows that Melody is going to miss the Jones family too.

Mrs Small says that Sarah will be celebrating her fifth birthday with her keeping family. Sarah wonders what kind of cake she will have. She hopes it is chocolate. Sarah hopes that she will be able to invite the Jones family to her birthday party. She and Melody are planning to talk to their keeping parents about that when they meet them. Sarah thinks she will have Melody ask them about that instead of asking herself.

242

4 When a child leaves care

Introduction

In this final section of the workbook we discuss what happens when a child moves out of care and into a situation that is intended to be permanent. We also give guidelines for helping children and families handle these moves. When a child moves out of care, he or she may be returning to the birth family or be emancipated to live on their own, or move into an adoptive family. We touch on the special aspects of each of these kinds of moves.

You will find that the material on moving a child into an adoptive home is more highly developed than the rest. This is because we did most of our early work in child placement with children who were in care and who were being prepared for adoption. We developed many of our principles and procedures through our work with these children. As you examine our suggestions on adoptive placement planning, we hope you will join us in our efforts to think of ways to incorporate these ideas into other parts of your work.

Before we discuss the three kinds of moves out of care – back to the birth family, into an adoptive home, or into an independent living arrangement – we mention one factor that is common to all such moves. When children move out of a foster home either to return to their birth families or to be adopted, they are vulnerable to the same wide range of feelings that they had when they moved in. They may be sad, angry, frightened or anxious, as well as eager, happy or relieved. However, when a child leaves, parents and workers tend to focus on the pleasant aspects of the move and ignore the fact that the child has ambivalent feelings about it.

In addition, the child's move out of care is often linked to the fact that he or she has done well in the foster home, and this may add to the child's confusion. The child may recognise that he or should feel happy about having done well and moving back to be with the biological family or into the adoptive home. Yet, he or she is apt to feel sad about leaving the foster home where they did well and to be angry about their impotence and their mixed feelings. By recognising the child's mixed feelings, acknowledging the appropriateness of them, and allowing their expression, parents and workers can help children handle these moves.

New forms of adoption are helping to ease the transition into adoption for many children. We briefly note two of these here – foster parent adoption and open adoption. Foster parent adoption is occurring with increasing frequency. The enormous advantage is that this protects existing attachments and prevents the trauma of separation. In undertaking such a plan the social worker should make a careful assessment of the child's needs; the foster parents' abilities to meet these needs on a long-range basis; and the degree of attachment between the child and parents and vice versa.

In addition, the social worker needs to explore with both the family and the child what their expectations are with regard to adoption. What does it mean to them? Will it change their relationship? Do the parents expect the child's behaviour to change following the adoption proceedings? Does the child expect the parents' behaviour to change?

In addition to allowing, and even encouraging, contacts between the adopted child and the previous foster parents, many agencies are now encouraging continuing contact with some birth family member. Continued contact between siblings who have been placed for adoption in different adoptive homes is the most frequent form of contact. However, in some cases continued contact with certain extended family members who have been psychologically important to the child is allowed.

When children come into or leave care, workers must always be watchful for the child's relationship with and attachment to family members other than parents. Many children are very attached to one or more siblings; in fact, these relationships sometimes have the intensity usually reserved for parent/child relationships. Every attempt possible should be made to avoid disrupting such attachments.

Open adoption in which there is some continued contact with birth parents or emancipated siblings is becoming increasingly popular. Most of the adopted children in such cases are adolescents and in many instances, have been adopted by their foster parents. In such cases, contact between birth parent and child had occurred during the foster placement and may continue following adoption.

In other situations in which a child has lived with their birth parents for a significant part of their lives, some adoptive families feel comfortable with some form of contact between the child and the birth parent during the adolescent years.

Contact between adopted children and their birth families should occur when things are going well between the child and adoptive family. The message to the child then is 'I want you to share your good times with your birth family. It is our job, not theirs, to work out problems between us.' Adoptive parents don't feel as threatened by contact between their child and birth parents when things are going well and the child is not put in the position where he or she is likely to try to get the birth parents to side with them against the adoptive parents.

Helping a verbal child move into adoption

Introduction
In this section we discuss moving the child over three into adoption, and in the next, we consider how this process must be adapted to help the child under three make the move into adoption. Although we use the age of three as the dividing line, in our discussion of the placement process it is the child's abilities to verbalise and to separate temporarily from the adults to whom he or she is attached that makes the real difference in the way the process is handled. Thus if we are dealing with a four-year-old who is developmentally delayed, we may proceed with the move in the fashion outlined for a two-year-old.

The process of moving a verbal child into an adoptive home will be discussed in stages. These stages include introducing the idea of adoption to the child, arranging the first meetings, getting a commitment to proceed, planning pre-placement visits, the day of the move, post-placement visits, and post-placement follow-up.

Introducing the idea of adoption to the child
In order to present a child with the possibility that he or she will be adopted, the social worker must first spend enough time with the child so that the two of them are comfortable together. Then, preferably in front of the foster mother, the social worker must tell the child about the difference between foster care and adoptive care in a way that he or she can understand.

When we explain adoption we often use the diagram and method

245

outlined in Section 1, on page 197. The basic facts we try to get across are that foster families take care of children until they can either return to their birth families or until an adoptive family is chosen for them. Adoptive families are 'keeping families' and are interested in raising children until they grow up. Once the adoption is completed the child no longer has social workers or judges who decide what will happen to him or her. The child shares the same name as the adoptive parents.

The social worker needs to explain that his or her job is to help find the family that will work out best for the child. We think children should be told that when the social worker finds a family that he or she thinks is the right one, a few visits will be set up so that the family and child can get to know each other.

We tell the child that it is the social worker's responsibility to make sure that the child and family are right for each other. However, we explain that everyone involved, including the family, the child, and the worker must agree that the child and family combination that the worker picked is the right one. If it is not, the worker will look for another family.

We take this approach because, on the one hand, we don't want the child to think that he or she is totally responsible for choosing a family. One experienced worker asked a six-year-old if the family he had met was the right family for him, and he responded anxiously, 'What if I pick the wrong family?' On the other hand, if the child lets us know by what he or she says or does that for some reason they are not hitting it off with this family, it is absurd to proceed with the adoption. Also, parents need to know that if they are uncomfortable proceeding with a child, the worker will take them off the hook and will accept the responsibility of looking for another family for the child.

Arranging first visits
Once the worker has selected a family for a child, the first meeting must be arranged. Some agencies sometimes permit families first to see the child without meeting him or her.

We are against such arrangements. Almost all children beyond the age of four, and some younger, know what is happening. They imply that the parents are choosing rather than that the decision results from mutual interaction. The rejection children experience from such an arrangement where they are not chosen seems greater than what they feel if they meet the family and it is decided that they are not the right combination. Videotape or home movie presentations of children to families do not have the same drawbacks and do allow prospective parents to get a clearer picture of children and their behaviour.

Since children usually feel most secure on their home ground, this is the best place for them to meet prospective adoptive parents. In most cases we think the child should meet only the parents during the initial contact. We recommend showing the child pictures of prospective parents before the visit, just as we show pictures of the child to the parents before the visit. Mental images are helpful prior to the meeting. Prospective parents should bring pictures of their home, other children, and pets to share with the child and to help him or her feel somewhat acquainted with what they will find when they visit.

Although the initial visit should occur on the child's home ground, it makes sense that the older child might also be taken on a brief outing with the prospective adoptive parents. Prospective parents should be advised against buying clothes for the child at this stage because a decision to continue placement planning has not been made. However, they may wish to buy the child an inexpensive toy.

During the initial visit in the foster home, the foster and adoptive parents have an opportunity to meet each other. In fact, there are some advantages to having the two sets of parents meet with the worker ahead of the meeting with the child. This type of meeting gives the foster parents an opportunity to share with the prospective adoptive parents the little bits of knowledge that are the real key to the parenting process.

We recognise that these suggestions are not compatible with our present system that discourages contact between foster and adoptive parents. We feel this posture encourages competitiveness between the two sets of parents and neglects the needs of the child. Foster parents are, at the time of the move, the most important persons in the child's life.

The social worker's role is that of facilitator, adviser, and director of the moving process. If the social worker is more attached to the child than the foster parents are, then there is something seriously wrong with one relationship, or the other, or both. If the foster parents can be helped to feel comfortable with the adoptive parents and sure that this family will do a good job of parenting the child, then the move will proceed with much less turmoil and disequilibrium for everyone.

The most important message for the child to receive at the time of the adoptive placement is permission to become close to and attached to the new parents. The child needs permission to transfer his or her attachment from foster to adoptive parents, and only the foster parents can give this permission.

It is important that foster parents have more than just a surface commitment to the child transferring attachment to the adoptive parents. Non-verbal messages are always more credible than verbal messages, if the two are not congruent. Thus, even if foster parents say they want the child to get close to the adoptive parents, but don't really mean it, the child will perceive this and will be confused about which message to obey.

Foster parents are very important in the moving process. This is a major part in the job of the foster parent, and it is one which we have too long neglected. During this period of preparation, the social worker is frequently called on to support the foster parents as well as the child emotionally. It is well worth the time and effort.

Getting a commitment to proceed
Most often the second visit should take place with the child visiting the prospective adoptive parents' home. The way the child reacts on leaving the prospective family on the second visit helps indicate how the child feels about this family. Ideally the child should be picked up from the visit by both the foster parent and the social worker. Who takes the child to the visit is less important. Sometimes the prospective parents come and get the child for the visit. At other times the foster parents take the child.

Following this second visit, the social worker can talk separately with the prospective adoptive family, the child, and the foster family. The social worker needs to get everyone's opinions about how things are going, so that he or she can decide whether to plan to move the child into the family. When the worker has this information at hand and finds it favourable, he or she should get the child and the adoptive parents together and ask each in front of the other, already knowing the answers, if they want to proceed with the move. Then, the plan for a further visiting schedule and the final move can be outlined.

We find this process is important because most children who are legally free for adoption these days have already experienced several rejections. It is a very healing thing for a child to hear from a prospective adoptive parent 'We want you to be our child'. Many children in care have not heard that kind of message before. Most adoptive families have been waiting a long time before a child is selected for them. They, too, derive great pleasure from hearing a child say 'I think these are the right parents for me'. Just the act of making this type of commitment in front of the social worker usually starts the bonding process between parents and child. It is a natural thing for them to want to hug and kiss or be physically close after such a commitment.

Setting up pre-placement visits
Most children over the age of three need two or three weeks to adjust to the idea of the move. Few children act up on the first visit or two. Everyone – child, foster parents, adoptive parents, and social worker – feels better if the child has done at least some minimal acting out during visits prior to the move. It prepares both the child and the adoptive parents for the reality of living together.

We realise that most adoptive parents do not see the need for a prolonged visiting schedule and that many children and foster parents appear to want to get the whole thing over. However, the slower the move is, within reason, and the more fully patterns of behaviour are transferred from one household to the other, the less likely it is that there will be extreme testing after the move. We have even seen cases where the visiting has taken place over very prolonged periods of time with great success. However, this is not meant to imply that very prolonged periods of visiting, over a month, are advisable for most children.

If the visits and the final moving day are marked on a calendar at the time of the meeting described above, it helps the child get a sense of the timing of the move. If the child is of pre-school age, he or she should visit the adoptive home at various times of the day during a two to three week period. Overnight, weekend or four to five day visits are also common during this period. The child and the family need to get used to each other in a variety of ways, but most of all in the day-to-day living situation.

It is important that the adoptive parents be able to ask the foster parents what works in terms of discipline for the child. The more that children are aware of considerable communication between the adoptive parent, the foster parent, and the social worker during the pre-placement visits, the more secure they will be that they don't have to worry about hiding things. If they think that everyone knows everything and is comfortable with that, it relieves them from the fear of saying or doing the wrong things.

The more that children are able to express their mixed feelings about the forthcoming move, the better. One must remember that no matter how much children like the prospective family, they also have other feelings – sadness at leaving the family they have learned to love and trust; fear and anxiety about the future; and anger that they have been put in the position of having such confusing emotions.

One very bright, verbal four-year-old girl was trying to explain what had happened in an adoptive placement that had disrupted after seven weeks. She looked puzzled and said, 'I was so sad when I moved, but I didn't cry because I wanted to be happy.' When this child was feeling sad and missing her foster parents, she did something 'naughty'. Her adoptive mother would spank her and she had permission to cry. However, getting permission to cry in this fashion did not help her develop any closeness with the adoptive parents. She and they were soon on a negative cycle of feeling lonely, acting badly, being punished and feeling even lonelier.

Figure 4

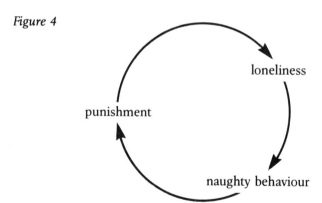

At the time of her placement in a different family, the child and her adoptive parents were helped to see the way this previous cycle had worked. The child was helped to learn that when she felt lonely for her foster mother, she could go and be close to her adoptive mother, and get extra loving then. The adoptive mother was helped to learn which of the child's behaviours were 'normal naughties' for this age, and which resulted from the child's loneliness. Thus, the negative cycle that was present in the first adoptive family was changed to a positive cycle that encouraged attachment in the second adoptive family.

Figure 5

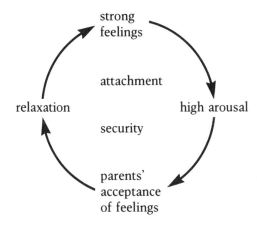

The day of the move

We do a lot of work with child and family on the day of the move. On this day we can open both the door to the past and the door to the future for the child and help him or her see that they connect and that one part of life cannot be walled off from the other parts. It doesn't mean that all the issues are dealt with once and for all on this date; they are just brought to the surface so they can be dealt with in the day-to-day living situation and in future therapy sessions with the child and the adoptive family.

Such sessions help the adoptive parents understand the relationship between the child and the foster parents. Once they understand this, they usually no longer need to feel competitive. They, then, are in a position to help the child deal with feelings of sorrow about the separation from the foster parents. The foster parents and the sadness about missing them becomes an acceptable topic of conversation, not one to be avoided at all costs. This session also provides an opportunity for the therapist or social worker to model ways to respond to the child's expression of feelings.

On the day of the move we try to include expressing feelings about the separation, setting up ways to build attachment between adoptive parents and child, and reviewing the child's life story with the child and adoptive parents. We encourage the adoptive family to have a celebration as part of the day. In the following pages we discuss each of these parts of the day of the move.

Expressing feelings at separation. If, for example, both sets of parents finish the packing together and load the belongings into the car, the non-verbal message is that everyone is in agreement on the move. Foster parents should not be discouraged from expressing sadness because the child is leaving. Children's great fear on leaving a home where they have been attached is often that the foster parents may not miss them at all, and that they didn't really matter.

One particular boy, a five-year-old red-head, wondered privately, 'Will Mum go behind the door and cry after I leave; that's what she did when Suzie left.' Should this child have to go through life wondering if his foster mother cried after he left, or should he see her cry? Which behaviour would give him the message that will raise his self-esteem? What says that missing people is all right? We don't miss people to whom we are not attached; we do miss those to whom we are attached.

In addition, if everyone must remain impassive or even cheerful about such an event then children soon learn they had best not ever become attached. It is too painful to separate and have to keep all the pain hidden and suppressed. When adults express their feelings, it gives children permission to do so as well.

Building attachment: practising getting close. At the time of the move, we talk to children about the way that people learn to love each other and explain that few children love their adoptive parents immediately. The children are asked if they want to learn to love their adoptive parents. If they say no, more work must be done around the separation. Most, however, say they do want to learn to love the new parents.

We then ask the children how they learned to ride a bike, read, or anything else that they have recently accomplished. All of these achievements required practising. Children from the age of three and up understand the concept of 'practising' very well.

It is possible to set up ways that a child may 'practise' getting close to the adoptive parents. We ask the child to practise calling his or her new parents 'mum' and 'dad' right away; to practise giving hugs and kisses at bedtime; and, for children eight and under, to practise sitting on mum's and dad's lap every day for ten minutes. During that time they can be read to, sing songs, talk quietly or whatever. It is to be a time when they can practise learning to be comfortable being close.

If the child is too old to sit on the parents' laps, they can practise having fun together by playing games or reading a story. Parents are given similar instructions primarily so that the child understands that learning to be close is a two-way process.

Reviewing the child's life story. During this session we also review the child's life story with the child in front of both sets of parents. This way the child learns that it is acceptable to share his or her past life with the new parents.

If the child has demonstrated any particularly bothersome behaviour during foster care, we try to get him or her to talk as completely as possible about this behaviour. It is important for children to learn that the adoptive parents know the worst of the worst about them and still want them. If children see acceptance on the faces of the adoptive parents in spite of their 'naughty' behaviour, they *may* not act out badly just to see if the adoptive family is going to keep them no matter what. If a child already knows that the family weren't turned off by the worst behaviour he or she was able to come up with in foster care, they are reassured that the family really wants *them*.

Case example: Steven

Steven was eight years old. He was to be placed for adoption with the Adams family. By the time he was two and a half, his mother had perceived Steven as an 'evil' child who was trying to kill her. He had incorporated that message and when he was four – he had already had several placements and returns to his birth parents – had tripped the foster mother down the stairs during the first half hour he was in the home.

The foster mother related that although she knew Steven deliberately tripped her since he was at the head of the stairs laughing, she also knew that if she behaved towards him as though he had done it on purpose, he could never learn to trust her. So, she merely commented, 'In this home, we don't laugh when someone is hurt.'

Steven had many severe behavioural problems. He soiled and smeared faeces; he raised a fire in the family room; he cut an electric cord that plugged in, shocking himself. He cut a hole in the living room carpet. The foster parents stuck with him through all his problems and asked for professional help to deal with Steven's behaviour. At one point in therapy Steven described himself as 'Satan' because he was so bad.

Most of his behavioural problems had subsided prior to the plan for Steven's adoptive placement with the Adams family. However, there was a recurrence of soiling as the social worker started talking about the plan for placement. Steven had a very prolonged pre-placement visiting period since the foster parents and the adoptive parents were acquaintances from church. The adoptive parents specifically applied to adopt Steven after getting to know him.

We were having a therapy session with the foster parents and the adoptive parents on the day of Steven's final move. We knew that for Steven the 'worst of the worst' was his tripping his foster mother down the stairs. However, we honestly weren't certain whether he remembered the incident or whether he had successfully used denial as a defence against this thought. However, the foster mother told us that she had overheard Steven relating the incident to another foster child just the week before.

During the session with both sets of parents present, we asked Steven what he had done the first day he had come to his foster home. He looked panic stricken. We said it had to do with stairs. He then haltingly whispered, 'I tripped Mum down the stairs.' As he said this, Steven did not look at the adoptive parents but at the floor.

We asked 'Do you know why you did that?' He answered, 'No!' We said we were certain he did not know why but that his foster mother knew why and he should ask her. He did. She replied, 'Because you wanted to find out if I could take care of you!' Relief flooded his face. There was a reason for his behaviour, and the reason was not that he was Satan!

We then asked if he had watched his adoptive parents' faces as he had talked of tripping the foster mother down the stairs. He said he hadn't. We asked that he repeat the statement and watch their faces. They knew, of course, of that incident as well as of all his other negative behaviour well before any decision about placement with them had been made. The adoptive parents commented, 'Yes, Steven, we know about that.' We then asked, 'Knowing that, do you still want to adopt Steven?' We asked this because we saw the question mirrored in Steven's eyes. We knew that the answer would be a part of his healing *process. The adoptive parents answered, 'Of course!'*

Although hopefully we do inform adoptive parents fully of the behaviour of the children we place with them and although we may tell the children that the parents know about their past, it is our experience that most children don't believe us. They feel that if the adoptive parents knew the worst they would not want them. One of the most healing things that can happen at the time of adoptive placements is for children to hear that the adoptive parents want them knowing 'the worst of the worst'.

Following this discussion with Steven, we commented that we were certain that there would be times when he wondered if the adoptive parents were able to take care of him. We wondered if he would need to trip them down the stairs, or soil and smear, or cut a hole in the carpet as a way of checking them out, or if he had learned new ways of checking people out while he was in foster care. He replied that he wouldn't need to do those things, but he would prefer to ask them if they loved him.

Interestingly, this child who had demonstrated so many very severe behavioural disturbances in foster care, has not had one serious acting-out incident in three years of adoptive placement. He has had age-appropriate naughty behaviour and has posed some disciplinary problems at school. He has demonstrated some problems getting along with peers, but there has been no soiling, no fire raising, and no destructive behaviour.

A *celebration.* Adoptive placement is a major event in a child's life. All too often it is not marked by any celebration or ritual. In fact, people seem to go overboard to minimise the occasion, pretending that this is just like any other day and not a day for strong emotion. Therefore, we encourage adoptive parents to have some sort of family celebration to mark the occasion of the child's entering the family. They may all go out to dinner; there may be cake and ice cream. Some celebration that can be repeated on the following anniversaries could begin at the time of the move. Sometimes families plan for some sort of religious ceremony to celebrate the child's admission to the family at a later date. Such ceremonies usually reassure the child that he or she, like other children in the family, has joined it in a spiritual way.

The major celebrations in our culture occur when people are leaving one way of life for another – at birth, graduation, marriage, and so on – and they are usually rituals. They encompass excitement for the future with some sense of loss for the past that is irretrievable. These same emotions are present on the day of the move, especially from the child's viewpoint. When a child has had a previous adoptive disruption, we must do something that signifies to the child 'this will have a different ending'.

Post-placement visits. It is important both to the child and the foster family to visit each other after placement. We often defer such visits for two to three weeks so that the child has time to make an initial adjustment. We have found that if adoptive children are allowed contact with their foster parents, they often come not to need it. If such contact is prohibited, the child's need for it intensifies and becomes disproportionate and may affect the way he or she bonds with the adoptive family.

The first visit, especially for younger children, should take place on the child's home ground, which is now the adoptive home. It also gives the child and foster parent a comfortable way to have conversation as the child shows the foster parent around. Future visits can then be scheduled to meet the needs of everyone concerned.

If the families live in the same community, the child should be allowed to contact the foster family when he or she wishes with one exception. If the child and the adoptive parents are having a problem, the child should not be allowed to contact the foster parent to seek solace or to make the foster parent take sides in the dispute.

Once the parent and child work out their hassle, then the child may call the foster parent. This encourages the child to work out problems with the adoptive parent rather than by draining off intense feelings on the foster parent. It is resolving intense feelings together that will help the adopted child become bonded to the adoptive parents.

Many children need to have a visit back to the foster home after several months. This enables them to re-process old information, like how they felt in the foster home, in the context of no longer being a member of that family. It can help children re-define their relationship to their foster parents.

Name changes. As children move into adoption, they need to be prepared to change their last name. This is very threatening for some children. They need to understand that members of the same family share the same last name and this is one of the ways that everyone knows who belongs to whom. From the child's viewpoint, one of the major differences between being a foster child and being an adopted child is that the adopted child has the same last name as the parents.

We believe that the situation is much different when it comes to first names. We are strongly opposed to changing a child's first name after he or she is six months old. A child's identity is strongly tied to his or her first name. Changing this first name implies that the child's identity is not acceptable.

If foster or adoptive parents insist on changing the child's name after they have been advised of its significance to the child, we must question the family's ability to see the child as a separate individual with needs that are apart from their own. If the family needs to have a child who matches the fantasies they've attached to a specific name, the chances of finding that child are very remote.

Case example

I met one child who, after a year in placement, was evidencing many signs and symptoms of lack of attachment. The parents were concerned about his lack of attachment and asked for help. This child had, on his own, one day announced, 'I have a new family and a new home, and I want a new name.' The family agreed to call him by a diminutive of his middle name that had been changed when he entered their family. However, this had not worked; it didn't make either the parents or child feel 'different' about their relationship. After one interview in which I did not confront the family at all about the name change, the mother decided that they should call the boy by his first name and told him this. He seemed relieved – and I was relieved that I did not make an issue of it.

There are, of course, exceptions to all rules and there are rare occasions when legitimate reasons exist for changing a child's first name. Occasionally, I have met a child whose birth parents were very hostile and selected a name with such negative connotations that the child would face long-term ridicule if he or she retained the name. A child with a very peculiar sounding name may feel very 'different' throughout his or her life.

Occasionally, I have met children whose first name alone might be acceptable but when it is combined with the adoptive parents' last name, it would make the child vulnerable to ridicule. In these cases the child's name may have to be changed. Sometimes too, a family may already have a child with the same name as the adoptive child, and in these cases, some alterations or adaptations must take place.

We do frequently advocate, however, that the child take on an additional name or substitute a middle name that has special significance to the adoptive family. This serves as part of the 'claiming process'. This sort of name change implies that adoptive placement modifies, but does not deny, the child's identity at the time of adoptive placement. This is exactly what we are trying to achieve when we place children for adoption.

Post-placement follow-up. After placement we are committed to work with the child and the family through the initial adjustment period. Parents are advised ahead of time that this will take three to six months. We are also committed beyond that time to help when either the parent or child feels they need it. Work with the family during this period will be to help them promote attachment and to help them identify problems early and create an environment that will correct these problems. This is presented to the family in a way that does not imply that they don't know about children or that their child has severe problems.

The family's potential need for assistance is explained in terms of family systems theory. The commitment must be to the family as a whole, not to the child. As Satir[4] points out, a family is like a mobile – it is constantly keeping itself in balance by moving in response to environmental changes. However, if one changes the mobile structurally by adding or subtracting a piece, it is put in a state of imbalance, and it must find a new equilibrium. So, too, when a family member is subtracted from or added to a family, the entire family experiences a state of disequilibrium and until it attains its new sense of balance, problems will emerge with little provocation. Adoptive parents must be prepared for the effects of a new child on their other children (Katz[5]).

In general, the child whose position in the family has been disrupted by the arrival of the new child is the one who will have the most problems adjusting. This does not mean that the child is 'disturbed'; it means that they may need help to define their new position in the family and to deal with their feelings about being displaced. If we are not prepared to anticipate that such help will be needed, recognise it and provide it, our success rate in placing older children will tumble.

If the family understands these dynamics and can receive help in dealing with the behaviour, that will help the situation. If prospective adoptive parents are incapable of asking for or receiving help, they should not be considered for adoption of a child with special needs. Refusal to get help is a way of saying that the need to be totally self-sufficient is more important than the child's right to have his or her needs met.

One of our key roles during this post-placement period is to teach the parent how to make use of any periods of discomfort, or stress, to promote attachment. This means that temper tantrums and sickness can be turned into times to build trust and enhance attachment rather than simply times to be dreaded.

If parents can view a child's temper tantrum as the two o'clock feeding they did not have to participate in (and two o'clock feedings are an important part of early attachment), then it reduces the likelihood of the parent behaving in such a way that the child perceives temper tantrums as a way to frustrate parents and keep them at a distance. It also teaches them the basis of handling temper tantrums.

Another role we play during post-placement is to give the child directions about things that he or she should do to get close to the parents. The child is less likely to resist an outsider; resistance is usually greatest with those with whom the child has day-to-day contact. In addition, it puts the parent in the position of helping the child meet expectations rather than placing demands, and in this helping process, bonding occurs.

We like to see the child and the adoptive family in their home at least once after placement, a procedure that is much more routine with social workers than with psychotherapists. Having a mental image of the home can frequently enable one to figure out environmental changes, such as changing someone's place at the table, that would eliminate undesirable behaviour.

One child, aged four, had recently been placed for adoption and drenched herself with a hose several times a day so that she needed to have her clothes changed regularly. While this is obviously not a serious problem, anything that causes the mother to feel impotent in dealing with the pre-schooler is going to have long-lasting effects on the mother/child relationship and should not be minimised. After looking the situation over, it was apparent that the easiest way of eliminating this source of recurrent hassle was for the parent to unscrew the hose when it was not in use.

The home visit also allows the child to show the worker around the home. This way one can see whether the child is identifying with the home and is feeling pride as he or she shows their new room, new toys, and new family. We frequently set up home visits to that we will be there for dinner where we can observe all the family interactions at one time. We often include the other children, at least part of the time, in post-placement treatment so they can be helped with their feelings of resentment of the new family member.

Case example

One memorable home visit was made to a family who had a nine-year-old boy and a six-year-old newly placed adoptive son. The parents were doing an excellent job of encouraging attachment behaviour in Timmy, the six-year-old. However, they were quite concerned about Mark's reaction to Tim.

On occasion, Mark refused to play with Tim and said mean things to him. The parents were told that, first of all, this was normal behaviour between brothers of this age, and second, it was likely that Mark was feeling somewhat displaced. The mother assured me that this couldn't be true because Mark had taken an active part in the decision to adopt a child.

I related to her a story told by Haim Ginott in Between parent and child. *Dr Ginott explained that the usual approach to dealing with the advent of a new child into the family was to explain to the older child that he or she was such a joy to us and that we liked being their parents so much that we wanted to have another child.*

Dr Ginott then asked, 'What would you say if your husband came home and said that you had been everything he could ask for and that he loved you so much he wanted to get a second wife?' This particular mother was still a little sceptical.

Shortly thereafter, Mark and his dad came home from a football game, and we all sat down to dinner. Mark make little comments that indicated that he thought I was interested only in 'dear little Timmy'. With everyone there at the table I said to Mark, 'I bet there are times when you wish that your parents had never decided to adopt Tim.'

Mark replied, 'Yes, I wonder how they would feel if I said I was going to get a second set of parents?' The mother looked at me with open mouth and my credibility went sky high.

20 minutes later the two boys were lying on the couch together comfortably watching TV. The parents commented that it was usual in the past for them to avoid being physically close.

It is important that other children in the family get the message that they don't have to like the adopted child all of the time, but that the adopted child is still going to be part of the family. The guilt that older children feel if they are successful in disrupting the adoption is extreme. In fact, if the adoption disrupts for any reason, the family must recognise how the other children will feel, and they must be given help in dealing with those feelings.

In the next exercise, you have an opportunity to think about ways to facilitate long distance moves. Following Exercise 5, the last part of this section considers specific suggestions for moving pre-verbal children into new homes.

Exercise 5:
Facilitating long distance moves

Instructions

Purpose:
To help identify ways of adapting the theories.

How to do it:
The case summary is given in parts, with some ideas for each task at hand. Read the case and add your own ideas at each step.

Suzanna, 13, and Robert, 11, are two of four siblings. They have been in foster care for three years now, in two different foster homes in the same city. Their younger sisters, aged six and seven, live in another foster home in the same city. The younger girls are to be adopted by their foster parents. A family who lives 850 miles away has been selected for Suzanna and Robert.

None of the children have had much contact with each other while in foster care. When Suzanna and Robert do get together, Suzanna tends to boss Robert and he calls her names and hits her. The family that will adopt Suzanna and Robert have four children: a boy, 19; two girls, 17 and 14; and a boy, 10. The social worker Mr Abrams, has been meeting with Suzanna and Robert weekly for two months now, working on life story books with them.

What other things would you to do increase contact between Suzanna and Robert before placement?

1 _____

2 _____

3 _____

4 _____

The Sterling family was selected for Suzanna and Robert in April. However, it was decided that the children wouldn't move until the end of the school year. The Sterling's social worker, Miss Phillips, had the family prepare a family album that included pictures of the family, relatives, the home, pets, a picture of the schools the children would attend and a picture of their church. In addition, the Sterling family made a cassette tape that went with the album explaining things in the pictures.

This was sent to Mr Abrams who shared the album and tape with Suzanna and Robert. Robert and Suzanna each had an opportunity to take the album and tape to their foster homes for several days so they could share it with their foster families and listen to the tape by themselves.

Then, Mr Abrams had Robert and Suzanna make tapes to send to the Sterling family. He helped them tell something about their past: what they liked best at school, what special interests they had, and some of their fears about adoption. Each child had an opportunity to ask questions they had thought of as they listened to the tape prepared by the Sterling family. Mr Abrams also made a short film of Suzanna and Robert. He made an audio tape at the same time. The tape and film demonstrated the type of hassles that Suzanna and Robert had with each other. These were sent to the Sterling family.

List other ideas for helping families and children learn more about each other before meeting.

_____

_____

_____

_____

The Sterlings are very active in their church. All of their children are involved in the church youth groups. Neither Suzanna nor Robert have attended church frequently with their foster families. The members of the youth groups that Suzanna and Robert will be enrolled in each

263

wrote letters to Suzanna and Robert in May and enclosed a group picture. Mrs Sterling registered the children for a week-long church camp at the end of July.

Do you have other ideas for helping children with bridging to new peer groups?

_____

_____

_____

_____

Mr and Mrs Sterling arranged to take a five-day trip to the town where Suzanna and Robert lived as part of the plan for the move. They arrived on the last day of school and had an opportunity to meet with the children's teachers. This gave them a clearer picture of the children's academic progress as well as their relationships with their peers at school.

Mr Abrams' supervisor was on vacation and arranged for the Sterlings to stay in her home for three days during the visiting period.

List your ideas for ways to structure the visiting time so that the parents have an opportunity to:
– get to know each child individually as well as to see ways they interact;
– meet each set of foster parents;
– meet the foster/adoptive parents of the younger sisters;
– make arrangements for continued on-going contact with younger sisters;
– share life story books;
– share worst of the worst for each child separately;
– have a final leave-taking of other siblings; and
– have a final leave-taking of foster families.

264

Plan for visit

Activity	Participants
day 1	
day 2	
day 3	

Helping a pre-verbal child move into adoption

Introduction

In this part of Section 4 we discuss procedures for moving pre-verbal children into their adoptive homes. Many children aged one to three are placed for adoption. While moving these children is often viewed as an easier task than placing an older child, there are some serious concerns that must be attended to in work with the younger age group. Children aged one to three are especially prone to having difficulties with separation from those to whom they are attached.

We strongly believe that it is easier to help the child and foster parents cope with the separation problems than to help the child's permanent family cope with the long-range effects of lack of attachment in the early years. However, this does mean that we must recognise the difficulties posed by separating a toddler and the person to whom he or she is attached, and do everything possible to minimise these problems.

In moving pre-verbal children, there is little margin for error in the way the move is handled. Workers and parents must pay close attention to detail – particularly non-verbal detail. While under-three children understand many more words than they can express, what they are really tuned into are the non-verbal signals. The attachment to the foster parents must be literally handed over to the adoptive parents; that means that there must be considerable contact between the two sets of parents. The ideal way that such a transfer occurs will be discussed in the rest of this part of Section 4.

Initial meetings

To start with we must remember that children feel most secure on their home ground. Thus, most of a child's contacts with prospective parents, and certainly the initial contacts, should take place in the foster home and in the presence of the foster parents. Also the adoptive parents must understand that during the first contacts with the child, the interactions between them and the child must occur at the child's pace.

If a child of this age is well attached to the foster parents, he or she may cling or hide a little when strangers enter the home. It is unlikely that he or she will immediately interact with them. It often works best if prospective adoptive parents just chat with the foster parents at first, almost ignoring the child. The child will sense that the foster parents feel comfortable and will begin to initiate interactions with the visitors. It is crucial that the child control the pacing of this encounter if he or she is to start to trust the prospective parents.

It is also wise for the adoptive parents to bring several toys to the visit. They will take these home, except for one cuddly-type toy that they leave with the child. When the child first visits the adoptive home, he or she will have toys to play with that they became acquainted with in the foster home. The non-verbal message in this is 'things that are okay for you to play with in your foster home are okay for you to play with here'.

We usually move pre-verbal children faster than we do children over three because of their poor sense of time. However, we must be careful not to move them too fast. Seven to ten days of visiting is usually about right for children of the toddler age, with two to three days of contact being all that is usually necessary for the child four months of age or younger.

Pre-adoptive visits

During the visiting period, the goal is to arrange for the most possible contact between the child and the new parents. The adoptive parents, especially the mother, should spend a lot of time in the foster home. The visits should occur at all times of the day. In part, this schedule allows the mother to learn the child's routine thoroughly. If the child is used to a crib, the adoptive parents should have one for the visits, even if it requires renting one. If the child is used to eating dinner at 5.30 and going to bed at 7.30, this is the routine that should be followed initially in the adoptive home, even if it is not convenient. As the first few weeks pass and the child feels more secure, then the changes in routine can be instituted gradually.

This type of extensive contact allows the child to receive the message from the foster mother that it is 'okay' to like, to take from, and to get close to the adoptive mother. If careful attention is not paid to giving this message, the child may not accept affection from the adoptive parents; he or she may not take notice of them.

How can foster parents go about giving this message to the child? They can do it in the same way that most mothers unconsciously work at transferring attachment to other family members. In the midst of feeding the young toddler, the mother says something like 'Oh, I need to check the cake in the oven, would you finish feeding her?' and hands the spoon to the adoptive mother. The message to the child is that the foster mother trusts the adoptive mother.

The foster mother needs to literally hand over all sorts of routine tasks to the adoptive parents during the visiting period. 'Would you please change him?' 'Come help me tuck her in bed.' 'Give your new mummy a big hug and kiss, too.'

Foster fathers and adoptive fathers have not had much of a role in the process just described. That is because it is usually the mother who cares for a toddler most of the time and is the person to whom the child is attached. However, if the foster father is an active caretaker for the child, he should be an active participant in the move.

Interchanges like this help the child realise that sometimes something unusual is going on because this type of behaviour is uncommon except among family members. The child's realisation that things are different is essential; we want the child to know that something big and important is happening in his or her life. Adults tend to protect children in ways that in the long run prove to be harmful, such as by not wanting to upset the child prior to the move.

We once worked with a child who had been moved as a toddler from a foster home where she was strongly attached to an adoptive family at the end of one visit. Several years later when we asked her where she thought people got babies, she responded 'anywhere they can'. She was deeply afraid that someone – anyone – might come and take her away from her adoptive parents. She did not trust that the parents would be able to prevent this. After all, her previous parents had not prevented these people from coming, visiting her, and then never taking her back to her foster home.

In general, it is more dangerous if children perceive a move as someone coming and 'taking' them, than if they perceive it as being 'given' to someone else after much preparation and many interactions between the two sets of parents. If children perceive a move as being taken away by relative strangers, they must live in a perpetual state of anxiety, fearing every knock at the door or every visit by acquaintances. If careful attention is paid to all details of the move, similar circumstances are not likely to recur in a child's life and trigger extreme anxiety.

During the second or third visit in the foster home, we often have the foster mother suggest that the child go for an outing with the new parent – either to a park, for an ice cream cone, or for some other short pleasurable outing. Even though this should be arranged in advance by worker, adoptive, and foster family, when it occurs it should be at the suggestion of the foster mother. This gives the child the message that 'I trust these people; they will take good care of you, and they will bring you back home'.

The visit following this one can include a visit to the new home, where the child can be re-introduced to the toys bought for the initial visit in the foster home and can become acquainted with the home. Prior to this visit, the adoptive parents should show the child pictures of the outside of the house, possibly a picture of his or her bedroom, and pictures of any family pets. If there are other children in the adoptive family, their pictures should be presented to the child at the first or second visit to their home.

For the pre-verbal child, overnight visits are not as important as they are for the older child. However, we like to include at least mealtime visits during the visits to the adoptive home and are not against an overnight visit.

The day of the move
At the time of the final move, the adoptive parents should come to the foster home, and both sets of parents should participate in some of the last packing together. The preparation for the move and the packing must not be done secretively. The child must get the non-verbal message that this is a very special day; something unusual is happening today. The foster mother may well be tearful and that is fine. If she is attached to the child, she is going to be sad, as well as happy, about the child moving. This is nothing to be concerned about or covered up.

At the final moment of the move, both sets of parents may load the car while one of the foster parents literally hands the child over to the adopters at the doorway. This should not occur on visits; during those, the foster parents may get the child ready and encourage him or her to leave with the adoptive parents, but should not pick up and hand over the child at the beginning of outings.

After kissing the child good-bye, the foster parents may cry, and the child may cry or cling to them. This should not be discouraged with sweet placations. Instead, the foster parents can say, 'We're going to miss you and you're going to miss us, but it's time to go now', and again literally hand the child over to the adoptive parents.

At the time of the move, the child should certainly take, not only his or her clothes, but also some special toys or bedding from the foster home to the adoptive home. Such transitional attachment objects are very helpful to children. Those who use them seem to be more, rather than less, attached to parent figures.

Post-placement visits

From three to six weeks after the move, we try to arrange for the foster parents to visit the child. Again, this should take place on the child's homeground, which is now the adoptive home. It is very important that the foster parents' other children, whether they be birth, adoptive, or foster, be allowed to go on the visit, too. The other children in a foster home often worry about what has happened to foster children who lived with them. These concerns easily become intertwined with guilt feelings.

Most children in a foster family occasionally wish that the others weren't there. Then, they feel guilty when the child moves and they stay. If they see that the child is happy in the new home, and that things are going well for him or her, it dissipates their guilt feelings. It also helps alleviate the guilt feelings that many foster parents have for not adopting foster children who live with them.

This is asking a lot of foster parents. We recognise this. We asked a foster mother who had worked with us in the move of a pre-verbal toddler to an adoptive home to write about her feelings about being an active participant in the moving process.

A smile and a wave
by Mary Ann Keifer*

In the past children would leave my foster home crying and reaching for me calling 'Mama, Mama!' Now they leave with a smile on their faces and wave goodbye. What has made this difference? Pre-placement visits.

My first experience with pre-placement visits was with Jennifer. She had come to us as a battered child when she was 17 months old. Her physical wounds healed rapidly, but her psychological scars lingered on. She had a very poor self image, threw terrible tantrums, held her breath and passed out. She was very frightened of men, strange people, and any

*Gene and Mary Ann Kiefer are foster parents in El Paso County, Colorado.

change in routine. With some professional help and a lot of patience, Jennifer finally came to love and trust our family. She became a happy toddler. She was, however, still very wary of change.

Jennifer was to be placed for adoption shortly after her second birthday. I was very concerned that she might regress to her earlier fears and problems. After considerable discussion with the social worker and with advice from Dr Vera Fahlberg, this is how it was done.

The social worker and I first met the adoptive parents at the Social Services Department without Jennifer present. We gave them some pictures of Jennifer and discussed her with them. We reviewed the problems she had in her early placement and how we had helped her through them. We discussed in detail her daily schedule, her eating and sleeping habits, and how we expected her to react in their home. Jennifer's first visit with the adoptive parents was in our home. Since Jennifer was still very wary of strangers, we decided that they should gain her trust before making any advances toward her. We just sat around and talked about the weather, the time of day, the trip to my home, anything but Jennifer. For the next week the adoptive parents made daily visits to my home. At first Jennifer would allow them to play with her but nothing else. She still looked to me to wipe her nose, wash her face, take her to the potty, or just to give her an occasional hug. As the week progressed, she needed me less and less. We started calling her adoptive parents her 'new mummy' and 'new daddy' and talked of when she would go to live with them.

The second week the visits moved to the adoptive parents' home. We took her there and stayed with her for her first visit in her new home. One day her new parents took her for an all day visit and they returned her the next morning. Toward the end of the second week Jennifer was happier to go with them than she was to come home with us. When they were around, she looked more and more to them for her care than she did to me. As if by miracle, she had transferred the love and trust she had in us to her new parents. We were the ones feeling rejected now. We knew she was ready to make the move. When the day came, both families and Jennifer helped in the packing. This was done in an exaggerated manner so she would know for certain that this was final. She left with a smile and a wave. I was the one crying.

This was three years ago and we still visit Jennifer several times a year. At first she called us mummy and daddy, but now she uses our first names. She had adjusted beautifully.

After a visit which took place about eight months after her placement, Jennifer told her mother, 'You and Mary Ann will always love me, but you're my mum and dad now'.

How did all this affect me as the foster mother? I felt very rejected and hurt when she no longer needed me. The end result of seeing her adjust well in her new home was worth it all.

Would I do it again? I insist on it! I now have a short-stay home for ages 0-2. The maximum stay in my home is 60 days. Many children go from my home to a regular foster home. Even with infants, I insist on pre-placement visits. I prefer the child to meet his or her new parents in my home. I take the child to visit in the new home. For most that is all that is necessary, but some require many visits like Jennifer did. I always look for the signs that the child no longer depends upon me but looks to the new parents for guidance. I know then that he or she is ready to leave.

Is all this trouble really worth it? Will it really make a difference to the child in a few years? Maybe not, but I'm not willing to take that chance. Are you?

Helping a child move back to the biological family
In most cases when children come into care, the plan of first preference will be to return the child to the biological family. There are a number of factors to consider when doing this.

Factors to consider in returning a child from foster care:
1 have the parents met the contractual agreements?
2 parents' ability to admit that there is (or was) a problem and willingness to work toward change;
3 parents' ability to ask for help;
4 stability in marriage, job, and/or living conditions has been attained;
5 parents have learned to make use of support systems;
6 parents have learned to trust someone;
7 child whose behaviour was disruptive has attained new behavioural controls.

The child's reaction to returning to the birth family is going to be strongly influenced by the length of time he or she has been in care; by the kind of experience they have had in the foster home; and the number and nature of visits they have had with the birth family. If the child is pre-verbal, and has been separated for any significant period of time from the birth parents, procedures such as those outlined for moving the pre-verbal child into adoptive placement should be used.

To get in touch with the child's viewpoint, it is helpful to think in terms of what percentage of the child's life has been in placement. If no pre-placement visits have occurred, visits aimed at transferring parenting from the foster parents to the birth parents should be set up. If the child has had regular visits with the birth parents while in foster care, then only such final steps as giving the child permission to go and to get close to the birth parents need to be emphasised.

If the child is verbal, a discussion aimed at the child's level of understanding should take place. This discussion should outline the gains the child has made while in care as well as the gains and changes that have taken place in the family during this period. Ideally the social worker, the child, the birth parents, and the foster parents would all participate in this discussion.

It is common for children in placement to express their feelings by behaving one way for one set of parents and in another way for the other set. This is not helpful to the child's adjustment in the long run. If the child has a discipline problem in the birth home but not in the foster home or if the child had behaviour problems that subsided while in care, then the foster parents should be actively involved in helping with the move.

For some older children an open discussion with both sets of parents present may be enough. However, for other children another more lengthy process is helpful. This process might begin by having the birth parents come to the foster home to observe the child's behaviour there. The foster parents might then begin to involve and support the birth parents in making demands on the child and in disciplining him or her. A final part of the process would include having the foster parents accompany the child on a visit to the birth home.

Children who usually behave well in the foster home but not in the birth home are then caught in a dilemma. Should they behave in the way they usually do for the birth parent? If they choose to behave badly, the foster parents can comment and give them permission to do well for the birth parent. The foster parent can also help the birth parents get the desired behaviour. If a child chooses to behave well, then both sets of parents can share their pleasure with the child.

We realise very clearly that many birth parents and foster parents do not want this kind of contact with each other. However, both sets of parents need to be helped to understand that lack of contact between them puts the child in the untenable position of having to choose one set of parents over the other. When this occurs, everyone loses because the child feel caught in a trap, acts out, and makes the move more difficult.

Ways to help children move:

— Birth parents need to observe what techniques worked in the foster home.
— Birth parents need to try these techniques out in their own home.
— Foster parents need to give the child permission to do as well at home as he or she has done in foster care.
— Social worker needs to support both the foster parents and the birth parents in the transfer process.
— In some cases, involving the foster parent with the child and the birth parent after the move may be helpful.

When a child returns to the birth home he or she should have a life story book that contains the pictures and information compiled while in foster care. The birth parents are more likely to accept the life story book if they were involved in putting together the pre-placement information and if pictures of the birth family were obtained for the child while in care. A picture of the child and the birth parents should be taken on the day of the move home and it should be incorporated into the life story book.

At the time of a move back to the birth home old unresolved feelings and issues are likely to emerge, both for the child and for the parents. Whenever family composition is changed by adding or subtracting a family member, the entire family system will undergo stress. Such stress should be expected when a child returns home after any appreciable time away from the birth family. It does not mean that the placement is going to fail. It does mean that increased social work services must be provided when children are returned home to help families clear up misperceptions and resolve issues.

The courts must be sensitised to the needs of both families and children so that court orders allow time for pre-placement visits. No child should return to the birth home precipitately if he or she has been out of the home for a significant period of time.

Leaving the system by emancipation

When adolescents leave care as emancipated young adults, we must remember that they need help to adjust to life on their own. Sometimes a social worker who has known an adolescent for a long time can provide some of this help and support. At other times, a foster family serves as a base from which an adolescent goes out into the world and to which he or she returns intermittently for advice and support. Sometimes adolescents can connect up with other types of adult supportive services. Some emancipated adolescents find that they can form or continue relationships with their birth families.

The important thing to remember is that few psychologically healthy young adults who grow up with their birth parents ever make a total break with their family at the time of emancipation. Most of us, as adults, depend on our family ties to support us in times of crisis and to share our successes and joys.

Since family ties are important to adults as well as to children, many of us advocate adoption for the older adolescent who wants to experience being part of a family over a life time. In cases where the plan is not to make the adolescent a permanent part of an adoptive family, the same type of needs must be recognised and met in some fashion.

Case example

We know of one social worker who, along with a foster family, carefully provided for these needs for a young man whom the worker had known for a number of years. The worker arranged for a college scholarship for this young man; she made frequent contacts with him to find out how he was doing in school; she sent him birthday cards and Christmas presents. The foster family continued to be available for the young man to return to during college vacations. He took an active part in their family life and was an integral part of their family holiday celebrations. His ties to the foster family were strengthened when he became the godfather of their youngest daughter.

This young man is now 30; he still considers himself part of the foster family. He has resumed contact with his birth parents whose parental rights were terminated years ago, and he continues to seek out and visit his social worker when he is in the area where she lives. These continued contacts have been rewarding and meaningful for all involved. This social worker has, in particular, had the opportunity to see how her continued interventions on behalf of this individual when he was a young adolescent have paid off. She can well be proud of playing a major part in helping this individual become a well adjusted adult who has been able to set many reasonable goals for himself and achieve them.

Steps in the move from dependency to emancipation include:
— learning basic skills such as budgeting, shopping, meal preparation, laundry, housekeeping;
— being responsible for self such as hygiene, dress, daily routine; and
— financial independence.

This process usually starts in a family setting as this is the usual place for learning and practising these skills.

A final exercise gives you an opportunity to plan a permanent placement for Merrilee.

Exercise 6:

Preparing the child for moving from a foster home to a permanent placement

Instructions

Purpose:
To help workers identify ways to minimise the trauma of moves out of care.

How to do it:
1 Re-read Merrilee's case history given at the beginning of this workbook.

2 Review your responses to events 4-12 in Exercise 1.

3 On Worksheet 1 provided for this exercise, in the left-hand column identify the underlying messages you would want to convey to Merrilee at the time of adoptive placement.

4 In the right-hand column, identify ways that you would go about conveying such messages, remembering Merrilee's age – two and a half years old.

5 On Worksheet 2 provided for this exercise, imagine that Merrilee, at the age of two and a half, is returning to her birth mother after eight months in foster care. Identify the underlying messages you would want to convey to Merrilee and how you would go about doing this.

6 At the end of this exercise are sample worksheets completed by one social worker for your comparison.

Exercise 6:

Preparing the child for moving from a foster home to a permanent placement

Worksheet 1

Merrilee at age 2½ is placed for adoption

Message to be conveyed	Strategy for conveying message

Exercise 6:
Preparing the child for moving from a foster home to a permanent placement

Sample worksheet 1

Merrilee at age 2½ is placed for adoption

Message to be conveyed	Strategy for conveying message
This is a planned and orderly move.	A number of visits and opportunities for Merrilee to deal with feelings about leaving her foster parents.
The people in Merrilee's past are okay.	Life story book with pictures of foster family, birth mum, places she lived, things she liked.
This is a 'keeping' family.	Go over life story book; talk about other families.
The foster family is okay and care about her.	Continuing contact after the move.
The foster family approves of her new family and wants her to have a permanent family.	Adoptive family visits to foster home; foster parents let adoptive parents do things for Merrilee (feed, dress); foster parents tell her they want her to have a 'keeping' family
Merrilee is as good as boys.	Placed for adoption in a family with boys.
Merrilee is the same girl even though she moves to a new family.	She keeps the same name; she keeps some of the same patterns and routines.

Preparing the child for moving from a foster home to a permanent placement

Worksheet 2

Merrilee at age 2½, returns home after eight months in foster care

Message to be conveyed	Strategy for conveying message

Exercise 6:

Preparing the child for moving from a foster home to a permanent placement

Sample worksheet 2

Merrilee at age 2½, returns home after eight months in foster care

---

Message to be conveyed	Strategy for conveying message
Merrilee can love both her birth mum and her foster mum.	Make a life story book for Merrilee to take with her when she goes home. Give her something to take with her from the foster home.
People who love her want her to go home to her mum.	Foster parents explain that they love her, but want her to go home.
Merrilee's mum loves her as much as her brother	Plan some things for her to do alone with mum.
This is an orderly and planned move.	Visits of the birth mum to the foster home and visits to birth mum's.
The foster parents give Merrilee permission to be taken care of by her mum.	Birth mum cares for Merrilee in the foster home - feeds, bathes, dresses.
Merrilee is the same child that she was in the foster home.	Foster mum gives birth mum list of things she does for Merrilee, and some of her likes and dislikes.

281

Appendix: Entering foster care in the USA

This text covers the same ground as Section 2, pages 204 to 211, but discusses it from an American viewpoint. UK readers will find useful pointers here to possible developments in practice.

Homemaker services: Though these services are probably the most common support services available to families who come into contact with the child welfare system, few communities have adequate numbers of homemakers. Homemakers may be used to motivate, instruct, and assist parents in developing better methods and routines for child care; for home management, food preparation, and health care. Homemakers encourage the family members to make use of community resources available to them. Working with the social worker, a homemaker may be able to provide help for parents to strengthen family relationships and learn more appropriate ways to relate to children and to discipline them.

In many parts of the country, homemakers are available only during regular daytime hours. If this type of programme is to be of maximum use, homemakers should be available to provide services druing the early morning or evening hours for working parents. In addition, emergency homemakers should be available to provide twenty-four hour a day care for short periods of time. Emergency homemakers could be used in a variety of situations, such as short-term hospitalisation of a parent, eliminating the need for foster care placement.

Family aides: These individuals help and support parents who are identified as being at high risk of abusing or neglecting their children or who have already abused or neglected their children. The family aide is usually a volunteer and works with a parent on a one-to-one basis. The aide's focus is on the parent, not the children. The aide acts both as a surrogate parent and a friend to the parent. This helps meet the parent's own needs and raises the parent's self-esteem.

Emergency caretakers: Providers of this service go into homes where children have been left unsupervised to provide care on an emergency basis. When emergency caretakers are available, children can remain in their homes rather than being abruptly removed to a foster home or shelter facility. The service is terminated when a parent or relative becomes available to supervise the children or when an emergency homemaker is assigned on the following day.

Day care services as an alternative to foster care: Day care services may be offered in a centre or a home. Either setting can provide a therapeutic day care programme if the staff are trained to understand the dynamics of child abuse and neglect and if they help to provide supportive and strengthening experiences for the children involved.

Nursery school and pre-school playgroups: Even typical nursery schools may help prevent family breakup because they can provide both relief for the parent and an opportunity for the children to relate to and learn from other adults. In a few places across the country, therapeutic nursery schools have been set up especially for abused and neglected children. Such nursery school programmes focus both on helping children learn new ways to relate to adults as well as on identifying and remedying the developmental delays frequently experienced by abused and neglected children.

In a few areas there are specialised nursery school programmes for children with developmental delays, emotional, auditory, or visual-perceptual problems. These school programmes can help by identifying perceptual problems or learning difficulties a child has and by remedying such problems so that the child's self esteem is not seriously damaged. Since children with these kinds of disabilities are often difficult to parent and may be prone to abuse, these programmes can be a useful support in maintaining a family.

Infant stimulation programme: These programmes are most often sponsored by child development clinics or by local community centres for the retarded. When young infants or toddlers have developmental delays, it is often difficult to determine whether the delays are due to organic retardation or to environmental problems. It is an indictment against the child care system that if these delays are seen in a child of a client, foster care is often the first solution to come to mind. Middle-class parents go to a private paediatrician where the automatic supposition is that the problem is organic.

Referral to an infant stimulation programme not only helps identify the nature and severity of the developmental delay, but also provides models of new ways for parents to work with their children since the programmes usually involve parents extensively.

Public health programmes: Health visitors are a first line resource for assessing and intervening in families who are identified as high risk for abuse when the mother is pregnant or at the time of birth of the child. They are particularly useful in following up cases where there has been minimal opportunity for bonding to occur in the hospital; for example, in cases of children born prematurely or who had health problems in the neo-natal period. A public health nurse can work directly with the parents on bonding once the child goes home from the hospital.

Since the health visitor sees the family in the home, she is in an ideal situation to assess the safety and stimulation provided for children. She can model new ways of parenting and help assess the parents' potential for change.

Parenting classes: Parenting classes are developing in the US and health clinics, pre-schools, church affiliated groups, hospitals, or military personnel or offered privately. These classes typically teach parents about normal child development and appropriate expectations for normal children of various ages as well as about non physical methods of discipline.

Although parenting classes alone may not be enough to help an abusive and neglectful family, they may be useful when a child is being returned home after the parents have given indications of change, or when the parents have some children without serious behavioural problems.

School programmes for the school-age child:

1. *School counsellors:* School counsellors or school social workers may be the first professionals to work with an abused or neglected school-aged child. Sometimes the types of intervention provided by such school personnel can be enough to help raise children's self esteem and modify their behaviour enough so that they can remain in their own home. At other times, children can be provided this support at their school while the parents can receive other supports.

2. *Special school programme for the learning disabled:* School programmes designed for children with varied learning disabilities are frequently indicated in child care cases. With the institution of a good school programme the child's self esteem may change enough that patterns of behaviour that were very troublesome diminish.

3. *Special school programme for the emotionally disturbed child:* With the increasing emphasis on providing education appropriate for the needs of all children in each district, most districts now have specialised classes for disturbed children. Again, when the child's behaviour is under control at school and school is an emotionally rewarding place for the child, we frequently see changes in the behaviour at home as well.

4. *Socialisation groups:* Some school social workers run programmes aimed at helping children with peer problems to improve their skills in relating to others.

5. *Special physical education programmes:* Some schools have now instituted special physical education programmes for children who have gross motor delays. Such children frequently have peer problems as well because they have difficulty competing with their schoolmates on the playground or in outside activities.

6. *Language problems:* Many schools not only provide traditional speech therapy, but also have language laboratories where a speech therapist works on all aspects of language development. Such services are especially important to the many abused and neglected children who have language delays.

7. *Special school programme for the mentally retarded:* The provision of community based schooling for the educable and trainable mentally retarded child has meant that many children who previously had to be institutionalised can now remain at home. In general, retarded children do best if they can live in a family setting.

8. *Special school programme for the blind and deaf:* In the past, blind and deaf children were institutionalised. Increasingly, special school programmes for such children, as well as for the physically handicapped child, are being provided within the child's home community so that the child may both remain with the family and receive appropriate schooling.

Outside sources of gratification for school-aged children:
Many school-aged children in abusive and neglectful families have few opportunities for gratification outside of school. They have few chances to develop special interests or to have friends outside the classroom. If the child is able to get gratification from school and outside activities, it lightens the burden on the parent. This is particularly important for single parents who often must keep up very demanding schedules. Potential sources of gratification for children include:

1. *Foster grandparents:* This programme provides simultaneously for the needs of the elderly and the needs of children. The children have an opportunity to form a special relationship with an adult and this builds self esteem.

2. *Big Brother and Big Sister programmes:* Such programmes may fill a void in the child's life by providing for an on-going positive relationshop with an adult of the sex of the missing parent in single parent homes. The Big Brother or Big Sister frequently has the same functions as the family aide has, but develops a relationship with the child rather than with the parent.

3. *Scouting, YMCA activities, Boys' Clubs, Girls' Clubs, church groups:* These programmes involve children in after-school and week-end activities that are supervised and planned which means that gratification for the children is more likely. In addition, they provide ample opportunities for interacting with peers in a setting outside the classroom.

4. *Sports activities:* Many school districts have varied afterschool recreation programmes such as swimming, soccer, gymnastics, basketball and so on. Such activities provide children with opportunities to increase their athletic skills and to interact with peers in a supervised setting. They also encourage team co-operation.

Therapy:
Therapy may be provided for the abused and neglected child, for the parents on an individual basis, for the marital couple, or for the family as a whole. Each form of therapy has its indications and its advocates. However, it seems to me that family therapy has not been used as much as it could or should be with the population served by the welfare system.

Group therapy has been successful in some areas. There have been groups for abused children, groups for sexually abused, latency-aged children, groups for sexually abused adolescents, groups for abusive parents, and for sexually abusive parents. All may be very useful adjuncts to keeping a family intact. Group therapy may be of either the traditional type with a trained psychotherapist as the leader or it may be of the self-help type such as that provided by Parents Anonymous.

Supervised parent-child modelling programmes:
In these programmes, parents have opportunities to interact with their own children and with other children. Parents learn new discipline techniques and ways of relating positively to children through modelling and through being supportively confronted by other parents involved. Such programmes tend to demonstrate that nearly all parents have some skills. The emphasis is on spreading the skills of each parent to the group as a whole rather than having a professional do all of the teaching or modelling.

Respite care:
Families who have children with special needs must be supplied with opportunities to meet the needs of the parental couple and the needs of the other children. They need to have occasional access to people who are trained to take care of their special child.

For example, a family with a developmentally delayed youngster may usually be able to meet the needs of their child but if another child becomes ill or hospitalised, respite care of some sort may be needed. The family of a retarded child may face parent burn-out if they have no opportunities for vacations with their other children. Such respite care may also be provided to foster parents who have such children in their homes to prevent foster parent burn-out.

Crisis intervention for abusive and neglectful families:

1. *Child abuse and neglect helplines:* Such telephone helplines are modelled after the community crisis intervention hotline. Their primary functions are to provide the caller with a non-judgmental and sympathetic listener and to offer information and referral services.

2. *Crisis nursery:* Such nurseries are frequently staffed with volunteers. They may provide both day care and 24-hour care, and usually handle the young pre-

schooler. Frequently, only parents who are involved in some other form of intervention i.e., who are involved in Parents Anonymous or are receiving counselling are eligible for the services of the crisis nursery.

3. *Crisis care in day care homes:* Some Protective Service units have provided specialised training for selected day care parents who then provide crisis care for children of potentially abusive and neglectful parents. Again, this care is usually limited to up to 48 hours at which time either the crisis is resolved enough so that the child may return home or the move to foster care is made. Such day care homes may provide crisis care for both pre-school aged children and for primary school aged children.

4. *Crisis shelter care:* In some communities this programme handles neglected children who are likely to be returned to their homes within a matter of a day or two. A similar programme is frequently set up for adolescents who are in a crisis situation with their family.

Residential programmes for abusive and neglectful families:
Some attempts have been made to treat abusive and neglectful families in a residential setting with both the parents and children receiving individual help as well as family therapy. Such intervention has usually been reserved for cases of severe abuse where there has been some indication that the parents are interested in, and capable of changing. Programmes that focused on less severe cases and aimed to establish new patterns of family interactions that could be supported by more traditional family therapy would seem to have exciting potential.

In-home therapists:
Programmes in which the therapist works in the family's own home might be expected to be more profitable than those where families are seen only in artificial settings such as clinics and offices. Some residential treatment centres have trained child care workers to go into homes where children are returning from residential care to help families make the transition. Although we know of no similar programme being developed to aid in the transition from foster care back to the birth family home, such an approach might help reunite families.

References

1 Jewett C *Adopting the older child* Massachusetts: Harvard Common Press, 1978.

2 Littner N 'The importance of the natural parents to the child in placement' *Child Welfare* LIV 54, 1975.

3 Hartman A *Finding families: an ecological approach to family assessment in adoption* Sage, 1979.

4 Satir V *Conjoin: family therapy* Palo Alto: Science and Behaviour Books, 1967.

5 Katz L 'Older child adoptive placement: a time of family crisis' *Child Welfare* 56 3, 1977.

WORKBOOK FOUR
The child in placement: common behavioural problems

CONTENTS

About this workbook

Children who enter foster care have a wide variety of problems. Some have never learned to trust parental figures; some have never learned appropriate autonomy; some have developmental delays. Most give evidence of these underlying problems by their behaviour. Birth parents, foster parents, and adoptive parents turn to their social worker for help in handling behavioural problems; yet many times the social workers themselves have received no training in the management of behavioural problems in children.

This workbook provides material about the management of behavioural problems that commonly occur among children in placement. The emphasis is on helping children with behavioural problems by creating an environment that meets their needs. Many times this means that children need to experience a new kind of relationship with parental figures.

There are two primary ways that people learn. The first is learning that comes through the repetitious experiences of daily life. The second occurs in extraordinary or unusual circumstances, such as at times of traumatic experiences.

The impact of children's day-to-day experiences on their behaviour is very powerful. They gain their perceptions of the world about them, of their own worth, and of the nature of parent-child relationships primarily from their day-to-day life. Events that cause emotional stress, such as separation, loss, or illness, have a significant potential for obliterating old pathways of learning and laying down new ones. However, if learning that occurs in these times of stress is not reinforced through day-to-day experiences, it is soon forgotten.

For example, children who face the loss of their parents and have strong reactions may for the first time express their true feelings if they are given support for doing so. However, if on a day-to-day basis those around them do not support their expression of strong feelings, the single experience will not have long-lasting effects.

Exercises have been interspersed throughout this workbook. They ask the reader to apply the material in the workbook to case situations. Sample filled-in worksheets are also included, although there is a danger that giving specific examples in this way may run the risk of encouraging 'closed thinking': it must be emphasised that they are not in any way directions for dealing with particular cases. They are included as one person's view and it is hoped that they will expand thinking along various possible lines. They may be used by an individual reader or serve as a basis for a group-training session.

This workbook has five major sections. The introductory one, Section 1, describes the perspective on behaviour management that is in this workbook. It also introduces the various child management techniques that will be discussed.

Section 2 provides a framework for analysis of behavioural problems. It is the heart of the book. A variety of underlying causes of behavioural problems are identified and paired with different behaviour management approaches.

Both Sections 3 and 4 deal with specific kinds of behavioural problems that are particularly common among children in placement. Section 3 deals with behavioural problems that reflect a child's attachment difficulties. Section 4 covers behavioural problems that stem from perceptual problems, including auditory problems, visual problems, and learning disabilities.

Section 5 discusses a large number of other behavioural problems that are seen among children in placement. The problems discussed range from fire raising to bed wetting. Each problem is analysed in terms of possible underlying causes and methods of management are suggested.

Before you begin the workbook, look at Exercise 1 that appears on the next page. Follow the instructions in Exercise 1 and return to it after you've completed reading the workbook.

Exercise 1:
Outlining a setting of boundaries approach to the behavioural problems exhibited by a specific child

Instructions

Purpose:
To help you outline a setting of boundaries approach to the behavioural problems of one child in your own caseload.

How to do it:

1 Think of a specific child in your caseload who exhibits behavioural problems.

2 Fill out the *Behavioural problem description* form on the following page.

3 As you read this workbook, make notes and comments on the form that you think are pertinent to this particular case.

4 After you have finished reading this workbook, review your notes and comments. Then, using the *Setting of boundaries worksheet* framework outlined in Section 2, outline a treatment plan for the management of your child's behavioural problems.

Exercise 1:
Behavioural problem description

---

1 Child's first name:

   Age: Length of time in care:

---

2 Briefly describe the circumstances leading to the child's placement.

---

3 Briefly describe the present involvement the child has with his or her birth family (visits and how often; rights terminated; how the child and family interact; and similar information).

---

4 Briefly describe the behavioural problem (or problems).

---

5 Briefly describe the disciplinary measures you have tried and the child's response to them.

Discipline   Response

6 Add any additional information that you feel will be helpful.

7 List the first names and ages of other children in the foster home.

Name   *Age*

1 Introduction to behaviour management

Perspective on behaviour management
Adults who are involved with children in placement often have concerns about specific behavioural problems the children exhibit and bring those problems to the social worker. This workbook is intended to help workers and parents develop effective approaches to these problems.

A single approach to the management of behavioural problems in children will not be outlined here. We believe that too many authors have advocated 'the method' to solve children's behavioural problems without defining the strengths and limitations of the method. Some promote behaviour modification approaches; others favour developing communication skills; yet others take a developmental approach and so on.

All these approaches are effective – sometimes. The critical issue for social workers is not so much if these approaches ever work; they do. The key questions are what problems does an approach solve, with what child, and when?

Behavioural problems in children have a variety of causes. Some behavioural problems begin as a way for the child to express feelings that he or she has difficulty expressing more directly. Some are evidence of the child's delayed development; for example, a child of five is expressing negativism in a way that would have been appropriate at two but is problematic at five. Some behavioural problems occur because of problems with the child's attachment to his or her parents; these problems are common in foster care where important attachments are often severed abruptly.

If a child does not correctly perceive the way the world works, he or she may exhibit behavioural problems. For example, undetected visual or auditory processing problems may cause a child to behave in undesirable ways. A child may exhibit a problematic behaviour because he or she is engaged in a control battle with the parents. Sometimes, behavioural patterns that begin for any of the reasons just described persist because the child has made them a habit. Finally, some children may have more serious psychological problems as evidenced by psychotic symptoms.

The management of a particular behaviour depends on the underlying cause. For example, if the child's behaviour occurs because he or she is 'stuck' at a particular stage of development, then the approach to managing this behaviour is to meet those earlier developmental needs. If it exists as an inappropriate expression of feelings, the child needs to learn new ways to express those feelings.

This analysis needs to be done carefully because a particular behaviour in one child may not have the same cause as that same behaviour in another child. In addition, a child's behavioural pattern may have more than one cause. The social worker needs to become expert in working with the family to assess the cause of behavioural problems and using this analysis to select the approaches with the best chance of success — and this of course includes referring the child and family to other specialists as appropriate.

A proper assessment of the child's needs is also critical in order to place him or her with a foster or adoptive family that can provide the most nurturing environment for that child. No parent can care for all children equally successfully. Each family has strengths and weaknesses in terms of parenting. A major part of the home study of foster and adoptive families should be geared toward identifying those strengths and limitations. If the aim of the child welfare system is to meet the needs of children, then it cannot continue to proceed as though considering a child's needs and a family's strengths and resources when making a placement is an unaffordable luxury.

General environmental needs

This workbook is devoted to helping adults understand behavioural problems of children in care and design approaches to those specific problems. However, before we go on, we must point out that the most helpful measure that can be provided for children with any type of behavioural problem regardless of the cause is a family environment in which the children's needs are recognised and met and their growth encouraged. Children's day-to-day living experiences provide opportunities for them to learn about themselves and for their needs to be met.

This does not negate the fact that many children in placement who have problems need other therapy as well. Some need psychotherapy; some need speech therapy; some need help in gross motor activities; and many need to be in a school environment in which their perceptual difficulties are recognised and remedied.

Ideally, every child would have a fine home in the best school district, and receive therapy from an excellent psychotherapist who understands the special needs of children in placement. However, we believe that the first priority for a child is a family that can meet the child's needs; the second, a good school setting; and finally, a good psychotherapist.

What must families provide for the children in their care?

All children need the family to hold appropriate expectations for them and to place controls on their behaviour. All children need love and nurturing from a family. Finally, they need the family to provide role models for them.

Though one may think that children detest controls, according to one expert in child development, 'No discipline feels like being on the wrong road without a map or directions' (Hymes[1]). It certainly has been our experience that reasonable limits are not only necessary, but indeed are welcomed by the child.

Several years ago one pre-school established a playground without boundaries. The pre-school staff wanted the children to be less inhibited. A small number of the pre-school children wandered off; they were determined to go until someone placed a limit on them. However, the surprising result of the experiment was not that a few children went an unreasonable distance, but that most of the children seemed to fear going too far and stayed much closer to the school than they would have had there been a fence.

Just as these children were reassured by visible physical boundaries on the playground, so all children are reassured if they know the limits that their parents are placing on their behaviour. Most children want to please their parents. They cannot do this if they do not know what their parents' expectations are. If they do not know where the boundaries are, they either find them by exploring beyond them or else they become inhibited, fearing that they will overstep them.

If appropriate limits are set by the parents, a great worry is removed from children's shoulders. They know they can move about, explore and try out new behaviour, and that if they get out of line, their parents will let them know. They are made freer, rather than more inhibited, by these limits.

In addition to needing limits, all children need to feel loved. It is the everyday happenings in children's lives that give them this feeling. When they are hungry, someone feeds them. When they are tired, they are tucked in bed. When they need comforting, they receive it. When they want to play, it is allowed.

All of these things happen, not because the children have been 'good' but because these things are good for children. Parents initiate many positive interactions with children. When children participate in these spontaneous positive interactions, they feel worthwhile and lovable.

One problem with behaviour modification programmes for children is that they depend on the child initiating interactions, either by 'good' or 'bad' behaviour. The child is in charge of what happens to him or her. However, the child who is always 'bad' needs more positive inter-actions and shows of affection than the child who is usually good, and a behaviour modification programme does not account for this.

In addition to needing love and limits, all children need parents who model appropriate behaviour. How can a child learn self control from a parent who has not yet mastered it? Parents teach children by their own behaviour.

The parent who makes a mistake with a child and says so, teaches the child that it is not the end of the world when someone makes mistakes and that most can be rectified. The parent who models appropriate ways to deal with frustration teaches the child how to cope with it. The parent who expresses both positive and negative feelings in a direct and appropriate way teaches the child about expressing the range of emotions. The parent who demonstrates love for the child physically and verbally teaches the child what love is and how to love in return.

Children who have been abused or neglected or in other ways have problems in their relationships to their parents need extra doses of good parenting. They are more susceptible to further damage from poor parenting practices than children who are well attached to their parents. Thus, we need to select families for these children that are capable of providing optimum environments for nurture and for positive interactions combined with reasonable limits.

Methods of managing behavioural problems

In addition to providing an environment that enhances the child's growth, sometimes families of children in care need to design specific approaches to behavioural problems. This workbook is about assessing behavioural problems and selecting approaches that are most likely to address them. As we have mentioned, we believe that workers should be familiar with a variety of approaches because certain methods work better than others for certain children and families or for certain problems. This workbook will refer to a number of behaviour management techniques that will not be covered here in detail. The techniques that will be referred to are noted here along with references to books that cover the methods in greater detail.

Good communication skills are invaluable to both social workers and parents. One of the most readable books in this area is *Parent effectiveness training* by Thomas Gordon[2]. This approach emphasises 'active listening' which is similar to Carl Rogers' reflective therapy[3]. It stresses the importance of using 'I' messages rather than 'you' messages to facilitate communication, raise self-esteem, and decrease defensiveness. A major section of the book is devoted to 'win-win problem solving' through which joint problems are solved in a way that meets the needs of all parties.

Communication skills are important in child management; however, they are not sufficient to address all problems, such as those stemming from unmet developmental needs or those that have become habits. One book that helps the reader understand developmental tasks and identify unmet developmental needs is *The child under six* by Hymes[4]. The book is referred to extensively in this workbook. Workbook 2, *Child development*, is another resource for identifying behavioural problems that stem from developmental delays.

Behaviour modification approaches have enjoyed great popularity in recent years. Behaviour modification approaches are most successful with those behavioural problems that have become habits. A common-sense approach to behaviour modification in the home and classroom is given in William Dobson's book, *Dare to discipline*[5]. He also does a fine job of describing behavioural problems that stem from control issues and the importance of handling these appropriately.

'Logical consequences' is an approach outlined by Driekurs in a book with this title[6]. The focus is spelling out the logical consequences of a child's behaviour for him or her. It is especially useful with school-age children and adolescents although variations can be used with younger children if their developmental capabilities and needs are kept in mind.

Like a logical consequences approach, giving 'two good choices' to the child helps teach him or her responsibility for their actions. An example of two good choices is 'Yes, I would like it if you could go to the party Saturday, but our rule is schoolwork has priority. It is your choice. If you get your homework done before Saturday, then you can go to the party.'

Open-ended discipline also fits in well with the concept of logical consequences. 'You will not go out to play until your room is cleaned' is an example of open-ended discipline. It helps the child feel more autonomous. It makes him or her more responsible for their own behaviour than does a statement such as 'Since you didn't clean your room, you can't go out for three days'.

Some behavioural problems stem from problems in the attachment between parent and child. Workbooks 1 and 3, *Attachment and separation* and *Helping children when they must move*, provide a basis for assessing and handling such problems.

In Section 2, we offer guidelines that help the worker and family select from among these approaches that we've just described.

2 Selecting an approach to behaviour management

Definition of discipline

This section is about selecting an approach to discipline. We begin by defining what we mean by discipline and distinguishing it from punishment.

Discipline helps children stay within reasonable behavioural limitations. Discipline does not harm children's self-esteem. In fact, their self-esteem is strengthened when they are able to meet appropriate expectations. When parents provide supportive control, they are meeting children's needs for both affection and discipline in a manner that conveys 'We want things to go well for you'. When a child loses control of his or her own behaviour, an adult supplies the external controls that are necessary until the child regains control. The underlying messages here are first, that it is too scary for anyone – adult or child – to feel they have totally lost control of their behaviour. The second message given is that the long-range goal is for the child to be able to control his or her own behaviour so that external controls will not be necessary.

The distinction between discipline and punishment is an important distinction to make. Punishment is usually initiated to alleviate the adult's frustrations while the primary goal of discipline is to help the child meet expectations. In selecting an approach to the management of behavioural problems it is important to remember that the goal is to help the child meet appropriate expectations. If the child succeeds, the parents will be less frustrated and be less likely to feel the need to be punitive. However, it is unlikely that any parent can always be therapeutic enough to use discipline and never be frustrated enough to lapse into punishment.

A reasonable goal is for parents to understand the difference and to work to maximise discipline and minimise punishment. On pages 304 and 305 is a *Setting of boundaries* worksheet. This worksheet an outline for assessing the cause of behavioural problems. It then pairs the different underlying causes of behavioural problems with the appropriate response.

As adults are faced with specific behavioural problems, they can use this worksheet as a basis for assessing the disciplinary needs and the disciplinary techniques that have the best chance of success. Mistakes in assessment usually become apparent when inappropriate disciplinary techniques are instituted. If adults listen carefully to what a child says by both words and actions, the child will usually help clarify the correct disciplinary needs.

In the rest of this section, each kind of disciplinary need is discussed.

Inappropriate expression of feelings

One of the most common causes of behavioural problems is a child's expression of underlying feelings in an inappropriate manner. Though one often thinks that a child who expresses feelings through undesirable behaviour must be angry or frustrated, he or she is just as likely to be sad, lonely, or afraid. Occasionally a child may even act out because of excitement or happiness.

The behaviour of children in foster care often reflects their feelings about separation from the birth family. Children who experience separation from one or both parents are going to have feelings about these separations. However, in many cases the children have not even identified their own feelings, much less expressed them appropriately. These feelings do not remain hidden; they pop out in various ways, frequently inappropriate ones.

In dealing with behavioural problems that stem from the child's inappropriately expressed feelings, the goal is to help the child learn new ways to express his or her feelings. According to Hymes[7], this is one of the functions of all disciplinary encounters between parent and child.

The child must be given permission to have strong feelings. Some children cope with their strong feelings by denying them. Such children may need to be given permission to express feelings in a structured situation such as a therapy session. Sometimes workers or parents can make use of a time when children can legitimately be angry in order to uncover their strong feelings.

It is important that families not only help children identify their feelings but also model appropriate ways to express them. It is possible to offer support for children's underlying feelings without supporting their behaviour. For example, say that a child tears up a picture of the

303

Setting of boundaries worksheet

Punishment is done to alleviate adult frustration.
Discipline is aimed at helping the child meet expectations.
Supportive control defines the adult-child relationship as an alliance
for the child's benefit.

Assess disciplinary need	*Respond appropriately*
Inappropriate expression of feelings	Give permission to have feelings Provide model of appropriate expression Support the feelings When denial is used, encourage the emergence of feelings, allowing the child the time that seems to suit his or her needs
– unresolved separation issues	Go back over facts and feelings about separation issues
Bad habits	Design behaviour modification approaches
Delayed development	Respond to developmental level, – not chronological age
– lack of experience	Teach Share Praise and support
Control issues	Sit Offer 'two good choices' Increase age-appropriate autonomy Hold
Attachment problems (lack of trust, over-competence, overaffectionate, withdrawal, aggression)	Work on building trust Re-parent
– delayed conscience (See Section 3)	Use stages of normal conscience development

Worksheet continued

Assess disciplinary need	Respond appropriately
Behaviours secondary to misperceptions	Identify misperceptions and help child deal with these
– learning disabilities	
Psychotic symptoms (See Section 2)	Demand psychiatric evaluation and treatment

birth parent after returning from a visit. If the foster parent says 'You shouldn't do that; that is naughty', the child receives the message that his or her feelings are bad. This response is quite likely to reinforce the child's egocentric ideas that he or she is bad and that it is their fault they are in foster care.

On the other hand, if the foster parent accepts the child's feelings but not the behaviour, he or she might respond, 'I know that you are angry about not being able to be home with your parents; that's understandable; I would be angry too. Tearing up the picture is not a very appropriate way to express your anger about it. What else could you do when you are angry about not being at home?' This response gives the child permission to have strong feelings but indicates that there are other, more appropriate ways to express such feelings.

Compiling or reviewing a life story book can help to pinpoint the child's unexpressed feelings about separation issues. It also provides opportunities to give the child permission to have feelings, to discuss ways that parent and child have expressed feelings in the past, and to talk about ways to express feelings in the future. Use of the life story book can also reveal misperceptions held by the child that influence his or her behaviour. For a complete discussion of how to create and use a life story book see Section 3 in *Helping children when they must move*.

Habits
Sometimes a behaviour problem occurs with such regularity that it seems to be a habit. In these instances the behaviour tends to be so

automatic that the child us unaware of it. These responses occur most frequently at times of anxiety (for example, stammering) or at times of boredom (for example, thumb sucking). Behaviour modification seems to be the most useful approach to a difficult behaviour that has become a habit. It is perhaps less useful when addressing behavioural problems that reflect unmet needs. If children themselves see a behaviour as a problem and want to change it, this provides a sound basis for behaviour modification efforts.

In general, behaviour modification works better to increase a specific behaviour in a child's repertoire rather than to decrease a behaviour. If a child gets rewarded for a behaviour, he or she has control over the amount of reinforcement they get. Using behaviour modification to decrease a behaviour requires establishing a time span during which a behaviour is not to occur for a reward to be earned. Also, it is simply easier for parents to praise a child's good behaviour than to comment positively on the absence of a bad behaviour such as 'Hey, I'm glad you're not spitting'.

This means that those devising a behaviour modification approach to change a child's behaviour must think creatively in order to devise a plan in which performance of a positive behaviour automatically precludes a negative behaviour. An example of this strategy follows.

Case example: Rachel
Rachel lived in a foster home when she was between one and two and a half. During this time her foster parents did not hold, carry, or rock her. She started to rock herself. This behaviour was liable to happen at any place or any time.

When Rachel was placed for adoption, the adoptive parents tried to satisfy Rachel's unmet needs by providing her with lots of close physical contact. The rocking behaviour disappeared during the daytime, but Rachel continued to get on her hands and knees and rock herself to sleep.

We determined that the rocking behaviour at bedtime now was a habit for Rachel. A behaviour modification approach to the problem was designed. Rachel's parents rewarded her when she remembered to cuddle her favourite baby doll as she went to sleep. Cuddling the doll precluded rocking because when Rachel rocked herself, she could not cuddle her doll comfortably. Thus, positive behaviour was reinforced, and negative behaviour altered.

Developmental delays

Many children who enter foster care are delayed in their development. Their behaviour seems immature, and foster and birth parents may feel they have problematic behaviours. In such cases parents need to respond to the child at the developmental level he or she exhibits rather than at the level appropriate to their chronological age. This is the only approach that will help the child outgrow such problems.

One of the most common areas of developmental delay among children in foster care relates to their fears. An example of a child with such a delay follows.

Case example: Rajiv

Rajiv was ten. He had been in and out of foster placements since he was four years old and had recently been moved to a new foster home. Rajiv had many fears of monsters and of the dark. His foster mother recognised that these fears typically occurred at a younger age. She decided to handle these fears as she would in a four or five-year-old and bought Rajiv a night light that she gave to him one evening at dinner. He was embarrassed rather than reassured.

The foster mother reported this to the social worker. The social worker suggested they review a summary of normal child development together. In the process of this review, the foster mother realised that although Rajiv had the fears of a four to five-year-old, he had the sensitivity about being singled out that is normal for ten-year-olds. Children at this age are very embarrassed when praised or reprimanded in front of others.

The foster mother apologised to Rajiv for embarrassing him at the dinner table and consulted privately with him about how she could help him cope with his fear of the dark. He decided that maybe the night light would help after all.

Children in foster care often have developmental delays because they lack experience. For example, although most children of ten understand very well what their parents mean by 'clean up your room', children in foster care may never have been taught how to make a bed or where to put dirty clothes. When this sort of delayed development is encountered in a child, the focus must be on teaching the child and on sharing responsibility with him or her. Positive behaviour should be praised and supported. In some cases a behaviour modification approach may be instituted to reward performance of the desirable behaviour.

Control issues

Parents should aim to define the relationship between parent and child as an alliance that benefits both of them rather than as a competition for control. Most disturbed families are very concerned with power. Such families look at relationships in terms of who has power over whom, rather than seeing them as ways for two or more people to get their own needs met simultaneously. If a social worker begins to view a relationship with a client in terms of power, then the worker/client relationship also becomes disturbed.

Many children who enter foster care come from families where the focus has been on who has power or control over whom. It is not surprising that many children in foster care have trouble with issues related to who is in control. In addition, many of the children in care were separated from their parents between ages one and two and a half when they were struggling to achieve autonomy. Others were separated around age four when they were prone to magical thinking. Separations at these stages of development may have effects manifested as control problems.

The approach to control issues is twofold. First, the adult must demonstrate to the child that he or she does not lose when they give up control to an adult and meet reasonable demands, but instead that everyone wins. Second, the adult should provide as many opportunities for the child to be autonomous as is appropriate, given the child's age.

Unfortunately, because such a child tends to see encounters with the parents as battles in which someone wins and someone loses, parents frequently begin to see them in the same way. Thus, parents fall prey to the desire to gain more and more control over the child and see the child's every attempt to assert his or her autonomy as a challenge or an attempt to manipulate.

Parents who know that they can take charge whenever the situation warrants it are not threatened when their children make decisions that do not work out well. If a parent does not know how to take charge when a child is out of control, the child senses this and becomes frightened. He or she keeps setting up opportunities for the parent to learn to take charge. If the parent continues to be unable or unwilling to control the child in such a situation, then the child's inappropriate behaviour usually escalates.

The same kind of escalating control battle is also seen when a parent always has to be in control of a child. Some children, faced with controlling parents, eventually give up and withdraw, never asserting age appropriate autonomy. Many abused children become inhibited, fearful, and withdrawn as a way to avoid overstepping the limits and incurring abuse. Although this defence may help a young child avoid abuse, in the long run such withdrawn children are as difficult to treat as children who are always engaged in control battles.

The management of control issues is covered more completely in Section 3 of this workbook.

Lack of attachment

Many of the difficult behaviours exhibited by children in foster care reflect their lack of attachment to their primary caretakers and their lack of trust that others will take care of them. These specific behaviours are also covered in Section 3.

Misperceptions

Some behavioural problems stem from misperceptions that the child holds about the way the world works. There are two types of misperceptions. Some are due to the visual and auditory perceptual problems that a large number of children in foster care have. The second kind of misperception results from the tendency children have toward egocentric or magical thinking.

When children have behavioural problems as a result of their misperceptions, someone must identify the misperceptions and help the child correct or cope with them. Careful observation and screening, which involves clinical and/or educational psychologists, can help detect visual or auditory problems, speech delays, or other learning disabilities. The life story book is a potent tool for identifying the type of misperceptions that result from egocentricity or magical thinking.

Case example: Odette

Odette's birth family considered her the 'naughty' child in the family. She and her mother got along very poorly. One day when Odette was five she misbehaved, her mother got angry, and Odette got angry back.

Later that day Odette's mother abandoned the children at the babysitter's. The mother did not follow through on any of the plans for returning the children to her care. Subsequently her parental rights were terminated. Odette and her siblings were placed for adoption.

In her adoptive home Odette never got angry at her adoptive mother. She was certain that her anger had caused her mother to abandon her, and she was not about to chance getting angry again. However, her underlying anger was manifested indirectly when she forgot to do her homework or her chores and when she was overly dependent on her adoptive mother.

Psychotic symptoms

Some children in foster care are very seriously disturbed and exhibit symptoms of psychosis. These children are not just immature; they behave in a way that is different from normal children of any age. According to Jay Haley[8], the schizophrenic individual behaves either as though he or she were not interacting with another person or as though the interaction was not taking place at the present time and place.

Communications with psychotic children frequently do not make sense. The child's responses have little to do with what is happening. Frequently, there is a predominant mood that is not appropriate to the situation. Such individuals do not exhibit the normal range of feelings.

Below is a list of symptoms that are frequently seen in mentally ill children. A child who demonstrates one of these symptoms is not necessarily severely disturbed; severely disturbed children usually have a cluster of these symptoms. A child who has several of these symptoms should receive a full psychiatric or psychological evaluation. (This is not to say that children who are not severely disturbed, but have a behavioural problem, would not benefit from psychiatric assessment. Child guidance is not only for the seriously disturbed.)

Exercises 2 and 3 that follow ask you to read the brief cases that accompany them and assess the needs of the children described. After each exercise, you'll find samples of completed worksheets.

Signs and symptoms requiring full psychiatric evaluation in children

Extreme withdrawal from interactions; behaving as though others are not present

Inappropriate expression of emotion, i.e. laughing, crying, or rage for no apparent reason

Fantasies so marked that they interfere with day-to-day functioning

Total lack of interest in interacting with peers; no normal peer interactions

Extreme lack of responsiveness to other people

Lack of appropriate fears and/or abnormal fears that interfere with day-to-day functioning

Auditory or visual hallucinations

Failure to develop speech or disappearance of speech after it has developed

Non-communicative speech

Persistent abnormal rhythm to speech

Abnormalities in reactions to stimulation; may be hypersensitive or hyposensitive to auditory stimuli, tactile stimuli, and the like

Peculiar posturing or persistent walking on tiptoe

Stereotypical finger and hand movements

Self-mutilation

Developmental delays combined with areas of normal or above normal functioning

Marked insistence on sameness, such as routines or object placement

---

Exercise 2:
Planning behaviour management

Instructions

Purpose:
To provide you with an opportunity to assess a child's behavioural problems and outline a plan for management of the most severe problems.

How to do it:

1 Read Susan's case history.

2 Answer the questions on the worksheet for Exercise 2. Then, compare your own answers with those of another social worker on the sample worksheet.

Susan's case

Susan is four and a half. As an infant she failed to thrive. She entered the foster care system, along with two siblings, at the age of two when her mother abandoned the family and her father could no longer care for the children.

As a result of her severe behavioural problems and her very demanding nature, Susan has been in five foster homes during the past two years. All reasonable requests on the part of parental figures are turned into major battles. At night, she gets out of bed repeatedly. Susan sometimes refuses to eat although the rule in her present foster home is: 'You must sit at the table until your plate is clean'. On several occasions when an issue has been made of her eating, Susan has vomited at the table.

She is bossy with peers. She seems seductive with men and generally tends to pay attention to father figures better than mother figures. All foster parents have seen her as 'phoney' and 'manipulative'.

When Susan is very angry with her foster mother, she stands looking at her and has a bowel movement in her pants. She talks back constantly. When she does not get her own way, Susan threatens to run away. Indeed on two occasions she was found several blocks from her foster home. Sometimes she seems very anxious and will bite her fingernails to the quick.

She also has marked fears of people in uniforms and of the swimming pool. Susan has got over her fear of taking a bath although she screams when her foster mother attempts to wash her hair while Susan is in the bath. Although she is sometimes reckless when climbing, Susan is terrified of merry-go-rounds and rides at the amusement park.

Exercise 2:
Planning behaviour management

Worksheet

1 List Susan's behavioural problems.

2 What other behaviour might you expect her to have as well?

3 What underlying needs does her behaviour indicate?

4 Outline a plan for behavioural management of the problems you consider to be most severe.

5 What problem areas might you choose initially to not treat directly while you focus on other areas?

Exercise 2:
Planning behaviour management

Sample worksheet

1 List Susan's behavioural problems. Control problems. Extreme fears and anxieties. Bedtime problems. Fingernail biting. Eating problems. Seductiveness. Recklessness. Bossiness.

2 What other behaviour might you expect her to have as well? Other food-related problems - e.g. eating between meals. Possibly poor attention span, poor personal hygiene. Problems in closeness with adults. Demanding behaviour.

3 What underlying needs does her behaviour indicate? She was extremely neglected from infancy. Her behaviour indicates need for protection, security, nurturing not met earlier on. She needs to trust adults and to have her dependency and need for autonomy met.

4 Outline a plan for behavioural management of the problems you consider to be most severe. Reparenting, to teach and nurture age-appropriate autonomy. Control issues and inappropriate expressions of feeling should be worked on first. Use of two choices might be helpful. Encourage expression of anger and help establish control. Use holding, affection, nurturing after outbursts. Encourage appropriate affection with care-givers. Work on life story book to help her gain understanding and sense of control over her life.

5 What problem areas might you choose initially to not treat directly while you focus on other areas? Eating and soiling. Peer problems. I'd take her fears seriously as a manifestation of her feeling out of control and not trusting adults to take care of her. This can be dealt with over time.

314

Exercise 3:
Using the 'Setting of boundaries' worksheet

Instructions

Purpose:
To give you an opportunity to use the *Setting of boundaries worksheet* in planning management of behavioural problems.

How to do it:

1 Read Debbie's case history. (We have met Debbie before, in *Child development*. Here her case is reviewed in terms of setting boundaries.)

2 Answer the questions on the worksheet for Exercise 3. Then, compare your own answers with those of another social worker on the sample worksheet.

Debbie's case

Debbie is 14. Her mother physically abused her, and her step-father started sexually abusing her when she was 11. Debbie reported the abuse to a school counsellor. When the police became involved because of the sexual abuse, Debbie's mother and step-father left the area, leaving Debbie with a neighbour.

Subsequently, the mother's parental rights were terminated. Debbie's birth father, who lives in another area, was contacted about having Debbie come to live with him. He expressed some interest but didn't follow it through. So, his parental rights were also terminated.

Debbie has had three foster care placements since she was 11 and a half. All of her foster parents have described her as a sexually provocative child. She is seen as wilful and disobedient with foster mothers although she usually obeys the foster fathers. She is also viewed as a manipulator.

During the past two years, her grades have dropped from primarily As and Bs to primarily Cs and Ds. She has peer problems; most of her friends are boys and girls who also have many problems. Most of them have been in trouble with the law.

Debbie says repeatedly that everything would be fine if she could live with her dad whom she hasn't seen for five years. She blames the judge and social worker for keeping them apart. She phones her father, and he always accepts her reverse charge calls. She tends to see her birth father as 'super' while she sees her birth mother as 'a rotten no good whore'.

Recently she ran away from her foster home after being punished for not coming home on time. The foster family has requested that she be moved.

A maternal aunt who lives about 100 miles away has expressed an interest in Debbie. There is also a local family who have expressed an interest in adopting an adolescent like Debbie.

Exercise 3:
Using the 'Setting of boundaries' worksheet

Worksheet

1 Make a list of Debbie's problem areas.

2 Using the *Setting of boundaries worksheet* on page 304, outline an initial plan for management of each problem area.

Problem   *Response*

3 Is there a recurrent theme to her underlying disciplinary needs?

4 How might this make a difference in your case planning with regard to placement with a family member as compared with a non-family member?

Exercise 3:
Using the 'Setting of boundaries' worksheet

Sample worksheet

---

1 Make a list of Debbie's problem areas. Low self-esteem
Inappropriate expression of feeling
Sexually provocative behaviour
School problems   Running away
Misperceptions   Control problems

---

2 Using the *Setting of boundaries worksheet* on page 304, outline an initial plan
for management of each problem area.

Problem	*Response*
Expression of feeling	Go over facts and feelings re sexual abuse and issues re birth parents.
School problems	Use praise, support and structure
Misperceptions	Give permission to have feelings. Help her do life story book.
Control problems	Increase autonomy by giving two choices and increasing decision
Running away	making in appropriate ways.

---

3 Is there a recurrent theme to her underlying disciplinary needs?
Unresolved attachment problems related to birth parent.
Fantasies about her dad and unresolved anger towards
her mum are keeping her stuck in control battles
and self-destructive behaviour.

---

4 How might this make a difference in your case planning with regard to
placement with a family member as compared with a non-family member?
Extended family should be rigorously explored,
recognising that the aunt may want her own needs met.
Whoever adopts Debbie will need to help her work
through her anger against her mother and fantasies
about her father. Possibly family therapy may be
needed during a predictable stormy adolescence.

318

3 Managing behaviour that stems from attachment problems

Many children in the child placement system have not developed normal healthy attachments to parental figures. Their problems in this area frequently date back to their earliest experiences with their birth parents. Unstable foster home placements and the series of moves that many foster children experience add to their problems in developing trust in others combined with an appropriate sense of autonomy.

As noted in Workbook 1, *Attachment and separation*, the signs and symptoms of attachment problems that children exhibit are the result of the way their parents behaved toward them, their environment, and their own particular psychological traits. In general, children who have been severely neglected are the most likely to suffer from a true lack of attachment. Children who have experienced less severe neglect, intermittent physical abuse, or emotional abuse are more likely to exhibit imbalance in their needs for dependency and their needs for autonomy. This section will deal with the management of behaviour that reflects attachment problems.

Most children with attachment problems do not trust that adults love them and will take care of them. Thus, the underlying theme in the management of all of these behavioural problems is building trust and attachment between the child and the parental figures.

In addition, children with attachment problems have learned not to trust themselves. Everything that is done to correct the child's behaviour must be aimed at helping him or her succeed and improve their self-esteem. Adults will not help these children by ignoring them, ridiculing them, or engaging in control battles over their behaviour. On the other hand, if the adults can maintain a sense of humour, particularly about themselves, it may save the day.

In the remainder of this section, specific behaviours that stem from attachment problems are discussed and suggestions for managing them are given. For more help in assessing attachment, see Workbook 1, *Attachment and separation*.

Withdrawal from interactions
Children who do not trust adults, or do not feel worthy of adult attention and affection, may withdraw from interactions with them. They may withdraw either physically or emotionally. Such children need to learn that their parental figures, and other adults, like them and value their company. They need gentle but persistent encouragement to be close to their parents. It is even possible to allow the child to earn 'withdrawal time' by first spending time with a parent. For example, when a child who always withdraws protests that he or she wants to be alone, the parents may say, 'Well, I'd like to play a game with you; then you may play in your room by yourself.'

Some children pull away or cringe when an adult reaches out to them.

Example
My usual response to a child who tightens up or withdraws when I hug him or her is to say, 'If you're pulling back I guess that means I haven't been giving you enough hugs lately. You must need two extra ones.' Then with a big grin I give two more quick hugs and go on about my business.

If the child 'wipes' my kiss off, I smile and redefine his or her behaviour. 'Umm, you're rubbing it off,' I respond. 'You may think you're rubbing it off, but I know you're rubbing it in,' and again return to business. If the child persists with verbal protests, I just reply, 'Well, I guess we have a difference of opinion.'

If exchanging physical affection becomes so much of an issue that the parents demand that the child admit that he or she likes it, they will be in trouble. Children have the right to decide whether or not they love their parents; however, they do not have the right to decide if their parents can show their affection. Such children need quick, physically affectionate exchanges during the course of the day. Prolonged periods of physical affection may be very difficult for them to tolerate initially.

Children who allow adults to be physically close but who seem to have a shield protecting them emotionally are likely to need longer term professional help. Frequently the emotional shield serves not only to 'protect' children from closeness with adults but also to 'protect' themselves from the intensity of their own feelings of sadness or rage. In other cases the presence of this emotional shield may indicate a severe psychological disturbance such as autism.

It is important to note that some children in placement withdraw not because they do not trust adults but because they are terribly depressed about separation from their birth parents. This type of problem is discussed in Section 5 of this workbook.

Many children with attachment problems withdraw from adults by avoiding eye contact with them. Frequently if the adult simply says, 'I like to have people look at me when we talk,' it works at least for a while. The next step is for the adult to remind the child non-verbally to maintain eye contact.

The least intrusive means of reminding that is effective should be used. The adult can give a simple non-verbal signal by moving his or her finger between their own eyes and the child's eyes. It is helpful if the adult and child sit relatively close together. If the child has difficulty maintaining eye contact from across a room, the adult should start out by asking the child to come closer and sit in an arrangement that is conducive to eye-to-eye contact; for example, facing one another in chairs that help overcome the difference in size.

If this seating and the finger movement are not enough of a reminder, then a finger under the chin of the child who is hanging his or her head and looking down, may work. If this is not successful – the child is then looking sideways – the adult can gently position their hands along the side of the child's head, blocking the child's peripheral view. If the adult says, 'I see that it's really hard for you to look at me as we talk; I wonder why that is?' it may yield valuable information.

Another tactic is to ask the child, 'Where do you think I want you to look when we are talking?' The response is often 'I don't know'. The adult can answer, 'Well, guess. I'll give you a hint – where am I looking as I talk to you?' The child usually will look at the adult to check this out, and even if the child does not answer verbally, he or she can be reinforced with 'That's it; that's where I like to look as we talk'.

Aggressive and hyperactive behaviour
Some children keep adults at a distance by behaving aggressively. If an adult is hit, kicked, scratched, or bitten every time he or she approaches a child, they will probably learn to keep their distance. Hyperactivity also may serve as a distancing mechanism. It is difficult to get close to a child who is always on the move. In such cases the parents and the child may profit from professional counselling. The parents need to learn

ways to physically manage the child without anyone getting hurt. Usually professional advice on ways to do this is necessary.

If the parent is afraid of the child's strong feelings, the child learns to fear them him or herself. One of the parent's principal tasks is to help the child recognise and deal with feelings appropriately. A more complete discussion of management of aggressive and destructive behaviour is included in Section 5.

Since many children in foster care have overwhelming feelings of rejection, it is important that the disciplinary techniques used with them do not reinforce these feelings. Although the average child over four is not overwhelmed when sent to his or her room after being naughty, children in foster placement, particularly soon after a move, may have their negative self perception reinforced by this kind of discipline. For such children, being sent to their room triggers and reinforces the idea that 'No one wants you if you are naughty: better watch out, or you might have to move again'.

Just having such a thought is enough to encourage some children to check it out by escalating their naughty behaviour. Messages that imply 'It's easier for you to be good and to be in control of yourself when you are close to me,' work better than ones that imply 'No one wants a naughty child'.

Indiscriminate affection

Children who are as affectionate with people outside their family as they are with family members are saying by their behaviour, 'No one is of special importance to me; I am equally close to everyone.' It is difficult for parental figures to feel close to the child who acts equally affectionately with everyone. The closeness seems phoney. This particular problem is more common in girls than boys. It is helpful to talk with the child about how she needs to learn to be close to one set of parents.

Example

I tell the child who tends to be indiscriminately affectionate that whenever she feels a need to be close to someone, she is to go and sit either next to her mum or dad or on their laps. I then ask the child, 'Will you remember to do that?' She usually assures me that she will, and I tell her, 'Good, but just in case you forget, I want your mum to remind you. Will you remember to do that, mum?'

When the mother sees the child clinging to someone else, she can just say, 'Do you remember what we talked about with Vee?' and hold out her arm to encompass the child. The mother can say to the other adult, 'Sally and I are just learning to get close to one another, and we're both working on practising that.' This avoids implying that there is something wrong with the neighbour or friend and hopefully prevents them from taking offence.

Over-competency or the self-parenting child

Some children with attachment problems have learned, usually through necessity, to take care of themselves. When they are placed in a foster or adoptive family, they behave as though they do not need parents. When such children need help, they do not ask for it, but instead they give the parental figures 'permission' to help them. For example, they might say, 'You may tie my shoes for me.'

In this situation parents need to feel comfortable parenting the child. Parents may need to be given permission to do this by the therapist or social worker. The child should not be allowed to determine how much parents can parent them. If the parent approaches the child with statements like 'I didn't have a chance to do things for you when you were little and couldn't do them, and mum needs to feel useful so I'm going to help you with this,' the child's self-esteem does not suffer. It also give the child the message that helping others is fun. This is a message that such children have never received before. The earlier message they received was 'I can't be bothered taking care of you. Do it yourself.'

There are several approaches to dealing with children who insist on giving parents permission to help them. If the child says, 'You may tie my shoes' in a demanding voice, the adult can respond, saying, 'I'd love to tie your shoes. I sure will be glad when you can just say "Would you please tie my shoes for me?".' If the child says, 'You may sit here,' adults can react as they would to a toddler. If that is where they wanted to sit anyway, they may sit down with no comment. If it isn't where they wanted to sit, they can simply say, 'No, I'm planning to sit here.'

Having discussions about whether the child has the 'right' to boss the adult around just increases the issue. Many children have learned that such comments are good ways 'to make mum mad', so to speak, and then they really are in control. When it is an older sibling who is always bossing a younger one, a light approach may work. For example,

'One mother is enough for any child to have to put up with at a time, and I was here as mother first. You'll get your chance when you grow up.'

It is important that the parents of such a child do not undermine their own statements by expecting the older child to be responsible for the younger child's behaviour. That, too, is the parents' responsibility. Sometimes the problem of a bossy sibling is not an attachment problem at all.

Case example: Shubi

One foster mother related to me that Shubi, her 12-year-old foster daughter, was always bossing her ten-year-old brother. I talked with Shubi about her perceptions of her foster home. She and her brother had been in this home for six years. No legal action had been taken, and the foster parents had become increasingly resentful because they had been told the children would be there for just a few months. I found that Shubi was afraid that if either she or her brother did anything wrong, they would be moved. Her bossiness grew out of her attempts to ensure that her brother would be 'good' so they could stay.

Lack of self-awareness

Some abused children seen very aware of people in their environment but nearly unaware of their own bodies. They may overeat to the point of bloating or vomiting. They may not react to pain or extremes of temperature in a normal manner. They may have problems with wetting. It is as if they never learned to pay attention to the signals from their own bodies or to what alleviates their own discomfort. A review of the way that children learn to recognise states of internal discomfort provides a basis for understanding why many children in foster care have this problem (see figure 1).

Infants do not come into this world recognising which state of discomfort is alleviated by which form of relief. It is the parents' response to the infants' needs that teaches them. With adequate parenting infants learn that there is a state of body discomfort that is alleviated by food; later, they learn that the word for this is 'hungry'.

As toddlers, they learn to recognise the state of discomfort occasioned by a full rectum or a full bladder. Early in toilet training children associate the feeling of discomfort with voiding only after they wet their pants. Gradually they become more aware of the feeling of a full

Figure 1

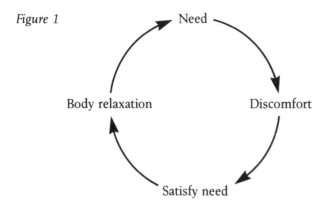

bladder and learn to go to the toilet to void. However, children learn to do this through developing the ability to pay attention to their own bodily states. Again, they develop this ability when their parents pay attention to their bodily states and supply the appropriate form of relief for their discomfort or appropriate teaching.

However, in neglectful and abusive families, children's states of discomfort are not alleviated on a regular basis; thus they do not associate specific forms of discomfort with certain forms of relief. Indeed, in abusive families children learn that expressing discomfort at all may lead to abuse. So they learn to ignore their own bodily discomfort, and focus all their attention on the caretaking adults. Such children are sensitive to the feelings and moods of the adults who take care of them, but not perceptive about themselves. They are frequently described as wary and watchful.

Such children need to learn to pay attention to their own bodily sensations. Parental figures can teach this. Comments such as 'It's nearly lunchtime, I'm hungry and I bet you are too – are you?' or 'Hey, you ate a good meal; I bet you're full,' help children focus on their own inner states. When such children fall and hurt themselves, parents could comment 'I bet that hurts; when I was a child and skinned my knee, I would cry sometimes.'

When a child overeats, the parent can be encouraged to allow the child to have a little more than is reasonable and then to say with a big smile 'Well, you can't be hungry for more food. You must be hungry for more loving. Come here and get some,' with arms outstretched to encircle the child. In addition, several foster and adoptive mothers have observed that such children gulp their food, and that once they start to chew, their appetites decrease. However, it is best not to make chewing a power struggle. It is possible to turn chewing into a game with the winner being the one that chews the most before the food is gone from the mouth.

A child who wets may need to be taken through toilet training. This problem is discussed in Section 5.

Control issues
Control issues are present when the parents' reasonable requests lead to major confrontations. As Dobson describes it, 'You have drawn a line in the dirt and the child has deliberately flopped his big hairy toe across it.'[9] Control issues are prevalent as children go through developmental periods when the surge for autonomy is great and there is an increase in stubborn and oppositional behaviour. This means that control issues are most noticeable during the toddler years, at age four, and during adolescence.

Children in placement are more prone to control issues than other children for two reasons. Frequently, they have been members of a family in which power struggles are a way of life. In addition, they often have experienced moves during the time of normal development of autonomy.

It is most important that the parental figures of children who instigate these control battles realise that underlying the child's apparent need to control everything is the feeling of not being in control of anything. If the parent feels threatened and needs to be in total control of the child, problems will increase. On the other hand, if the parent backs off from the task of helping the child learn that 'minding does not mean losing', control battles will escalate, and the child will 'run' the family.

When parents have made a reasonable request and find that there is a major battle ensuing, they need to stop, look, and listen. They must quickly assess whether the request is reasonable; whether there are extenuating circumstances that prohibit the child from obeying the request; and what the issue is.

If the parent determines that it is a control issue, then there is a need to quickly devise a strategy that allows the child to obey the request without feeling that he or she has lost. Two major supportive disciplinary techniques are used in this kind of setting. The first is called 'logical consequences' and the second, 'two good choices'.

An example of 'two good choices' might occur when a child refuses to tidy up his or her room and is given the choice of sitting in a chair until ready to tidy it up or tidying it up immediately. Such choices must be given in such a manner that implies that the parent does not have a strong need for the child to select one over the other, but that the choice is truly the child's.

Establishing rules that have consistent and logical consequences is also a useful way to handle control issues. A family rule that says, 'If you want dessert, you must eat all your meat and vegetables,' is much more effective in overcoming control issues around food than one that says, 'You must stay at the table until your plate is clean.' In the latter case the child has merely to sit passively until the next meal to 'win'. Some children will eat and then vomit the food back onto their plate to 'win' over this issue.

It is best for parents to avoid control battles from developing in certain areas. We have developed the 'rule of two ends'. This rule warns parents not to make a control issue over anything that goes into or out of either end of the child. The child is much more in control of his or her two ends than the parent will ever be. A parent can say, 'Yes, you will go to bed now,' and enforce it by taking the child to bed, but the parent cannot say, 'You will not wet the bed,' and enforce this order.

Frequently, physical action works better than repeated verbal chastising in control battles. Most children who are prone to control battles have learned to manipulate their parental figures by constantly arguing or reasoning with them. Usually, they have learned these approaches from the parents themselves, who use them to handle their children. Thus, if a child is annoying another child at the table, the parent might remind the child once to stop. If the behaviour continues, the parent should get up and lead the child away from the table to a chair, saying 'Let me know when you are ready to come back and eat instead of annoy.'

Since children who frequently engage in control battles usually perceive themselves as having little control over their lives, it is important that parental figures help them develop more age-appropriate autonomy by selecting areas where they can legitimately have control. This can be done either by delegating an entire area to the child; for example, 'You are in charge of your toys,' or by defining limits over which the child does not have control but delegating control within these limits; for example, 'It is bedtime. You may either put yourself to bed or I will put you to bed.' Remember the goal is to teach children that they can influence outcomes by changing to meet parents' reasonable expectations.

Delayed conscience development

The foundation for children's conscience development is their trust in others and their attachment to someone. Thus, the task of developing trust and attachment must be addressed with children who exhibit signs of delayed conscience development. With active work on the part of the parents, the child, and usually a therapist, it is usually possible to retrieve conscience at least up to the age of ten and frequently up to the early teens. This is especially true if the child will accept nurturance from parental figures.

The most common obstacle to conscience development in a family setting is the parents' notion that they have to be able to trust children before they can really nurture them. This is just the opposite of the truth. Children must first learn to trust the parents; they need to trust that the parents really care about them; that the parents will protect them from making serious mistakes; that the parents' limit-setting will be out of consideration for the needs of the child, not because they have to be in control of everything to satisfy their own needs; and that the parents will stick up for the child when he or she needs it.

While the child builds up this sense of trust, the parental figures need to keep their eyes and ears open. If the child is in school, his or her parents and teacher need to keep in frequent contact. The child needs to be under the supervision of one adult or another most of the time. If the child is enrolled in extra-curricular activities, then parents must have sufficient contact with the organisers to know what is going on.

This does not mean that an atmosphere of 'constant chatting' must prevail. Instead, the child can learn to trust that the parents know what he or she is doing at school. This should include knowledge of behaviour that indicates growth as well as instances of undesirable behaviour. If the teacher feels uncomfortable calling the child's home to find out information, such as 'Your Johnnie and another child are arguing over a pound coin. Did Johnnie have a pound when he left home?' hours of wrangling and inquisitions at school can be eliminated.

This kind of communication can also prevent the child who is being honest from being put in a defensive position. The teacher can then go back to the classroom and say to the children, 'Johnnie, I called your mother and she said she forgot to give you the money for the field trip. This money must belong to Mark.' The teacher then drops the subject and lets the parents pick up on it when the child returns home.

In this situation parents should not set the child up to lie by asking, 'How did your day go at school?' When parents do this, the child wonders if the teacher lied about calling the parents, or if the parents are lying by implying that they do not already know about the child's day. Instead the parents should greet the child at the door with a no-nonsense air and say, 'I got a call from Mrs Jones today about a pound coin, I want you to tell me what happened.'

Case example
This was particularly important in one particular case because the child had told the mother the day before that he needed a pound, but then in the before school rush, both had forgotten. This child needed to learn that his mother could take her share of the blame, and that, more importantly, they could talk about the ways that this situation could be avoided in the future.

This child, who tended to be impulsive, chose the quickest means at hand to solve his problem – stealing from a classmate. However, if he had known that a telephone call to his mother would have resulted in the pound being delivered to school and if he had trusted her that much, the situation could have been avoided.

Most children with delayed conscience development give them-selves away when they are lying. A useful question to ask parents is 'How do you know if your child is lying?' Some children who normally have good eye contact have difficulty looking at the parent when telling a lie. Others constantly lick their lips while others may move other parts of their body in characteristic ways. Parents need to focus on the child's body when one or more of these 'lie detectors' are present.

Case example
One child, who usually had reasonably good eye contact, developed very direct, piercing eye contact whenever she told a lie. Her parents started focusing on her 'truthful eyes'. When she lied to them, they would comment, 'Your mouth is saying one thing, but your eyes are saying

another. I have learned that you have very truthful eyes.' The child's self-image of herself as 'a liar' started to change. Within a short period of time they progressed from the 'What are your eyes saying?' stage to the 'Pay attention to your eyes, Barbie' stage.

As children learn to stop themselves from lying, they need praise for developing this inner control. Consider Steven's experience.

Case example: Steven

Steven was an eight-year-old who had problems with delayed conscience development but was making good progress in this area. One day, while his mother was putting clean clothes away, she glanced out of the upstairs window and noticed that Steven was starting to tease the dog – a behaviour for which he had been disciplined on numerous occasions. Then, he glanced at the front door of the house and stopped himself.

Later, when Steven came in to wash for dinner, his mother commented, 'I noticed that you were able to stop yourself from teasing the dog. Good job!' Thus, she not only reinforced Steven for improving his behaviour, but she also gave him the message that 'I care enough about you to know what you are doing and if you could not have stopped yourself, I would have helped you stop.'

Parents of children with delayed conscience development need not only to have 'big eyes and big ears' but also be exceptionally truthful themselves. They need to give the children very straight messages about what their expectations are. They might say, 'I like it when you do this' or 'I don't like it when you do that.'

Consequences that have something to do with the infraction are much more meaningful than unrelated discipline. For example, working to repay stolen money relates better to the behaviour of stealing than does being restricted to the house for a week. It also teaches alternative pathways to the child for getting his or her needs met. The solution for a child wanting extra money is for the child to find a way to earn it, and not to be restricted to the house for a week.

Some adolescents who appear to have conscience problems in reality have too much conscience rather than too little. These young people may sometimes lie and steal. However, they constantly promise themselves, or others, 'I'll never do it again.' This is a very weighty promise. When they are unable to live up to their own expectations, they 'dump' on themselves and see themselves as 'rotten and no good'. These children need help setting more realistic goals for themselves; for example, 'I'm not going to lie to my parents *today*.' These more realistic goals enable them to build up their self-esteem.

Some children have problems that are more serious than delayed conscience development. Children who have true sociopathic tendencies frequently do not give themselves away when they may not only be deceiving adults by their lies, but they may be deceiving themselves. Individuals with this problem frequently convince themselves that their lies are the truth. Chances of successful work with these children are reduced considerably.

In Exercise 4, you have an opportunity to look at the case of an eight-year-old girl who has a number of behaviours that stem from attachment problems.

Exercise 4:
Managing behaviour that stems from attachment problems

Instructions

Purpose:
To give you an opportunity to suggest behaviour management of problems that are the result of lack of attachment.

How to do it:

1 Read Sharon's case history on the next page. (You will recognise Sharon from previous exercises in the other workbooks where we looked at different aspects of her development.)

2 Answer the questions on the worksheet for Exercise 4. Then, compare your own answers with those of another social worker on the sample worksheet.

Sharon's case

Sharon, aged eight, will move into an adoptive home within the next month. She has a past history of considerable emotional and physical deprivation, rejection, and physical abuse from her birth parents. She has been in and out of foster care since she was four years old. She has had seven moves since then, including two moves back to her birth parents.

Her current foster parents report that Sharon has problems with both daytime and night-time wetting. A medical examination did not reveal any physical cause.

Sharon is very sexually provocative. She pulls her dresses up in front of men and boys and asks them openly if they want to go to bed with her. She has many fears, especially of the dark and of sirens. She becomes very upset when family members tease or become boisterous with each other. Sharon is seen as demanding and manipulative by the adults with whom she has had close contact although she can be quite helpful.

Academically she is at her age level. She seems to be quite intelligent; however, she does not always complete her school work. She has poor play skills and is rarely able to keep friends for any length of time. In spite of acceptable academic performance, Sharon's logical thinking skills and sense of cause and effect, in terms of the day-to-day living situations, seem to be severely impaired.

Sharon has problems telling the truth. Sometimes she lies about her misbehaviours; at other times she tells meaningless lies, such as saying that peas are her favourite vegetable when she hates them. She has very poor eye contact when lying about her misbehaviours; when lying about her likes and dislikes, her eye contact is normal. She also brings home many small things from school that she either states she has found or have been given by friends. When she wets her pants or doesn't pay attention, Sharon does show signs of guilt.

Sharon is a very affectionate child. Sometimes she is inappropriately affectionate with relative strangers.

Exercise 4:
Managing behaviour that stems from attachment problems

Worksheet

1 How would you present Sharon's behavioural problems in a way that the prospective adoptive family could understand their origin?

2 What advice with regard to behavioural management would you give adoptive parents for early in the placement period?

3 Which problems should they confront promptly in the placement and with which ones can they use a 'wait and see' attitude?

Exercise 4:
Managing behaviour that stems from attachment problems

Sample worksheet

---

1 How would you present Sharon's behavioural problems in a way that the prospective adoptive family could understand their origin? By explaining Sharon's early neglect, probable abuse and series of rejections, whilst moving back and forth, all of which has resulted in her having trouble trusting adults. She has problems in attaching to parent figures and delayed development. She doesn't feel good about herself or think she's worth very much. She needs her parents to understand and to be willing to work hard at the sort of parenting that would normally be done at a much earlier age.

---

2 What advice with regard to behavioural management would you give the adoptive parents for early in the placement period? That the central job for them is building Sharon's attachment to them, working on trust and self-esteem, starting with the relationship with the adoptive mum. For example:
 - encourage Sharon to be close to mum, offering her practice times and helping her stop indiscriminate affection
 - deal with lying and stealing by knowing what she's doing at school and making her aware of her 'truthful eyes'
 - give her lots of praise and help her meet expectations
 - take her through toilet training by getting her in touch with her body's needs

---

3 Which problems should they confront promptly in the placement and with which ones can they use a 'wait and see' attitude?

Confront the trust issues - lying, stealing, being close - and the bed wetting to help her gain some control over herself. The fears, peer problems and logical thinking problems in school will improve over time.

---

4 Management of perceptual problems

Many children in placement experience perceptual problems or learning disabilities. What appear to be behavioural problems often have their roots in perceptual or learning difficulties. In this section, management of these types of behavioural problems is discussed.

Every child who enters foster care after the age of three should be screened for visual or auditory problems, speech difficulties, and gross motor delays. This is particularly important with children who exhibit signs of any developmental delay.

In general, children with perceptual problems have difficulty handling changes in their environments or routines. Like all children who have been in care, they need a home life that is reasonably well organised, with parents who prefer to plan ahead and lead a rather scheduled life.

If a child has visual problems, then describing what is happening will help the learning process. If the child has auditory perceptual difficulties, then visual demonstrations must accompany verbal instructions.

Auditory problems

Children with auditory perceptual difficulties have normal hearing, but they have difficulty processing the spoken word. It is a little like someone who has a general knowledge of a foreign language but is not fluent. They must pay very close attention to what is said and can easily hear a word incorrectly. Such incidents often change the entire meaning of a sentence. When speaking, they may have to struggle to find just the word they want.

Many children with auditory perceptual problems demonstrate marked auditory distractibility as well. As a result they have difficulty discriminating between distant and nearby sounds, and the world may become a very confusing place. We have seen children with childhood schizophrenia who showed evidence of extremely sensitive hearing.

Case example: Danny

A schizophrenic child named Danny had strong fears of loud noises, especially vibrating sounds like those made by vacuum cleaners, power mowers, and power saws. As he left his schizophrenic world and became part of 'our world' more of the time, he was able to explain his perceptions to us.

When he was a toddler, Danny's family lived close to a large airport. When he was ten, he explained to his mother that 'Everytime one of those planes went over, it was so loud that it felt like it was inside my head and was going to bust it open!' No wonder this child blocked out the world and withdrew into schizophrenia.

Danny's auditory fears confused his other perceptions as well. When he was 11, he was finally able to tell his mother more about the origin of his fear of vacuum cleaners. Danny reminded his mother of one occasion when she was vacuuming with an old, disabled vacuum cleaner. The bag blew off the cleaner, spewing dust all over the house. His mother became very upset about the mess, and she 'blew up' verbally. This event was very frightening to a pre-school child who was having trouble sorting out his perceptions. The noise of the vacuum cleaner became confused in Danny's mind with his mother's anger.

Another case example is included here to demonstrate how a child's disability may affect others as well as ways people can help a child compensate for his or her difficulties.

Case example: Tom

Tom had been abused and neglected by his birth family. He had been in numerous foster homes and had been hospitalised at a children's treatment unit. Finally, Tom was placed in our assessment centre. He had a tendency to have violent temper tantrums and to abuse himself.

It rapidly became apparent to Tom's teacher that he had a problem with auditory distractibility and with localisation of sounds. Tom heard things before the rest of us did. If he said 'What's that?' we soon learned to listen, rather than to look.

One day, as Tom was getting better, I took him shopping in the town centre. We were in a shop that had no other customers; in fact, it was deadly silent. As we stood at the counter, Tom commented 'It's very noisy in here.' The woman at the counter gave him a 'smart alec kid' look. I knew I should listen. Sure enough, I could hear the sound of a jack-hammer a block away pounding on the pavement. 'That jack-hammer makes a lot of noise,' I said.

Tom replied, 'Yeah, I wonder what they are building.' At that point the woman's expression changed from one of marked disapproval to one of admiration of his perceptiveness.

No wonder the world is a confusing place for Tom. Others don't share or understand his perceptions and react to him in what must seem to be very unpredictable ways.

Parents of children with perceptual problems must observe them carefully to become aware of the way they perceive the world. The parents must help clarify the children's perceptions and help them to cope with the world.

Speech problems
Children with speech problems need to learn to watch faces; watching people talk and observing facial expressions helps them hear and understand better. Children with speech delays often need parents who can provide speech stimulation, rather than formalised speech therapy, particularly in the pre-school years.

Pre-school age children are not used to talking in unfamiliar places with strangers. The speech therapist who goes to a child's home and observes his or her speech can make a better assessment and is in a position to tell the parents what they can do to encourage speech in the home. Alternatively the speech therapist can work with the child in this familiar setting initially. Stimulation by parents provides children with many more hours of speech therapy in a week than they receive in two, half-hour sessions a week. Of course, more traditional therapy may be useful with children who speak freely in front of strangers.

Sense of time
Many children with perceptual problems lack an internal sense of time. Many such children have difficulty learning to tell time; even learning the names of the days of the week and months may be difficult for them. A sense of distance is often confusing to such children as well.

Most children begin to acquire a sense of time long before they are ever asked to tell time on a clock. They begin to learn the sequence of the days of the week and to develop internal awareness of how long a few minutes, an hour, or a half-day lasts. Children gradually learn this sense of time between ages three and six. Helping a child of this age learn a sense of time usually requires just responding to his or her interest in the subject.

We have found that if children get beyond about nine without learning to tell the time, they often become adept at covering up this lack of knowledge. They are unlikely to express an overt interest in learning about time.

People who are in day-to-day contact with a child with perceptual problems need to figure out what it is the child does and does not know. If the gaps in the child's knowledge are not identified, they cannot be filled in.

How do children learn a sense of time? Parents of pre-school children usually talk about days of the week and help the child learn them by rote. Calendars that identify special events help the school-age child. For example, parents can use a calendar when they respond to the often-asked question, 'How many days until my birthday?' Using a calendar is much more helpful than simply saying 'three months' or 'It's too early to start thinking about your birthday yet.'

Parents can teach a child a sense of time by talking about time as they go about their daily business. For example, they may say, 'Come and wash up, dinner will be ready in five minutes,' or 'It's half an hour until bedtime.' When children ask, 'How long is half an hour?' the answer can be related to daily occurrences. Half an hour can be equated to a favourite TV programme; ten minutes to the trip to the corner shop; and so on.

Use of a timer can help a child internalise a sense of time. It a parent says, 'You have ten minutes to get dressed,' and sets a timer, a child will rapidly learn to 'beat the clock'. If this sequence is repeated daily, the child will learn to 'beat the clock' without looking at a timer.

Before children can learn to tell time on a conventional clock, they must be able to count in fives. Until they learn this, they will only be able to identify the hour and the half hour. After they have this capacity, parents can start to ask children what time it is. Devising games to use these skills makes learning to tell the time much more fun than if parents respond with disgust or ridicule to children's learning efforts.

Most children develop a sense of past and future time by the kind of conversation that occurs in the normal course of family living. Comments like 'We moved to this house two years ago,' or 'You can have pierced ears when you become a teenager,' give children an understanding of past and future and help them gain a sense of continuity in life. This type of time sense is poor in many children in foster care even if they have no perceptual difficulties.

Two factors contribute to this. Too often foster parents do not have the information that helps the children sort out their past. They may know that a child was in another foster home but not know where, when, or for how long. In addition, there is a tendency for both foster and birth parents to feel uncomfortable when a child starts to talk about the past with which they are not familiar. The non-verbal message parents give to the child may be 'Don't talk about your past; I don't want to hear about it.'

The future poses even more of a problem for children in foster care. No one can tell them where they will be living in the future. Since foster children are denied so much in this area, it is critical that they be given all the information about their past that is available.

Learning disabilities

Many children with learning disabilities have a medical syndrome now recognised as 'attention deficit disorder', characterised by a short attention span, hyperactivity, auditory and/or visual distractibility, impulsiveness, and emotional lability. Children with this disorder tend to be very easily distracted. For this reason, an environment that is not over stimulating is helpful. Such children do poorly in a household where the television or radio is on constantly. Although they certainly need a place to play with toys, they also need a place to which they can retreat that is not so stimulating.

This may be particularly important at bedtime. It makes sense to keep the toys of an extremely distracted child in a box outside his or her room or in another room of the house. An occasional very young hyperactive child will get up after going to bed and try on all of the clothes in the chest of drawers in the child's room. So it, too, may have to be removed.

Easily defined spaces help such children learn limits. A fence around the garden makes it easier for children to understand and recognise the boundaries they must observe when their parents say 'Stay in the garden.'

Since children with attention deficit disorder tend to be impulsive, it is helpful to make them focus on what they are going to do next, and to make them responsible for choosing what they are going to do. With this kind of child the parent does well to say 'Sit down here a minute until you can decide what you want to do next.' Once the child is verbally committed to a specific activity, it is easier for him or her to focus on it. When parents give verbal instructions, it often helps to ask such a child to describe what he or she is going to do before doing it. This step gives the parents a chance to clarify instructions if the child is confused and give the child some positive reinforcement if he or she is clear about what is to happen.

Daily routines help any child become more secure. Routines associated with meals are important. With such children little things, like putting their clothes for the next day out at bedtime, are helpful. Doing this gives parents an opportunity to talk briefly with the child about the next day's activities and expectations.

With a child with attention deficit disorder it is important to break learning tasks into parts that the child can understand and achieve more easily. It is also important to provide day-to-day experiences at home and at school that enhance the child's self-esteem.

Hyperactive children may be helped by dietary restrictions suggested in the Feingold diet. This diet restricts the intake of food colourings and food additives. Although double blind studies attempting to demonstrate the efficacy of this approach have not, to date, yielded conclusive results, some families we have met have felt that the diet helped their children significantly.

There are some children who seem to become more hyperactive after eating sweets. In such cases, foods containing simple sugars, called glucose, should be limited. Fructose, which is the sugar contained in fruits and more complex carbohydrates, does not seem to cause the same problem for these children. Snacks of fruit, nuts, popcorn, and natural fruit juices can be substituted for glucose-rich snacks like sweets, chocolate, or cake.

Exercise 5 on the next page describes the behaviour of Ronnie, a seven-year-old with typical minimal attention deficit disorder. Read his case and follow the instructions for suggesting a plan for management of Ronnie's problems.

Exercise 5:
Managing perceptual problems

Instructions

Purpose:
To give you practice in planning management of behavioural problems that result from attention deficit disorder.

How to do it:
1 Read Ronnie's case history.

2 Answer the questions on the worksheet for Exercise 5. Then compare your own answers with those of another social worker on the sample worksheet.

Ronnie's case
Ronnie is seven years old. He reads at his age level or above and does well in maths when he completes his work. His handwriting, however, is poor. Although he rarely gets out of his seat at school unless it is appropriate, he constantly twists, turns, drops things, and picks them up. Ronnie also frequently talks out in class.

He has great difficulty switching from one subject to another, particularly if he hasn't completed the work. He is apt to direct a verbal outburst at the teacher when this happens.

Ronnie has difficulty getting along with his peers. If someone accidently brushes against him, he is likely to verbally, and possibly physically, lash out at that person. He seems socially immature.

His foster parents state that Ronnie is very messy at the table. He never sits still and frequently drops food from his fork. He falls asleep promptly at night and is a very sound sleeper. He wets the bed two or three times a week.

Ronnie wakes up early and promptly goes to the kitchen where he gets into whatever food is available, leaving the kitchen in a mess. He occasionally has daytime wetting problems. This occurs most frequently at weekends or on outings. Ronnie is very hard on his clothes, and frequently he misplaces or loses coats, hats, and sweaters.

Ronnie is very good at gross motor activities. He is a very agile child. He much prefers outdoor to indoor activities. Although he does like playing with small cars and trucks, he dislikes models and other arts and crafts activities.

Worksheet

1 Make a list of Ronnie's behavioural problems. Group together the ones that are indicative of attention deficit disorder and that would encourage you to recommend that the family seek assessment from an expert.

2 Apart from the medical management, what would you suggest as a plan for behavioural management of the problems?

Exercise 5:
Managing perceptual problems

Sample worksheet

1 Make a list of Ronnie's behavioural problems. Group together the ones that are indicative of attention deficit disorder and that would encourage you to recommend that the family seek assessment from an expert.

Attention deficit disorder
Impulsivity Problems with attention span
Difficulty with changes in routine   Fidgetting
Developmental delays in fine motor skills
Other
Day and night-time wetting
Possible morning loneliness
'Aggressive' outbursts

2 Apart from the medical management, what would you suggest as a plan for behavioural management of the problems?

Helping him to become aware of his environment and to focus on 'what next' may help him with impulsivity and difficulties with changes.
His environment, especially at weekends, should be more structured.
Opportunities for him to succeed and to help out at home should be provided to build self-esteem and desire to anticipate more positive interactions with others.
When is bedtime? Is he reminded to use the bathroom during the day and at bedtime?
Help him become more aware of his body's needs.
Give him some alternative behaviour when he's angry or frustrated.
Is he lonely in the mornings? Setting out his breakfast in advance might help.

5 Management of other common behavioural problems

This section addresses a number of problems that social workers have encountered in children in placement. These problems stem from a variety of causes. Some are inappropriate expressions of feelings; some are bad habits; some result from developmental delays; and some are related to the attachment and perceptual problems discussed in Sections 3 and 4 of this workbook. In any one child, more than one of these dynamics may be at work. In addition, a behavioural problem in one child may have different roots from that same behavioural problem in another child.

In this section we attempt to analyse the likely causes of a number of behavioural problems, and we use the *Setting of boundaries worksheet* to suggest approaches to the management of these problems.

Aggressive behaviour

Children who are very aggressive toward others or very harmful to themselves need to be physically prevented from carrying out such aggressive acts. Some people use a 'time out' procedure and put such children in an area by themselves where they cannot hurt anything. But there are serious problems with this approach. A child who is that much out of control is extremely anxious. Anxious children need to be close to others.

Having an aggressive child take a seat in the same room as the parent may be a helpful course of action. If the child is being so aggressive that he or she cannot contain themselves in a chair, then the parent must physically contain the child in a way that does not harm either of them.

If children hit or bite themselves when they are frustrated but are not totally out of control, a different technique may be quite successful. An adult can approach such children face-to-face, and tell them that if they are feeling so frustrated that they need to hit something, they may slap the adult's hands until they don't need to hit themselves.

Handslapping hurts both people's hands equally; there is not a puncher and a punchee. It encourages children to have face-to-face contact when they are frustrated. It gives children the message that the parent cares about them, wants to help them relieve their frustration, but does not want to see them hurt. Finally, children can end the activity because they can stop as soon as they do not 'need' to hit themselves anymore.

It is even more helpful if the parents at the same time use words to help a child learn how to express his or her strong feelings verbally. Such words might be 'You must really be mad about something' or 'You're really frustrated today.' Many times these words open the door for the child to discharge anger or frustration verbally. The parent gives the child the message that 'I care about your strong feelings, and I am not afraid of them.'

Bed wetting and daytime wetting

Bed wetting has a variety of causes. Physical causes are relatively infrequent while anxiety is a common cause. Children are most apt to wet the bed prior to or just after moves or other events that upset them. Children who do not pay attention to their body states frequently wet the bed. Other children who are very heavy sleepers may not respond to stimuli that tell them their bladders are full.

In general, making bed wetting a big issue is not helpful. If it is distressing to the child, then the parent can offer to help the child find a solution to the problem. If the parent can identify when the wetting usually occurs during the night, a solution frequently becomes apparent. For example, the parent can get the child up if the wetting occurs in the early evening, or can set an alarm for early in the morning if that is when the wetting occurs.

Having the child take a reasonable part in coping with the extra work that bed wetting necessitates is helpful. One mother illustrates two unreasonable approaches to bed wetting. Her son was six years old. The mother put him in a nappy at night because he was 'acting like a baby' and also made him totally responsible for stripping his bed, washing and drying the sheets, and then remaking the bed. Both of these extremes are unreasonable for a six-year-old. Asking the child to strip his bed and help his mother remake it after she washed and dried the sheets would not have been unreasonable.

Wetting in the daytime is a stronger indication of a need for a medical examination to determine if the child has a bladder or kidney abnormality. However, there are many children in foster care who have problems with daytime wetting because they are not aware of their own states of discomfort. Such children frequently overeat, and they may be insensitive to heat, cold, or pain as well. The way this syndrome develops is discussed more completely in Section 3.

Once adults recognise lack of self-awareness in children in foster care, the remedy becomes apparent. The goal is to help teach children to pay closer attention to their body signals. In the case of the daytime wetting, the parent may need to help the child go through the usual stages of toilet training, even though the child may be seven, eight, or even older. The child should not be punished for wetting, but instead should be reminded to go to the bathroom on a regular schedule and to pay attention to how he or she feels before and after voiding.

Children with this problem may urinate right after they get up in the morning. They may be sitting on the bed or standing on the rug in the bedroom. Parents often see this behaviour as intentional and a sign of anger; while in reality, it is frequently due to lack of self-awareness. Such children need to be reminded to go to the bathroom as soon as they awaken in the morning. Some children who have solved a wetting problem revert to either daytime or night wetting when they are particularly anxious such as after a move or during times of crisis.

Child too good

Children who have experienced frequent moves sometimes try to become 'perfect' since they assume that the reason for the moves was their bad behaviour. It is hard for parents or siblings to live with a child who is always trying to be perfect. It is also pretty hard on the child. All the child's energy goes into maintaining a perfect facade, and little is left for developing relationships or continuing intellectual and emotional growth.

The 'perfect' child is a real challenge to treat. When one is treating a child who exhibits naughty behaviour, one only has to worry about failures. However, with the 'perfect' child, one may fear that the child will go overboard when taught to be normally naughty. In reality, this rarely happens.

The child has to have permission to have a normal repertoire of negative feelings and then permission to express these feelings in age-appropriate ways. However, often just giving permission is not enough.

Children who strive to be perfect maintain their facade by working at a slow pace, even in circumstances when they could be legitimately frustrated or angry. They frequently talk very softly, and they may mumble or leave out words. When asked, 'What would you like to do?' they respond with 'I don't know,' or 'Whatever you decide.' Such children are frequently withdrawn.

Since one of the major defences such children use is moving and talking at a slow pace, 'rhythm' control is an effective way to interrupt their perfection. Talking rapidly with a demanding voice and getting them active by running or exercising with them frequently helps these children assert themselves and say 'No' or 'I'm mad at you.'

Case example: Tracy

Tracy was a child who never asserted herself. She got up in the morning and quickly made both her own and her birth brother's bed and tidied up both rooms. When given choices, she always responded, 'I don't know.' She was so good that it was difficult for her adoptive mother to feel close to her.

Her younger brother started to dislike her because, in his words, 'She never gets into trouble.' Her teachers thought she was wonderful and had made 'such a good adjustment' to her recent adoption. However, they were concerned that she worked so slowly in school that she was falling behind. Whenever her mother asked that Tracy sit on her lap, she did so in a stiff manner, with a plastic smile on her face.

My goal in treatment was first to encourage Tracy to express some appropriate anger toward me in her parents' presence and some anger about the past events in her life as we constructed her life story book, again with her parents' participation. In this way Tracy had a chance to see that her parents could both accept and understand her underlying anger.

We then set up some 'homework' whereby if Tracy could show some appropriate autonomy, such as by saying 'I don't want to do that,' she didn't have to do what she was asked. We arranged that one parent would confront Tracy, and the other parent would support her in her appropriate assertion of autonomy.

Interestingly, her younger brother's behaviour improved as Tracy learned to be normally 'naughty'. Her adoptive brother was delighted when he could tell me, 'Guess what? Tracy got in trouble for not tidying up her room this week!'

Child good in one setting, but not another ('let's you and him fight' syndrome)

Some children behave acceptably for one parent but not for the other or behave well at home but not at school. In these cases the children need to be encouraged by the person for whom they usually behave well to behave well in other situations. For example, the child who always takes notice of the father but not the mother needs to be told by the father, 'I want you to take notice of what Mum says!' Or, the father might overhear the child not taking notice of the mother and ask, 'What did your Mum just say? Well, then, what do you think I want you to do?'

Such children have frequently lived in families where the child was used as a party to parental disagreements, or where the child was given the message 'You don't have to take notice of anyone but me.'

If the child's behaviour is acceptable at home but not at school, then the parents need to work closely with the teacher so that the child knows that he or she is pleasing the parents by taking notice of the teacher. The child who behaves well at school but acts out at home is more typical. In the case of young, school-aged children, it often seems as if they expend all of their energy maintaining their behaviour at school and are just too tired to continue this control once they get home. Of course, on occasion it means that the teacher is more consistent in expectations and that the parents do not follow through.

Clinging

While clinging usually reflects some early unmet needs, there is also a habit quality to this particular behaviour. The child needs to learn that he or she will receive at least as much attention when they do not cling as when they do. In working to change clinging behaviour, the parent may focus on one recurrent bothersome situation in which the child tends to cling. For example, one child clings to the mother whenever a neighbour comes over for a cup of coffee.

In this situation the mother might approach the child with 'I know that you want attention when Mrs Jones comes over. However, this is my time with her, and I find that I get angry with you when you cling and interrupt. I would rather spend fun time with you than nagging you. How about making a bargain? The next time Mrs Jones comes over, we will see how long you can go without clinging or interrupting? Then, I will pay you back that much time playing a game with you as soon as she leaves.'

Pre-schoolers may have trouble with this approach as their needs are frequently too great to allow for postponing attention even this long, but older children can frequently respond to such an approach positively.

The approach allows the child to choose whether to get attention negatively or positively. The parent can help the child take responsibility for the choice by asking 'Did you make a good choice or a bad choice about getting attention today?' and 'How do you feel about the choice you made?'

Destructiveness

Identifying what the child destroyed, and when, frequently leads to understanding the underlying cause of destructive behaviour. Children who destroy a sibling's toys when they are angry with the siblings are expressing anger inappropriately. Children who destroy only objects from their birth families usually have unresolved feelings about the birth family or separation from that family. Some children are destructive only when they are lonely. Some hyperactive children seem to have periods of nearly driven destructiveness related to their impulsivity and inability to control their feelings. Many children who are destructive are developmentally delayed. They are stuck at the early toddler stage when their behaviour would have been considered undesirable but normal.

Clearly the destructive child needs closer supervision than other children so that the bouts of destructiveness can be prevented or interrupted as soon as possible. At the same time such children usually need help in learning to express their feelings more appropriately. The ones who have problems with impulsivity are most likely to need more intensive counselling or psychotherapy as well.

'Don't know' syndrome

If a child's usual response during an interview is 'I don't know', I usually comment 'I have found out that when children say "I don't know" lots of times, what they really mean is "I don't want to answer your question." I wish you would tell me "I don't want to answer," if that's what you really mean.' I then make sure that the next few questions are of the kind where it is okay with me if the child responds that he or she does not want to tell me the answer.

Then I ask an important question, and when the child says 'I don't want to answer' my reply is 'I know that's a really difficult thing for you to talk about, but it's important for me to know how you feel about it if I am to be able to make the best decisions about how to help you.' What this does is to set up a mini-parenting experience. It gives the child the message 'I care about you, and I respect your right to not share everything with me, but there are reasonable limits which I will place on your behaviour.' This, of course, is what all parenting is about. This helps convince the child that I truly have their best interests at heart.

Encopresis (faecal soiling)

Children with encopresis usually chronically stain or soil their clothing rather than have regular large bowel movements. Encopresis commonly indicates repressed anger. It occurs most frequently in children who tend to be stubborn or withholding.

When this behaviour occurs, the parents must be advised about the psychological connection between unexpressed anger and faecal soiling so that they can help the child express his or her anger more appropriately. It is important that parents remember that the child is usually not aware of the connection between faecal soiling and anger. The child does not engage in the behaviour 'on purpose'.

Behaviour management techniques can be used to help the child overcome his or her problem; however, if the parent is terribly disturbed by the behaviour, they may not work. If someone, other than the parent, can get the child to agree to work on the problem, then it is possible to set up a behavioural programme.

Physically speaking, it is easiest for children to have a bowel movement right after eating. Children with encopresis need to be encouraged to go to the bathroom directly after each meal and to try to have a bowel movement. They should be positively reinforced every time there is any stool in the toilet. If the child over five has an accident, he or she should be responsible for rinsing out their underwear and putting it in a specified place. For children under five, the parent can provide a nappy pail in which the child can place the soiled underwear.

It is not uncommon for children with this problem to hide their soiled underwear. It is helpful if the parent asks the child each day if he or she remembered to put any soiled underwear into the wash. If children see the parents as helping them to attain their goal of stopping soiling, it improves their relationship with the parents.

Many children with encopresis have difficulty delaying gratification. For this reason it may be best to reinforce the child immediately for his or her success with something like food. The more stools the child has in the toilet, the more frequent the reinforcement, and the less likely he or she is to soil. It is then possible to move to an accumulative reinforcement; for example, to have the child earn enough stars to get a special toy. It is best to establish a reward that can reasonably be earned in one or two weeks.

Using the *Setting of boundaries worksheet*, it becomes obvious that control of encopresis involves a combination of approaches. Encouragement for appropriate expression of underlying feelings of anger is combined with a behaviour modification approach to the habit of soiling.

Excessive concern about small injuries

Children of about age six are prone to excessive concern about small injuries. This concern emerges after they become aware that people die and that they too someday will die, but they do not yet know what kinds of illnesses or injuries are likely to result in death. Children in foster care may display this behaviour at a later age. Frequently it indicates a delay in the child's emotional development.

Case example

Recently, a social worker at a conference asked me about an eight-year-old boy who had recently begun to exhibit this problem. I talked about why the problem usually occurred and that I assumed that there might be a relatively mild developmental delay in this case. The worker commented, 'It all makes sense now; his foster grandmother died just a few months ago, and he had been quite close to her. This was his first experience with a death in the family.'

Fake smile

This smile usually is an inappropriate expression of an underlying feeling. Most often the fake smile expresses anxiety, uncertainty, or embarrassment. Some children smile to cover up sadness or anger as well. Such children need to have permission and encouragement to express their feelings more appropriately. Many of them are not yet truly aware of their underlying feelings, however, and they may need to be taught to identify their feelings as well as to express them.

Fire raising

Although traditionally fire raising has been linked to underlying anger, our work with a number of young children who had a history of raising fires showed that most of them were very lonely and depressed at the time of the fire raising incidents. In cases of children with this history, we begin by exploring with the children in minute detail what occurred immediately before they raised the fire. We try to let them know that if we can identify how they felt just before the incident and during it, then we can usually help them with the problem.

In general, it does not help to ask children why they raised a fire or for that matter, to ask 'why?' about any negative behaviour. Children's reaction to this question is defensive. They will say whatever they think will get the adult off their back quickly. 'I wonder if you know why you did that,' or 'Do you know why you did that?' are much better than the accusatory 'Why did you do it?'

If a child says he or she does not know why they did it, we can then suggest we work together to figure it out. We ask the child where he or she was just before raising the fire, what they were doing, and how they were feeling about it. Were they happy? Sad? Lonely? Angry? Scared?

We have been amazed how often children who raise fires did so when they felt alone and unloved. It certainly is a behaviour that is guaranteed to get attention rapidly; however, this attention rarely helps the child feel less lonely or more loved. If the child raised fires when he or she was lonely, the intervention needed is obvious. When children are lonely, they should be close to people.

Case example: Paul

Paul was eight. He had been in foster care for several years. His parents' rights to him had been terminated. His foster parents were considering adopting him, but they hesitated because they were concerned about several behavioural problems he exhibited. For one thing, Paul had come home from school on several occasions and raised small fires in the garage.

Paul had fairly severe learning problems. School was not very rewarding for him. His foster mother had a part-time job and usually was not home when he came home from school. An elderly woman babysat for Paul after school; however, her favourite television programme was on just at the time he returned home.

When we asked Paul about his feelings the last time he raised a fire, he looked very sad, started crying, and talked about how he 'did not belong at school or at home'.

Once the foster mother found out that Paul was especially vulnerable to feelings of loneliness right after school, she rearranged her work schedule so that she usually could be home right after school. On days that this was not possible, she gave Paul extra attention in the morning and left an 'I love you' note with a special after-school snack for his return.

Paul raised no more fires. Subsequently his foster parents adopted him. Since the family had been able to help Paul get over this fairly serious problem, they felt confident in their ability to work together to overcome any future problems that might arise.

Food hoarding

Some children steal food and hide it. This distresses parents because the child seems accusatory. The message appears to be that the parents won't give the child enough to eat. In addition, the food is generally found under a bed or behind a cushion, or some such location and is wasted.

When children hoard food, it rarely has anything to do with their nutritional needs. It often is a sign that they feel they cannot count on others to nurture them and that they must take care of themselves. Food hoarding is usually related to lack of attachment, loneliness, or jealousy of attention received by others. The child who eats excessively but does not grow is often involved in the same sort of dynamics as the child who hoards food.

To solve food problems it is important to meet the child's underlying needs while at the same time using environmental controls. Such controls might involve delineating which foods may be eaten at will and which ones may be eaten only when the parent gives permission.

One thing should be noted here. Many children who hoard food seem to crave sweets. They hoard chocolate, biscuits, cakes, and so on. Such children should be watched closely to see if eating of excessive sweets makes them more hyperactive or more irritable.

If such a relationship does exist, the child and parents can work on the problem together. The parent can approach the child saying 'You know and I know that every time you eat a lot of sweets we seem to have more problems. Some people have that difficulty, others don't. Apparently you are a person who is affected by eating a lot of sweets.

What do you think would be a good choice – to avoid eating too many sweets or to eat them and get into trouble?' Then the parent is in a position to ask the child, 'What can I do to make it easier for you not to eat a lot of sweets?' The child can see the parents as helping rather than accusing and rejecting him or her.

Lying

In assessing the child who lies, it is important to know when the lying occurs and what it is about. In some cases, lying indicates a developmental delay; at other times, it is an indication of a different problem.

Some parents describe a child's exaggeration about him or herself or the birth family as lying. If this behaviour is exhibited by a child in placement, then he or she probably needs help with separation issues. For some other children lying about certain behaviours has become a habit, and in these cases a behaviour modification approach is best.

However, the most common cause of lying seems to be related to delayed conscience development. Attachment to a parental figure is essential for conscience development so children with attachment problems may have difficulty with lying. Approaches to supporting conscience development are outlined in Section 3.

Masturbation

Although most children masturbate in private occasionally, some children masturbate excessively sometimes in private and at other times in public. Children who are prone to loneliness at bedtime or night-time fears, may masturbate excessively to relieve their lonely feelings. The problematic aspect of excessive masturbation is that the child is relying on him or herself rather than others to provide feelings of nurturance and closeness. The child who masturbates occasionally or in an exploratory way is in no such danger. If the masturbation has become of habit proportions, then a behaviour modification approach to it may work.

Nailbiting, handwringing, hair pulling, picking at face or fingers

Nailbiting, handwringing, hair pulling, and picking at the face or fingers are behaviours that are all common signs of anxiety in children. This anxiety most often stems from children's lack of trust in what is going to happen to them. Such children need to be helped to resolve past issues about separation from their parents and to clarify what the future holds for them. It is unlikely that the signs and symptoms of anxiety will diminish until a permanent plan for the child has been achieved.

Children who live in homes where the expectations are very high may exhibit the same symptoms because they are anxious about living up to those expectations. In such cases more work needs to be done with the parents than with the children. A behaviour modification approach to this group of problems may be combined with efforts to alleviate the child's anxiety. For example, one foster mother made a pair of puppet mittens for her daughter to wear to bed so that she would not pull her hair. The daughter was rewarded for keeping the mittens on at night.

Night roaming

Some children get up during the night and roam through the house getting into things and being destructive. Children who roam at night are often depressed and lonely. These feelings may relate to a child's separation from the birth family.

The principal way to deal with this problem is to work to alleviate the underlying feelings. However, with young children who tend to get themselves into dangerous situations at night, it may be necessary to prevent them from leaving their room. There are plastic objects that fit over doorknobs and make it difficult for some children to open the door. However, like most childproof things, these devices are often more easily mastered by children than by adults. With some children it is necessary to put a simple hook lock on the outside of the bedroom door for a period of time while the underlying problem is worked on.

These measures are somewhat extreme. They have worked when they have been presented in a supportive fashion and used for a relatively short period of time. The parent might say 'I worry when I find that you have been up at night by yourself. Also, you get into things then. I get mad in the morning, and then, both you and I feel badly, and things don't work out well for us. So, until you learn to feel more comfortable with us, I am going to fix your door so you cannot get out at night by yourself. If you wake up, you can play with your toys in your room or you can call to me if you need something.'

Some parents have used an intercom system to alert them when the child is awake. Many times some extra positive attention during the daytime helps alleviate the child's feelings of loneliness and helps the problem subside.

Night terrors

Night terrors differ from nightmares in that they seem to take place in an altered state of consciousness such as that experienced by sleep walkers. Children with night terrors may scream and seem to be in a panic. They may have their eyes open but not be awake. Even if they do wake up while being put back to bed, they often have no memory of these events or feelings. When children who have had a nightmare wake up in the morning, they usually remember having a bad dream although they may not remember the content of the dream unless they make a conscious effort to do so.

Night terrors tend to be associated with the chronic fears and anxieties of children who have experienced traumatic events, such as moves, for which they were not adequately prepared. Preparing children for potentially traumatic events is essential. In addition, timely permanent planning is essential.

Nightmares

Nightmares are most common in children between the ages of four and six years. This is the age when the child has developed an imagination and has a propensity for magical thinking. Nightmares at this age do not mean that there is a serious psychological problem. Some children in placement have nightmares at later ages. These often reflect delayed development.

Nightmares are also common when the child is anxious; for example around visits with birth parents or near the time of moves. When a child awakens or cries with a nightmare, the parent figures should comfort him or her for a short period until they can be tucked back into bed again.

Automatic response of 'No'

Some children automatically respond 'No' to any request. Such children must be taught that the automatic 'No' gives them no more choice than the automatic 'Yes'. When adolescents have this problem, it is possible to demonstrate to them how much control they give to others. Children between four and six are also prone to this problem. With them it may be possible to ignore what they say and respond to their behaviour. If they say 'No', but follow the request, then they can be praised for doing what they are asked to do and the 'No' that they spoke may be ignored. Again, finding ways to increase age-appropriate autonomy is a necessry part of the treatment of this problem.

Peer problems

Peer problems are very common among children in placement. They occur most often when children have not had their early needs for dependency and autonomy met. Such children frequently have not learned to share or to play with others. They need to be actively taught how to relate to others.

Children who have difficulty with peer relationships need practice in making those relationships, not protection from them. The helpful parent will encourage a child to invite others over. The parent can then be watchful and if things do not go well, can help the child alter his or her behaviour to produce a desirable result. The parent can play games with the child who has difficulty losing. This is much more helpful than discussions about the virtue of being a graceful loser. Many school social workers run groups with the primary purpose of teaching children with peer problems some interpersonal skills.

Setting self up for punishment

Setting themselves up for punishment is a common, normal problem for seven to eight-year-olds who tend to have very high expectations. It is as though they alternate between extremely high self-esteem and extremely low self-esteem.

It is hard for parents to handle children who set themselves up for punishment. On the one hand, they do not want to fall into the trap of reinforcing a child's negative self-image; on the other, they cannot ignore the child's behaviour. If the parent tries to ignore the behaviour or listen to the child's feelings, the child may escalate the negative behaviour until the parent becomes angry and punitive. In such cases it is important to increase the child's responsibility for his or her own behaviour. The child may be given the message that change is possible and expected by comments like 'I'll be glad when you don't need to set yourself up in this way anymore.'

Rage reactions

Rage reactions are similar to temper tantrums but are more related to anger than frustration. It is sometimes necessary for the adults to physically control children so that they cannot hurt either themselves or anyone else. At such times the message must always be 'You are clearly out of control of yourself. That is uncomfortable and dangerous so I will control you only until you are back in control of yourself.'

Periodic rage reactions may be associated with a physical condition called temporal lobe epilepsy. This possibility should be explored through a neurological consultation with children who are prone to rage reactions.

Running away

Many children in placement run away. Anyone who has worked with runaways knows that no one approach is successful in helping them. Since the reason underlying the behaviour differs widely from child to child, the approach to the problem also varies.

The first question to ask is 'Is the child running from something or to something?' If the child is running to the birth family, it usually indicates an unresolved separation issue.

Children run away for a variety of reasons. Some children run away to express their feelings. They run away when they become angry or when they feel sad or lonely. Some children, particularly adolescents, need to get away from people whenever they have strong feelings. In these cases the family and child can decide together where the child can go; for example, out to the tree-house or to his or her own room. Some children have run away so frequently that it has become a habit; however, this pattern is relatively rare.

Running away may indicate that the child feels that he or she is caught in an intolerable control battle.

Case example

A mother once called asking what she should do about her ten-year-old daughter who had just run away. Frankly, my first thought was 'Why aren't you going after her rather than calling me?' When I asked about the events leading up to the daughter's departure, the mother said, 'Well I told her she could either do the dishes or get out of the house and she left.'

The preceding situation gives an example of the danger of presenting a child with one good choice and one bad choice: what is the parent to do if the child takes the bad choice? The child is in a position of giving in, or taking the bad choice and asserting his or her autonomy.

This mistake is not the same as offering a child a good choice and another choice that the parent considers less preferable but not harmful. Such choice could have been given in the preceding example. The girl could have been told 'You have a choice; you can either do the dishes now and then be free to play, or you can sit in a chair right here until you are ready to do the dishes which means you won't have as much time to play – it's up to you.'

Some children who run away, particularly small children, are giving the parent a 'love' test. The test is 'Do you love me enough to stop me from going? Do you really want me here?' For this reason parents should always try to retrieve the child. Children who run away usually have poor self-esteem, and they doubt that anyone really wants them.

Sexually provocative behaviour

Young children who have been sexually abused in one home often attempt to interact with new parental figures in the same way that they interacted with the sexually abusive ones. This is particularly true if the child viewed the sexual interactions as demonstrations of caring and affection. Sexually provocative behaviour can be viewed to some extent as a developmental problem. The child has not had experience with appropriate parent-child interactions.

In general it is best if the parent of the same sex as the child takes the primary role in handling the problem. The implication of this strategy is 'I will teach you how to be close to your other parent; I, too, had to learn this as a child so I know what to do.' A foster mother might physically place a young foster daughter on her husband's lap in a way that is not provocative. If the child is sexually stimulated by this type of contact, the appropriate response might be 'Right now, it is too uncomfortable for you to sit on daddy's lap. You can sit next to him or on my lap for now. As you get to know us better, it won't be so uncomfortable for you, and you may try again.' This message does not imply that there is something bad about the child or about being physically close to the parent of the opposite sex. It does convey that the child's feelings can and will change.

Foster parents need to know that many children in foster care do exhibit sexually provocative behaviour. They need to be able to talk about this behaviour without one of them thinking the other is jealous of the child. Some experienced foster parents have said that they were able to recognise, talk about, and help a young foster daughter only because they had heard a discussion of sexually provocative behaviour in foster parent training classes.

Children with this problem are especially good at dividing and conquering parental figures. They can get the parent of the opposite sex to stick up for them and the parent of the same sex to reject them. This is especially true when children have experienced separation from parents during the Oedipal stage of development.

Stealing
Some children steal only from family members; others steal only from people outside the family, while others steal from both. Some steal food; some steal insignificant articles; and others steal things of value. The dynamics of each of these situations differ.

Stealing sometimes accompanies lying and delayed conscience development. Some children pick up many small things that they have 'found' at school or on the playground. This is a normal developmental stage for six to seven-year-olds and is sometimes seen in older children who have delayed development.

Children who steal only from family members, particularly from parents, are usually expressing their feelings in an inappropriate fashion. Stealing may be their way of saying that they are not getting enough love or attention from the family. Some children in foster care steal and give the stolen things to members of their birth family. This behaviour usually indicates a need to resolve feelings about separation from the birth family.

Shoplifting is quite common among children between the ages of ten and 12. One or two episodes of shoplifting in children of this age does not indicate a serious underlying problem. Parents who meet this behaviour with disapproval and who insist that the child return or pay for the merchandise can usually stop the problem at this stage. However, more drastic measures need to be taken when an adolescent is involved in frequent shoplifting. Such teenagers frequently have all kinds of explanations for their acquisitions. They may say they found them, borrowed them, or received them as gifts.

When an adolescent has problems with shoplifting, the parents need to give the clear message that 'We know this is a problem for you and we are going to have to work together to make it easier for you not to be tempted to take things.' One foster mother approaches the problem with 'It will be easier for us both if you show me a receipt for everything you bring into this house. That way I can't unjustly accuse you if you really did buy something. It will be easier for me to trust you and for you to trust me.'

For such a child, rules that prohibit borrowing or keeping things that have been 'found' help avoid constant hassles between parents and children. Parents place responsibility on the child for proving that he or she has acquired things honestly rather than shouldering the responsibility of making sure that the child is not lying.

Some children and adolescents steal because they want things and have no other way to obtain them. Even young children need an allowance to spend on things they want. Older children, and particularly adolescents, should have opportunities to earn money so that they can purchase the things for which they are willing to work.

Temper tantrums

People have temper tantrums when they have a great need or desire, an inability to achieve this need, and no capacity to appropriately express their frustration. Everyone experiences unfulfilled needs; however, most learn to appropriately express the frustration without having temper tantrums. Abusive parents have adult tantrums in which child abuse is the manifestation of their frustration.

Temper tantrums in children are most likely to occur between ages one and three and ages five and a half and six and a half. At these ages children's perceptions of the world and their ability to cope with it do not mesh well, and they experience considerable frustration. The focus of the parents' efforts should be on helping the child learn to express this frustration appropriately.

However, when children are in the throes of a tantrum, they cannot process additional input well so it does little good to talk to them then. If they are not hurting themselves or anyone else during the tantrum, then the parents might ignore it. If they are hurting themselves or someone else, then a parent must physically control them.

At the end of a tantrum children are open to being close and to learning other ways to express their frustration. A parent can talk to a child about alternative behaviour and then have the child practice the behaviour right then and there. Some parents are hesitant to be close to a child at the end of a tantrum for fear of reinforcing the negative behaviour. However, at such a time the child has a desperate need for acceptance as a person.

No one would tell a marital couple not to kiss and make up after a fight because it reinforces fighting; yet for some reason we take that approach with children. Obviously if a marital couple can only be close after an argument, they are in trouble. If a parent and child can be physically close both after a tantrum and at other times, the closeness will not reinforce the tantrums.

Unreasonable fears
Unreasonable fears often originate in events similar to those that cause night terrors. Many children with unreasonable fears have been subject to frequent moves for which they were inadequately prepared. Children who experienced precipitous moves during the stage of the development of autonomy between ages one and three are particularly vulnerable. These experiences have given them the feeling that they have limited control over what happens to them. They feel that things have been 'done to' them.

Trying to dispel such fears by exposing the children to reality, such as taking the child who is afraid of sirens on a visit to the fire station, usually is not helpful. Instead the underlying problems must be recognised, and the child must be helped to become as autonomous as is appropriate for his or her age level.

Such children should be given many opportunities to make choices and to learn to count on themselves. The choices they should be encouraged to make may have nothing to do with their fears. Choices such as 'Do you want milk or juice?', 'What would you like me to fix for your lunch?', or 'Do you want to take a bath tonight or have me help you wash?' are all relevant. Defining areas where the children have control, for example, their own toys or the selection of their clothes, is helpful in overcoming the problems associated with unreasonable fears.

Whining
Whining is usually a habit and thus changing this behaviour is usually best done with a behaviour modification approach. Sometimes it is necessary for parents to tell the child what they are doing. For example, they might say 'I've told my ears I don't want them to listen to your whining voice. They only listen to your other voice.'

The principle is to help the child learn that a normal voice is going to be more successful in getting what he or she wants than a whining one. However, some children whine only when they know perfectly well that they cannot have what they are asking, no matter how they ask. In these cases, give the child two good choices, such as, 'If you want to whine, fine; you may do so in your room. If you want to be near me, then stop whining.'

Exercise 6 that follows gives you an opportunity to plan the management of a number of behavioural problems for a six-year-old boy named John. After you've completed Exercise 6, go back to Exercise 1 at the beginning of the workbook and finish your behaviour management plan for the child you selected from your caseload.

Exercise 6:
Practice in planning behaviour management

Instructions

Purpose:

To give you practice in planning behaviour management for a child with multiple problem behaviour.

How to do it:

1 Read John's case history.

2 Answer the questions in the worksheet for Exercise 6. Then compare your own answers with those of another social worker on the sample worksheet.

John's case

John is six years old. He has been in and out of foster care since he was a toddler. His background includes a history of moderately severe abuse and neglect. He was often left alone in a locked room for several hours at a time while his single mother was out.

In his present home, John has demonstrated many behavioural problems. He pokes holes in furniture with any sharp objects that he can find; draws on the walls; he sometimes smears faeces on the walls, as well as lipstick, paint, or anything else he can get his hands on. He is easily frustrated and difficult to control.

According to his foster parents, John seems to 'just ask for spankings'. They were concerned about the frequency of spankings so they decided to avoid all forms of physical discipline. Several weeks later, after John had misbehaved, he was found trying to cut his wrists with a table knife.

Of particular concern to the parents is the fact that recently John started two small fires – one in the basement and one in his bedroom. The foster parents have become increasingly frustrated, and feel that everything they have tried has been unsuccessful.

Exercise 6:
Practice in planning behaviour management

Worksheet

1 What is John's behaviour indicative of in terms of his underlying needs?

2 Outline a behaviour management plan for the foster parents to implement, based on these needs.

Exercise 6:
Practice in planning behaviour management

Sample worksheet

---

1 What is John's behaviour indicative of in terms of his underlying needs?

He has experienced neglect and abuse, repeated moves, rejection and periods of isolation. His behaviour indicates pent-up anger, frustration and loneliness and a need for closeness and affection. There is also some evidence of developmental delay in the way he acts and the objects he uses in his destructive behaviour.

---

2 Outline a behaviour management plan for the foster parents to implement, based on these needs.

Focus on being ready to anticipate antecedents to John's acting-out episodes and help him expose his feelings in other ways. He needs close supervision and to be interrupted as soon as the inappropriate behaviour begins.

Most of all, John needs lots of opportunities to be close to parents and to increase appropriate autonomy and build self-esteem.

References

1 Hymes J L *The child under six* New Jersey: Prentice Hall, 1969.

2 Gordon T *Parent effectiveness training* New York: Peter Wyden Inc, 1971.

3 Rogers C *Client-contact therapy* Boston: Houghton Mifflin, 1951.

4 See 1 above.

5 Dobson W *Dare to discipline* Wheaton, Illinois: Tyndale House and Regal Books, 1972.

6 Dreikurs R and Green L *Logical consequences* New York: Meredith Press, 1968.

7 See 1 above.

8 Haley J *Strategies of psychotherapy* New York: Greene and Straton, 1963.

9 See 5 above.

Further reading

In addition to the references listed at the end of each workbook, the following books will be of interest to workers. BAAF can supply more extensive reading lists on demand. Other sources of invaluable material are BAAF's journal *Adoption & fostering* and the National Foster Care Association's *Foster care* magazine.

Adcock M and White R (eds) *Good enough parenting* BAAF, 1985.

Aldgate J and Simmonds J (eds) *Direct work with children* Batsford Academic/BAAF, 1988.

Batty D (ed) *Working with children* BAAF, 1986.

Bower T *The perceptual world of the child* Fontana, 1977.

Bowlby J *The making and breaking of affectional bonds* Tavistock Press, 1979.

Bretherton I and Waters E *Growing points in attachment theory and research* Chicago: Society for Research in Child Development, 1985.

Jewett C *For ever and ever* BAAF, 1982.

Jewett C *Helping children cope with separation and loss* Batsford Academic/BAAF, 1984.

Melina L *Raising adopted children* Harper and Row, 1986.

Ryan T and Walker R *Making life story books* BAAF, 1985.

Stern D *The first relationship: infant and mother* Fontana, 1977.